The Pilgrim's Guide

C. S. Lewis and the Art of Witness

Edited by

DAVID MILLS

WILLIAM B. EERDMANS PUBLISHING COMPANY
GRAND RAPIDS, MICHIGAN / CAMBRIDGE, U.K.

© 1998 Wm. B. Eerdmans Publishing Co.
255 Jefferson Ave. S.E., Grand Rapids, Michigan 49503 /
P.O. Box 163, Cambridge CB3 9PU U.K.
All rights reserved

Paperback edition 1999

Printed in the United States of America

03 02 01 00 99   7 6 5 4 3 2

Library of Congress Cataloging-in-Publication Data

The pilgrim's guide : C. S. Lewis and the art of witness /
  edited by David Mills.
       p.   cm.
  Includes bibliographical references.
  ISBN 0-8028-4689-0 (pbk : alk. paper)
  1. Lewis, C. S. (Clive Staples), 1898-1963 — Religion.
  2. Christian literature, English — History and criticism.
I. Mills, David, 1957-   .
BX5199.L53P55   1998
230'.092 — dc21   98-22482
                             CIP

THE PILGRIM'S GUIDE

To my father

Contents

The Character of a Witness

The Work of a Witness

Introduction

HAVING NOW SPENT several months in the Lewis literature, I must admit to sharing many readers' weariness of the Lewis cult, and to feeling slightly irritated when someone prefaces a statement on almost any question with "It's like Lewis says." *The Pilgrim's Guide* is yet another book on C. S. Lewis, and you may well ask (I did): Why should the editor and his writers take the time to write, Eerdmans publish, and I read yet another book on C. S. Lewis? The simple answer is that he was an extraordinary man, an extraordinary Christian, and an extraordinary writer. Not perfect, certainly, not infallible, but extraordinary.

To deny this would be to fail very badly in gratitude for a gift God gave the church in this century. Lewis answered many of the questions Christians must answer, often with a clarity and insight rarely matched. Many writers have written well on a few subjects, and many more have thought well but written badly, but only Lewis (and G. K. Chesterton before him) has thought so well and written so well on such a range of subjects.

The Pilgrim's Guide is intended for the serious general reader, though academic readers should find it helpful. The book explores the art of Lewis's witness, which was both a moral art, in the formation of his character, and an intellectual art, in knowing how to speak the Word so that it would be heard. The distinction is a poor one, in some ways, because, as Lewis himself knew, one can only communicate what one knows, and one only knows what one sees, and one sees well or badly depending on one's character.

The first three essays (those by Mitchell, Blamires, and Edwards) explore what in Lewis's faith and life made him such a witness, and the others explore the ways in which he witnessed to the people, lay and academic, of his day. Some (Ware and Patrick) examine the sources of his thinking and his engagement with his teachers, ancient and modern; others (Macdonald and Shea, Duriez, Caldecott, Smith, Myers, Mills, and Harmon) examine how he presented Christian truths to people who did not know or could not understand them, or thought they did not want to hear them; and still others (Howard, Peters, Root, Fairfield, and Gilley) examine his response to some of the alternatives our century presents to orthodox Christianity.

The appendices are included to help readers better understand Lewis's work. Dr. Glyer's essay surveys the best and worst of the available works on Lewis, and the timeline places him in the context of his time, giving readers an idea of how his work relates to the events, thought, and culture of his day. The book includes (at some expense) extensive quotations from Lewis to help readers understand him as completely as possible, paraphrasing Lewis being, almost always, to lose something of his meaning. The notes have been made as helpful as possible. To do this, the form has been simplified ("Eerdmans" for "Eerdmans Publishing Company," for example), the number reduced by not giving notes for books in which the average reader could find the reference (especially the Narnia Chronicles), and references to additional useful works included.

All the writers are concerned with Lewis's engagement with the challenges to the Christian mind, vision, imagination, and under-standing in the late twentieth century, and most tend to emphasize his standing against the stream (the title of the lecture from which Dr. Blamires' essay was taken) but also, to adapt the metaphor, his floating happily and without worry down the historic Christian main-stream. Lewis opposed much that went on around him, but only because he accepted something much greater. He was not a reaction-ary, or was so only in the sense that a man about to hand another a glass of wine reacts when he sees the other about to drink a glass of poison.

Perhaps surprisingly, almost all the writers emphasize that Lewis is a humanist, concerned not only for the restoration of man from the degradation he has chosen, but also for his glorification. This is why so many refer on the one hand to *The Abolition of Man, The Great*

Divorce, and *That Hideous Strength* and on the other to the salvation scenes in the Narnia Chronicles and (especially) the closing of his sermon "The Weight of Glory."

*   *   *

Most of the essays were written for this book, but I have included a few reprints not easily available to the average reader. Bishop Kallistos's essay, for example, has for several years been passed around among Anglican and Orthodox readers in increasingly degraded photocopies, and is the best short study I know of Lewis's use of the church fathers. The authors of the reprinted essays, especially Prof. Myers, Mr. Duriez, and Mr. Caldecott, have substantially revised and expanded their contributions. I am grateful to the authors and their editors for permission to reprint the essays. I would also like to thank Mr. Walter Hooper for letting me include what seems to be the source of Lewis's use of "mere Christianity," which he discovered through the hard work of reading through the works of Richard Baxter.

As is (rightly) traditional, I must thank many people for their help. Jennifer Hoffman and Anne Salsich at Eerdmans were very helpful, and, more strikingly, patient. They provided a model of gracious editorial manners in finishing a book under a very tight deadline. Maxine Moore, our dean's secretary, made time in her day or stayed late to help with this book. My authors were gracious and usually accommodating. Finally I must thank my wife, Hope, and our four children, for their kindness in bearing the costs even the relatively simple project of editing a book puts upon a family's life. Sarah in fact served as an editorial assistant.

Readers may notice a few unusual typographical conventions, in particular printing "Heaven" and "Hell" with initial capital letters rather than the usual "heaven" and "hell." They are printed so because Heaven and Hell are places, like, say, Oxford and Grand Rapids. Or perhaps more to the point, to Lewis's point, they are destinations.

Ambridge, Pennsylvania   David Mills
The Feast of the Annunciation, 1998

Contributors

DR. HARRY BLAMIRES, who studied with C. S. Lewis in the mid-1930s, is the author of *The Christian Mind* (Servant Books) and many other books in theology, including *Recovering the Christian Mind* (Inter-Varsity Press) and *Knowing the Truth about Heaven and Hell* (Servant Books). A literary critic, he has written *The New Bloomsday Book* (Routledge), *A Guide to Twentieth Century Literature in English* (Routledge), *A History of Literary Criticism* (St. Martin's Press), and books on Romantic and Victorian literature, Milton, and T. S. Eliot. "Standing against the Stream" is adapted from the inaugural lecture of the Irish Christian Study Centre, which he delivered in 1983. Omitted is his discussion of the history of specifically Christian literature.

MR. STRATFORD CALDECOTT is the director of the Centre for Faith & Culture in Oxford, assistant editor of *The Chesterton Review,* and publisher with T & T Clark. He is the editor of *Beyond the Prosaic: Renewing the Liturgical Movement,* and with John Morrill the editor of *Eternity in Time: Christopher Dawson and the Catholic Idea of History* (both published by T & T Clark). He was for several years senior editor for HarperCollins-UK. His "Speaking the Truths Only the Imagination May Grasp: Myth and 'Real Life'" is a revised and expanded version of an article that originally appeared in *Epiphany*.

MR. COLIN DURIEZ is general books editor for Inter-Varsity Press in England, and author of *The Lewis Handbook* (Baker Book House) and *The Tolkien and Middle-earth Handbook* (Monarch). He is currently writing a book on the Inklings with David Porter, to be published by

Baker. He is also a consultant editor for the forthcoming *Dictionary of Biblical Imagery,* to be published by InterVarsity Press. "The Romantic Writer: C. S. Lewis's Theology of Fantasy" is an abridged and revised version of "The Theology of Fantasy in Lewis and Tolkien" from *Themelios.*

DR. BRUCE L. EDWARDS is the associate dean of the College of Arts and Sciences and professor of English at Bowling Green State University in Bowling Green, Ohio. He is the author of *A Rhetoric of Reading: C. S. Lewis's Defense of Western Literacy* (Center for the Study of Christian Values in Literature), editor of *The Taste of the Pineapple: Essays on C. S. Lewis as Reader, Critic, and Imaginative Writer* (Bowling Green University Press), and a contributor to *C. S. Lewis: A Reader's Encyclopedia,* edited by Jeffrey Schultz (Zondervan).

THE REV. DR. LESLIE P. FAIRFIELD is professor of church history at Trinity Episcopal School for Ministry in Ambridge, Pennsylvania. He has written on the English Reformation and is finishing a book on the healing of the modern schisms.

DR. SHERIDAN GILLEY is reader in theology at the University of Durham. He is the author of *Newman and His Age* (Christian Classics), with W. J. Sheils he is the editor of *A History of Religion in Britain: Practice and Belief from Pre-Roman Times to the Present* (Blackwell's), and he is the editor of two collections on the history of the Irish in England. "The Abolition of God: Relativism and the Center of the Faith" is an abridged and revised version of the 1985 C. S. Lewis lecture given at the Irish Christian Study Centre in Belfast and published in the *Journal of the Irish Christian Study Centre.*

DR. DIANA PAVLAC GLYER is associate professor of English at Azusa Pacific University in Azusa, California. Her publications focus on the interaction of C. S. Lewis and the Inklings. She chaired the 1998 C. S. Lewis Centenary Celebration sponsored by the Mythopoeic Society and is a contributor to *C. S. Lewis: A Reader's Encyclopedia* (Zondervan).

THE REV. DR. KENDALL HARMON is theologian in residence at

St. Paul's Episcopal Church in Summerville, South Carolina. He graduated from Trinity Episcopal School for Ministry in 1987.

MR. WALTER HOOPER, C. S. Lewis's last secretary, is the author of *C. S. Lewis: Companion and Guide* (HarperCollins), now the standard reference work on Lewis's life and writing. He is the editor of Lewis's *Narrative Poems* (Harcourt Brace Jovanovich) and *Collected Poems* (HarperCollins) and of the revised and enlarged edition of Lewis's *Letters* and his letters to his childhood friend Arthur Greeves, *They Stand Together* (Macmillan). He has also edited several posthumous collections of Lewis's essays, including *Studies in Medieval and Renaissance Literature* (Cambridge University Press), *Of Other Worlds* (Harcourt, Brace & World), *Christian Reflections* (Eerdmans), *Selected Literary Essays* (Cambridge University Press), *God in the Dock* (Eerdmans), *The Dark Tower* (Harcourt Brace Jovanovich), and *On Stories* (Harcourt Brace Jovanovich). He has also written a study of the Narnia Chronicles, *Past Watchful Dragons* (Macmillan), which includes Lewis's "Outline of Narnian History" and early drafts of some of the stories.

DR. THOMAS HOWARD is professor of English at St. John's Seminary, the seminary of the Roman Catholic archdiocese of Boston. He is the author of *C. S. Lewis: Man of Letters: A Reading of His Fiction, Chance of the Dance?, Evangelical Is Not Enough,* and other books (all republished by Ignatius Press). His latest book is *On Being Catholic* (Ignatius Press).

DR. MICHAEL H. MACDONALD is professor of European studies and the director of C. S. Lewis Institute at Seattle Pacific University, and editor (with Andrew Tadie) of *The Riddle of Joy* and *The Permanent Things* (both published by Eerdmans).

DR. CHRISTOPHER W. MITCHELL is director of the Marion E. Wade Center and associate professor of theology at Wheaton College.

MR. DAVID MILLS is director of publishing at Trinity Episcopal School for Ministry and editor of the school's journal *Mission & Ministry.* He is also an associate editor of *Touchstone: A Journal of Mere Christianity.*

DR. DORIS T. MYERS is professor emeritus of English at the University of Northern Colorado and the author of *C. S. Lewis in Context* (Kent State University Press). She is also the author of *Understanding Language* (Boynton-Cook). "Growing in Grace: The Anglical Spiritual Style in the Narnia Chronicles" is a revised and expanded version of "The Compleat Anglican," which appeared in *The Anglican Theological Review,* and is used here by permission.

DR. JAMES PATRICK is the provost of the College of St. Thomas More in Fort Worth, Texas, and the author of *The Magdalen Metaphysicals* (Mercer University Press), a study of C. S. Lewis and his philosophical peers in Oxford in the 1930s and 1940s. He is the editor, with Andrew Walker, of *A Christian for All Christians: Essays in Honor of C. S. Lewis* (Regnery Gateway), which includes his essay "C. S. Lewis and Idealism."

DR. THOMAS C. PETERS is the author of *Battling for the Modern Mind: A Beginner's Chesterton* (Concordia) and *Simply C. S. Lewis* (Crossway), and serves on the staff of the University of California, Riverside. He is working on a book comparing the worldviews of H. G. Wells and C. S. Lewis.

MR. JERRY ROOT is assistant professor of Christian education at Wheaton College in Wheaton, Illinois, and with Wayne Martindale the editor of *The Quotable C. S. Lewis* (Tyndale). He has taught and written extensively on C. S. Lewis, and contributed several articles to the *C. S. Lewis Encyclopedia* (Zondervan) and an essay "C. S. Lewis and the Problem of Evil" to *C. S. Lewis: Lightbearer in the Shadowlands* (Crossway Books). He is currently a doctoral candidate at the British Open University.

MR. MARK P. SHEA is a freelance writer and speaker. In addition to writing the column "Heaven and Earth" in *New Covenant,* he is the author of *By What Authority?: An Evangelical Discovers Catholic Tradition* (Our Sunday Visitor Books) and *This Is My Body: An Evangelical Discovers the Real Presence* (Christendom Press).

DR. STEPHEN M. SMITH is professor of theology and ethics at

Trinity Episcopal School for Ministry and a frequent contributor to its journal *Mission & Ministry*. His "Worldview, Language, and Radical Feminism" appeared in *Speaking the Christian God* (Eerdmans).

BISHOP KALLISTOS WARE is Bishop of Diokleia and Spalding Lecturer in Orthodox Studies at Oxford University. A convert to Orthodoxy as a young man, he is the author of *The Orthodox Church* and *The Orthodox Way* (both published by Penguin) and an editor of *The Philokalia* (Faber and Faber). "God of the Fathers: C. S. Lewis and Eastern Christianity" is adapted from his "C. S. Lewis: Anonymous Orthodox," which appeared in *Sobornost,* the journal of the Society of St. Alban and St. Sergius, and is reprinted here with permission.

The Character of a Witness

Bearing the Weight of Glory:
The Cost of C. S. Lewis's Witness

CHRISTOPHER W. MITCHELL

WHAT IS IT THAT motivated C. S. Lewis, a comfortable academic with more than enough to do, to direct so much of his time writing and speaking toward the conversion of the unbelieving of the world? What made him sacrifice not only the regard of many of his colleagues but his own academic advancement to defend the faith? The answer will no doubt appear quite obvious once it is stated. But since it says something important about Lewis and something quite profound about the human drama viewed through the lenses of the Christian faith, and because I do not recall anyone having yet called specific attention to the connection I propose (though some have hinted at it),[1] it seems appropriate to present the matter here.

To state the case most plainly, the vividness with which Lewis perceived the potential eternal destinies of every man and woman compelled him to direct a great part of his energies toward the saving of souls. Lewis perceived evangelism to be his lay vocation, and the means by which he expressed this evangelistic impulse were his writing and speaking. The particulars of his ministry are generally well known. However, a summary of them in the context of his life

---

1. See, for example, Patrick T. Ferry's fine essay "Mere Christianity Because There Are No Mere Mortals: Reaching beyond the Inner Ring," in *C. S. Lewis: Lightbearer in the Shadowlands,* ed. Angus Menuge (Crossway, 1997), pp. 169-90, where he suggests that the motive behind Lewis's sermon "The Weight of Glory" unites Lewis's idea of "mere Christianity" and evangelism.

will be necessary in order to appreciate the significance of his motivation.

Lewis's bent toward evangelism began to assert itself within the first year of his conversion in 1931.[2] He "felt it was the duty of every Christian," observed Owen Barfield, "to go out into the world and try to save souls."[3] In an essay on "Christianity and Culture" Lewis stated plainly that "The glory of God, and, as our only means to glorifying him, the salvation of the human soul, is the real business of life," and in another place admitted that most of his books were "evangelistic."[4] Speaking of the fundamental difference between the Christian's and the unbeliever's approach to literature, and by extension to any of the great works of human culture, Lewis said without qualification that "the salvation of a single soul is more important than the production or preservation of all the epics and tragedies in the world."[5]

His vision for employing his own fiction as a means of evangelizing came quite unexpectedly and quite early. When in 1939 he became aware that most of the reviewers of his book *Out of the Silent Planet,* the first book of the space trilogy, failed to recognize its Christian theology, the idea struck him that the gospel could be "smuggled into people's minds" by means of fiction.[6] It was a vision he sustained

2. George Sayer, *Jack: C. S. Lewis and His Times* (Harper & Row, 1988) p. 138.

3. Oral History Interview, conducted by Lyle W. Dorsett, Kent, England, July 19 and 20, 1984, for the Marion E. Wade Center, p. 61.

4. "Christianity and Culture," in *Christian Reflections* (Eerdmans, 1992), p. 14; "Rejoinder to Dr. Pittenger," in *God in the Dock* (Eerdmans, 1993), p. 181. According to the poet and novelist John Wain, who had been one of Lewis's students, "Lewis used to quote with approval general Booth's remark to Kipling: 'Young man, if I could win one soul for God by — by playing the tambourine with my toes, I'd do it.' Lewis did plenty of playing the tambourine with his toes, to the distress of some of the refined souls with whom he was surrounded at Oxford." "A Great Clerke," in *C. S. Lewis at the Breakfast Table,* ed. James Como (Harcourt Brace/Harvest Books, 1992), p. 69.

5. "Christianity and Literature," in *Christian Reflections,* p. 10. Similarly, he wrote in the midst of a sharp argument against T. S. Eliot, that "I agree with him about matters of such moment that all literary questions are, in comparison, trivial." *A Preface to "Paradise Lost"* (Oxford University Press/Galaxy Books, 1961), p. 9.

6. Letter to Sister Penelope, July 9, 1939, in *Letters of C. S. Lewis,* rev. and enl., ed. Walter Hooper (Harcourt Brace & Company, 1993), p. 322. It is not the purpose

throughout his career. Less than six months before he died, in answer to the question, asked by an American evangelical: "Would you say that the aim of . . . your own writing is to bring about an encounter of the reader with Jesus Christ?", he replied, "That is not my language, yet it is the purpose I have in view."[7]

Lewis, whose literary output was enormous, has been aptly called a "literary evangelist."[8] Before his death in 1963, he wrote forty books and edited three. Since his death, nearly a dozen volumes of his essays have been published. In addition, he wrote thousands of letters (many of them published). Add to his writing (most of which was evangelistic) his speaking, praying, and discipling,[9] and one begins to sense Lewis's enormous drive to save souls.

It is important to notice, however, as Michael Ward has recently pointed out, that Lewis's brand of evangelism never involved the kind of direct appeal that bids people to "come to Jesus."[10] Lewis saw himself not so much as a reaper of souls, but as one who prepares the soil, sows the seed, and weeds out what hinders growth. His job, as he understood it, was on the one hand to seek to break down the intellectual prejudices to Christianity by detecting and exposing the fallacies of current objections to belief in such a way as to make faith in Christianity intellectually plausible, and on the other to prepare the mind and imagination to receive the Christian vision.

His evangelistic genius was not in his ability to inspire faith (this he flatly disavowed), but to create and maintain an atmosphere where faith could be possible — rationally and imaginatively plausible — and

---

of this essay to go into how Lewis dealt with the problem of communicating traditional Christian content by using modern literary forms such as fantasy. Those interested in this aspect will find help in Doris T. Myers's *C. S. Lewis in Context* (Kent State University Press, 1994) and in Meredith Veldman's treatment of the subject in *Fantasy, the Bomb, and the Greening of Britain: Romantic Protest, 1945-80* (Cambridge University Press, 1994).

7. "Cross-Examination," in *God in the Dock*, p. 262.

8. Lyle W. Dorsett, *The Essential C. S. Lewis* (Colliers/Macmillan, 1988), p. 8.

9. Philip Ryken has nicely summarized the various aspects of Lewis's ministry of evangelism under teaching, writing, praying, and discipling in "Winsome Evangelist: The Influence of C. S. Lewis," in *C. S. Lewis: Lightbearer in the Shadowlands*, pp. 55-78.

10. Michael Ward, "Escape to Wallaby Wood: Lewis' Depictions of Conversion," in *C. S. Lewis: Lightbearer in the Shadowlands*, p. 143.

where it could grow and even thrive. He was happy to prepare the way for those who were gifted to reap what had been sown — who could successfully bring the direct appeal to the heart.

The well-known preacher Stephen Olford tells of an experience he had with Lewis during a "This Is Life" crusade, held in London, when he found himself on the same platform as Lewis. Lewis spoke first, brilliantly arguing, according to Olford, the case for Christianity before an audience of approximately 3,000. Following Lewis, Olford picked up on a motif that came through Lewis's message and used it to lead into his own message and ultimately to an invitation for an open commitment to Christ. After the meeting, Olford remembers Lewis coming up to him, shaking his hand, and saying, "That was so impressive and effective. Thank you for that." "I hope you didn't mind my taking up on what you said," replied Olford. "No," said Lewis, "That was magnificent!"[11]

Lewis's prominence as a representative of the Christian faith began initially in 1940 with the publication of his book *The Problem of Pain,* rose in 1941 as a result of his series of broadcast talks over the BBC, and reached new heights with the publication of *The Screwtape Letters* in 1942. Other avenues for speaking of the faith included such diverse settings as Britain's RAF, the weekly meeting of the Oxford University Socratic Club, Christian groups on university campuses, and the occasional sermon.

A Hated Man

Lewis's evangelistic impulse not only brought him public acclaim, but also created tensions and hostility among friends and colleagues. Owen Barfield, who was one of Lewis's closest friends, honestly

11. Oral History Interview with Stephen F. Olford, conducted by Lyle W. Dorsett, Oxford, England, July 26, 1985, for the Marion E. Wade Center, Wheaton College, pp. 6-7. Lewis said that his intellectual approach was the result of the *limitations* of his own gifts and valued the more emotional or "pneumatic" appeals he had seen work so well. He thought a pair of evangelists would be ideal, one to make an intellectual case for Christianity and the other to then appeal directly to the heart. "Modern Man and His Categories of Thought," in *Present Concerns,* ed. Walter Hooper (Harcourt Brace Jovanovich, 1986), p. 66.

admits that Lewis's zeal for the conversion of unbelievers bothered, even embarrassed him at times.[12] He could appreciate Lewis's faith as a private matter, but found it difficult to accept his determination to take it public with the aim of converting others.

Barfield was not alone. The amount of ridicule and scorn it fostered among his non-Christian colleagues was especially virulent. His theological books and his standing as a Christian apologist that made him much loved also spawned a great amount of ill-feeling. According to his student and friend Harry Blamires, Lewis was acutely sensitive to the fact. He recalls that Lewis once told him with great feeling, "You don't know how I'm hated."[13]

One of the reasons for this hatred is that Lewis's use of his training as a scholar in the work of Christian apologetics was viewed by many of his colleagues as a form of prostitution. In an attempt to explain to Walter Hooper the reason for Lewis's unpopularity among so many dons in Oxford, J. R. R. Tolkien observed: "In Oxford, you are forgiven for writing only two kinds of books. You may write books on your own subject whatever that is, literature, or science, or history. And you may write detective stories because all dons at some time get the flu, and they have to have something to read in bed. But what you are *not* forgiven is writing popular works, such as Jack did on theology, and *especially* if they win international success as his did."[14]

Lewis's work on a popular level, which appealed to vast audiences outside the university, defied academic protocol. It was felt by some to be a misuse of his scholarship and academic status for less than worthy ends. "In the eyes of some," said Blamires, "he was using a

12. Oral History Interview, conducted by Lyle W. Dorsett, Kent, England, November 19, 1983, for the Marion E. Wade Center, p. 9.

13. Harry Blamires, "Against the Stream: C. S. Lewis and the Literary Scene," *Journal of the Irish Christian Study Centre* 1 (1983): 16. A. N. Wilson wrote that the *Oxford History of English Literature,* published in 1954, "established Lewis as a giant among pygmies of the Oxford English Faculty, which made their failure to promote him to a professorship all the more surprising." *C. S. Lewis: A Biography* (W. W. Norton, 1990), pp. 244-45.

14. Quoted in a letter from Walter Hooper to Christopher W. Mitchell, February 8, 1998. Lewis himself noted that having written imaginative books was used against a writer if he then wrote theology or literary criticism. *English Literature in the Sixteenth Century, Excluding Drama* (Oxford University Press, 1973), p. 185.

donnish knowledge to mesmerize the innocent masses with dialectical conjuring tricks."[15] Moreover, he chose to express his faith in the vernacular rather than in the language of the scholar. Although he did so in order that he might make the faith accessible to all, this was viewed by many in the university as a thing not proper to his profession. Besides, it was thought that a Professor of English Literature should teach literature, not theology. It appears that Lewis's growing fame as an amateur theologian contributed to his being twice passed over for appointments to much coveted Chairs in English Literature at his university despite his scholarly claim to the appointments. Some certainly objected to his Christianity in itself, but apparently also suspected, along with perhaps even some sympathetic colleagues, that his commitment to the salvation of human souls would not allow him the time to fulfill the duties and responsibilities the position would require.[16]

Lewis was himself, however, clearly uncomfortable with the publicity his success brought. As early as 1941 he was already feeling the sting of hostility and the crush of popularity. Responding to a point made by Dom Bede Griffith in a letter in October of that year concerning his growing public persona, he acknowledged the growing tension within himself: "As for retiring into 'private life', while feeling *very* strongly the evil of publicity, I don't see how one can. God is my witness I don't *look* for engagements."[17]

A particularly burdensome outcome of this growing popularity was the ever increasing amount of correspondence he felt obliged to answer. One of the reasons Lewis chose to terminate the radio broadcast talks was that he could not face the increase in the number of letters that would certainly be generated if he didn't.[18] Already he was spending countless hours responding to the correspondence he was

15. Blamires, "Against the Stream," p. 17.

16. Walter Hooper, *C. S. Lewis: A Companion and Guide* (HarperCollins, 1996), p. 65.

17. *Letters of C. S. Lewis,* p. 369. Lewis was "a rare case of the don who is forced into the limelight by the demands of his own conscience," noted Wain. "I believe he would never have bothered to court the mass public at all had he not seen it as his duty to defend the Christian faith . . . against the hostility or indifference that surrounded it." "A Great Clerke," p. 69.

18. Sayer, *Jack,* p. 170.

receiving. When describing, in his autobiography *Surprised by Joy,* what he considered the perfect day, he made a special point of noting that an essential element of the happy life was that one "would have almost no mail and never dread the postman's knock."[19]

Yet the number of letters continued to increase as the years went on. There was a time, Lewis told a young correspondent in 1956, when he was apt to delay responding to letters. But that was when there were fewer of them. "[N]ow that I have such a lot to write," he said, "I've just got to do them all at once, first thing in the morning."[20]

For, unlike most in his position, Lewis felt a commitment to answer every letter that required a personal response. (His brother Warren, who in 1943 took on the role of secretary for his brother, routinely answered those letters not requiring Lewis's personal attention.) Although there were moments when he complained about his vast correspondence, he continued the practice to the end of his life. A letter dated March 26, 1963, just a few months before his death, provides a vivid picture of both his reluctance and commitment to letter writing. The letter is addressed to Hugh, a young man and the eldest of eight children who had been corresponding with Lewis since 1954: "Don't get any more girls to write to me," he wrote, "unless they really need any help I might be able to give. I have too many letters already."[21]

Lewis's Evangelistic Drive

Now here is the question: *Why* did Lewis willingly persist in the kind of evangelistic activity that created obvious tensions and hardships in his personal and professional life and that increased an already heavy workload?[22] He did not have to do so. He could easily have avoided

19. *Surprised by Joy* (Harcourt Brace & Company, 1984), p. 143. Walter Hooper states that if all the extant letters of Lewis were published today the entire collection would run to at least a half-dozen volumes.

20. *Letters to Children,* ed. Lyle W. Dorsett and Marjorie Lamp Mead (Touchstone Book, Simon & Schuster, 1995), p. 60.

21. Ibid., pp. 106f.

22. Lewis typically had a heavy tutorial load each term, frequently lectured, and was often occupied in the afternoons with domestic duties at home. See W. H. Lewis, "Memoir of C. S. Lewis," in *Letters to C. S. Lewis,* p. 37.

such problems and still lived an active and fruitful, enormously fruitful, Christian life. Admittedly, no single factor can account for his actions at any given moment, and certainly in the case of his commitment to evangelize several other factors could be suggested. For example, in one place he explained his passionate and forceful defense of the Christian faith in terms of Donne's maxim, " 'The heresies that men leave are hated most.' The things I assert most vigorously are those that I resisted long and accepted late."[23]

Yet I would propose that the primary driving force behind his evangelical impulse is best summed up by his conviction that "there are no *ordinary* people."[24] The line comes near the conclusion of his sermon "The Weight of Glory," which was preached in Oxford at the University Church of St. Mary the Virgin on June 8, 1941. Coming when it did, just about the time his ministry as a herald and defender of the Christian faith was taking off, the sermon may reasonably be assumed to express an early fundamental and guiding conviction. The sermon's beauty, force, and clarity seem to suggest this as well.

Lewis began the sermon with the startling assertion that "if we consider the unblushing promises of reward and the staggering nature of the rewards promised in the Gospels, it would seem that Our Lord finds our desire not too strong, but too weak. We are half-hearted creatures, fooling about with drink and sex and ambition when infinite joy is offered us. . . . We are far too easily pleased."[25]

He went on to argue that there is reason to believe that such infinite joy does in fact exist — indeed, our deepest longings suggest that it is so. At the moment, however, we all are on the wrong side of the door, leaving us with two possibilities: we can choose to be "left utterly and absolutely *outside* — repelled, exiled, estranged, finally and unspeakably ignored" or "we can be called in, welcomed, received, acknowledged." But to *get in* we must choose to follow Jesus Christ, who has opened the way and who invites us to follow him inside. We have a choice. "We walk every day," said Lewis, "on the razor edge between these two incredible possibilities." Consequently it is hardly

23. *Surprised by Joy,* p. 213.
24. "The Weight of Glory," in *The Weight of Glory and Other Addresses* (rev. and exp. ed., Macmillan, 1980), p. 19.
25. Ibid., pp. 3-4.

possible, he concluded in the crowning paragraph of the sermon, to think too often or too deeply about my neighbor's potential glory.

> The load, or weight, or burden of my neighbour's glory should be laid on my back, a load so heavy that only humility can carry it, and the backs of the proud will be broken. It is a serious thing to live in a society of possible gods and goddesses, to remember that the dullest and most uninteresting person you can talk to may one day be a creature which, if you saw it now, you would be strongly tempted to worship, or else a horror and a corruption such as you now meet, if at all, only in a nightmare. All day long we are, in some degree, helping each other to one or other of these destinations. It is in the light of these overwhelming possibilities, it is with the awe and the circumspection proper to them, that we should conduct all our dealings with one another, all friendships, all loves, all play, all politics. There are no *ordinary* people. You have never talked to a mere mortal. Nations, cultures, arts, civilisations — these are mortal. . . . But it is immortals whom we joke with, work with, marry, snub, and exploit — immortal horrors or everlasting splendours.[26]

A Burden of Glory

Why was Lewis willing to sacrifice his own pleasure and comfort, risk alienating friends and colleagues, and jeopardize possible career opportunities? Because of the enormous magnitude and weight of the possible eternal destinies of human beings: "[A] weight or burden of glory which our thoughts can hardly sustain."[27] According to Tolkien, Lewis knew the price of such popularity, he knew he would be hated, yet "he was driven to write popular works of theology because of his *conscience*."[28] Lewis was convinced that one of these two destinies was true for all humanity, and it compelled him to make the saving of souls the chief end of his earthly labors.[29] To put it most plainly, Lewis

26. Ibid., pp. 18-19.

27. Ibid., p. 13.

28. Quoted in a letter from Walter Hooper to Christopher W. Mitchell, February 8, 1998.

29. Patrick Ferry does a compelling job of linking this idea with Lewis's notion

preached what he believed, and practiced what he preached. As he said to Dom Bede Griffith in the same year he delivered this sermon, he did not know how anyone could do otherwise.

This is not to say that Lewis never struggled with his commitment (he would have been happy to have avoided the public notoriety), nor that he felt himself more saintly than other Christians who did not share his sense of urgency in the matter. Rather, he simply did not see that *he* had a choice. The possibilities were plainly too momentous to be ignored. But Lewis did not do the work of evangelism simply out of a feeling of duty either. For it was also a labor of love.

Dorothy Sayers gave memorable tribute to this side of Lewis's evangelistic person in a letter addressed to him in May 1943. Sayers had herself by this time become quite well known in Britain for her creative and effective presentation and defense of orthodox Christianity. And like Lewis she had attracted a growing number of correspondents who wrote to her about religious concerns. Speaking of one particular pesky atheist, she wrote to Lewis:

> Meanwhile, I am left with the Atheist on my hands. I do not want him. I have no use for him. I have no missionary zeal at all. God is behaving with His usual outrageous lack of scruple. . . . If he reads any of the books I have recommended, he will write me long and disorderly letters about them. It will go on for years. I cannot bear it. Two of the books are yours — I only hope they will rouse him to fury. Then I shall hand him over to you. You like souls. I don't.[30]

Sayers recognized that Lewis "liked souls" in a way she did not. In other words, viewed from the perspective of eternity, he worked

---

of "Mere Christianity": "A respectful regard for the glory of eternity finally must overcome factionalism for the benefit of those who are still outside the faith. . . . As long as there are people who are numbered among those who comprise the communion of saints, the *una sanctu* remains in need of a 'mere' Christianity — because, as C. S. Lewis reminds us, there is no such thing as a 'mere' mortal." "Mere Christianity Because There Are No Mere Mortals," in *Lightbearer in the Shadowlands,* pp. 170-71.

30. *The Letters of Dorothy L. Sayers,* vol. 2, chosen and edited by Barbara Reynolds and published by the Dorothy L. Sayers Society (Carole Green Publishing, 1997), p. 413. Sayers is having a bit of fun at her own expense here, for as Barbara Reynolds noted, Sayers continued the correspondence for at least another year and even permitted the atheist to call on her twice (p. 413, n. 8).

sacrificially and without complaint for what he understood to be the soul's ultimate good. This is not to say that he liked all the people with whom he associated. Lewis was, as are the rest of us, possessed of a particular social disposition. Although he was typically pleasant and courteous to all those with whom he had contact, he maintained that his temperament was such that he tended to shy away from the company of others beyond the close circle of friends he maintained in and near Oxford. Nonetheless, in spite of the fact that he did not always like people, he valued them enough to risk directing his unique talents and the majority of his energies toward their spiritual good.[31]

"But heaven forbid we should work in the spirit of prigs and Stoics," Lewis declared, writing of the ultimate purpose of love in his book *The Four Loves.* "While we hack and prune we know very well that what we are hacking and pruning is big with a splendour and vitality which our rational will could never of itself have supplied. To liberate that splendour, to let it become fully what it is trying to be, to have tall trees instead of scrubby tangles, and sweet apples instead of crabs, is part of our purpose."[32] In his fiction, theology, apologetics, and correspondence Lewis can be seen hacking and pruning with the hope that his efforts might be used to produce "everlasting splendours."

I am reminded of the vision expressed by the Apostle Paul to the Corinthians: "We do not lose heart. Even though our outer nature is wasting away, our inner nature is being renewed day by day. For this slight momentary affliction is preparing us for an eternal weight of glory beyond all measure, because we look not at what can be seen but at what cannot be seen; for what can be seen is temporary, but what cannot be seen is eternal" (2 Corinthians 4:16-18). Although Lewis never refers to this text in "The Weight of Glory," its spirit and truth pervade the work, and all his work.

Lewis longed above all else for the unseen things of which this

---

31. Once again, Patrick Terry's treatment of the connection between Lewis's concept of "Mere Christianity" and his idea of the "Weight of Glory" provides a compelling illustration of this point. One further qualification is in order. I do not mean to leave the impression that Lewis's ministry was limited to the written word. See, for example, his brother Warren's estimate of Lewis's sense of charity in "Memoirs of C. S. Lewis," in *Letters of C. S. Lewis,* pp. 41-42.

32. *The Four Loves* (Harcourt Brace & Company, 1988), pp. 117-18.

life offers only shadows, for that weight of glory which the Lord Christ won for the human race. And knowing the extraordinary nature of every human person, Lewis longed for and labored for their glory as well.

Teaching the Universal Truth:
C. S. Lewis among the Intellectuals

HARRY BLAMIRES

IT WAS IN the inaugural professorial lecture he delivered at the University of Cambridge in 1954 that C. S. Lewis presented himself boldly as a surviving relic of Old Western Man, a breed rapidly becoming as extinct as the dinosaur; and he suggested that, as such, he ought to fascinate his contemporaries as a rare specimen of how the civilized mind once worked and what it once contained.[1] It was of course a brilliant stroke on Lewis's part thus to parody the assumption of his enemies that he was out of date. But the claim was something more than an ironic countershaft. It had real substance for him.

I want to reflect on the validity of the image of the lonely embattled leftover in relation to the two sides of Lewis's output: his literary output and his theological output. I accept that the division is clumsy and inadequate. One of Lewis's greatest works, *The Screwtape Letters,* is at once a little masterpiece of imaginative literature and a telling moral and theological tract. Indeed, Lewis once made clear to me that he saw himself as being about the same task in writing the Narnia books as he had been about in writing *Mere Christianity.* But Lewis the writer plainly has a standing in both literary and theological circles; and any sense of his being the odd man out no doubt had reference to both.

---

1. *"De Descriptione Temporum,"* in *They Asked for a Paper* (Geoffrey Bles, 1962), pp. 9-25. Lewis's declaration of his position comes in the last three pages, after an explanation of "the greatest of all divisions," what he calls the "un-christening" of Western culture.

In the literary world secular propaganda would naturally try to persuade us that the works of Lewis and other writers of his circle are museum pieces. In Lewis's later years and after his death it became fashionable in literary journals and critical books either to ignore him, and Charles Williams too, as literary figures, or to give them grudging recognition as freaks. The Christianity they represented might have its interest for a closed circle of reactionaries, but in terms of twentieth-century literary history in general it was something of an oddity and a throwback. As fashionable criticism saw it, the mainstream of twentieth-century literature flowed on its way, reflecting the values and concerns of a post-Christian society.

Twenty years ago that was the assumption you would have encountered had you been bold enough to raise the names of Lewis and Williams in some quite influential academic circles. It was a totally false assumption, but it was the kind of thing Lewis's antennae accurately registered when he burlesqued himself as a dinosaur.

If the image of C. S. Lewis as the last surviving dinosaur does not fit his historical standing as an imaginative writer, what about his theological standing as a Christian apologist? There is no doubt that he suffered from *odium theologicum* to a painful degree. He was acutely sensitive to the fact that his theological books made him much hated as well as much loved. "You don't know how I'm hated," he once said to me with great feeling.

The Student Who Read *Pilgrim's Regress*

Perhaps I should say a word at this point about my own connection with C. S. Lewis. I went up to Oxford in 1935 and, by an odd coincidence, I had read *The Pilgrim's Regress* soon after it came out in 1933. I reread it carefully, pencil in hand, when I learned that C. S. Lewis was to be my tutor.

You must remember that this book was coolly received and sold few copies. I did not find any fellow-student who was aware of it. I do not recall how soon or in what way I made it clear to Lewis that I had read it and enjoyed it; but naturally I did not waste this opportunity to get in with my tutor, and the point was made. I mention this because it is possible that I was soon marked in his mind as "The student who had actually read *The Pilgrim's Regress.*" Be that as it may, we got on well together and Lewis was always ready to chat when the business of the tutorial was over.

It was some years after my student days were over that I came back into Lewis's orbit as a young writer. He helped me generously over my first books to be published, and from time to time I went to spend a night at Magdalen College for dinner, an evening's conversation, and breakfast with him. When my trilogy of theological novels — *The Devil's Hunting Grounde, Cold War in Hell,* and *Blessing Unbounded* — came out in 1954 and 1955, Lewis read them and wrote to me encouragingly about each in turn.[2] So his letters at that time tended to be about my books. But of course sometimes something was said that threw light on his own, and, in this connection, one memory is worth recalling.

I should explain that my trilogy is a sequence of journeys on the Dantean pattern through regions of the afterlife, though not exactly Purgatory, Hell, and Heaven. The narrator is guided by his guardian angel. To spice the books and to suggest the element of judgment on the human soul, I gave my angel the idiom of the bureaucrat and the pedant — a mixture of the two, I suppose.

Lewis questioned me about this. He thought it very funny, but he also seemed a little apprehensive lest I was not taking angelhood seriously enough. He told me that when he wrote *Screwtape* his first idea had been to combine letters between the two devils trying to ensnare the human soul, with corresponding letters between two angels looking after the young man on the other side.

But then he hesitated to enter the angelic mind, as though it might be too presumptuous. Now this — put in the friendliest possible way — certainly carried a probing point to cause me grave reflection. It appeared that I had rushed in among the angels where Lewis had feared to tread.

The Oxford Attitude and Lewis's Logic

But my purpose here is to say something about the Oxford attitude to Lewis the theologian, which no doubt helped to give him his sense

---

2. Published by Longmans, Green and Company.

of standing against the stream. In *The Inklings* Humphrey Carpenter has said some interesting things about it.[3] Oxford dons objected to Lewis, not for becoming a Christian, but for advertising the fact. His way of putting intellectual and moral pressure on people in print for the purpose of converting them was an offense against academic etiquette. Unspoken rules of academic decorum required one to be decently secretive about religious convictions.

Lewis had no degree in theology and was therefore, in the eyes of some, trespassing into other people's rightful territory, an amateur taking on the experts. Professional academic theologians could not be expected to enjoy having their thunder stolen. Lewis appealed to a vast audience, over the heads, as it were, of the university establishment and in defiance of academic protocol. In the eyes of some, he was using a donnish know-how to mesmerize the innocent masses with dialectical conjuring tricks.

As Christians we know that Lewis was right to do what he did. The message of the gospel is unmistakable in this respect. The disciples were ordered to preach the gospel throughout the world, and there was no mention of their need to graduate in theology first. By comparison with what Lewis had to tell his generation the academic protocol of even the most exalted university was trivial and petty.

Nonetheless the offense was an irritating one for the Oxford academic mind. It was all very well to use the machinery of rigorous logic in playful exercise. It was good fun to manufacture syllogisms in the privacy of the tutorial room to sharpen and discipline the mind. And it was high sport to bring the artillery of logic into play in a spirit of semi-mockery in public debate in the Union on such propositions as: "This House believes that a woman's place is in the home." In these circumstances dialectical battle could be sportively joined and a thumping good time had by all.

But here was a man, Lewis, who took the machinery of logic and soberly, devastatingly, proved that Naturalism was the implicit creed of half his academic colleagues and (worse) that it was nonsense. He told dons and workers alike that they were miserable sinners and that Almighty God was calling upon them to confess themselves such, to

---

3. *The Inklings: C. S. Lewis, J. R. R. Tolkien, Charles Williams, and Their Friends* (Houghton Mifflin, 1979), pp. 207-8.

cut the cackle and get down on their knees, for everything else they were involved in, even academic work, was trivial by comparison.

That was one of the most unpalatable home truths of all. They'd got their priorities wrong. Wasn't Lewis as good as telling most of them that they had no sense of proportion, no awareness of what mattered supremely in life, being obsessed with the peripheral and the ephemeral? Wasn't he insisting that if they were not moving into the Christian way, they were lost in the mists of error, the unwitting agents of the evil one?

The man had a perfect right to believe this secretly and share his strange notions with his friends in decent privacy. But he had no right to enter the public arena and use the verbal and dialectical equipment of the Oxford scholar and philosopher to press such a message upon others. The take-it-or-leave-it attitude was vulgar. The either/or dichotomy was a lapse from good taste.

In the field of religious argument into which Lewis had entered, the polite method was to express every opinion tentatively, to begin every crucial sentence with expressions like "It could be argued that," "A case might be made that," or "It is possible to hold that." And instead of indulging in such civilized exchanges of unruffled urbanity, here was a man who brandished the tool of learning like a battle-ax, and who brought his weapon crashing down to cleave the sheep from the goats in the name of God himself.

An Irish, Not English Mind

The intensity and coherence of Lewis's Christian understanding of life and thought provided one of the most formidable instances of Christian synthesis in our country; and it thrust Lewis into collision with the Oxford establishment. No doubt the collision could be identified as a collision between the Christian mind and the secular mind.

But perhaps there would be justification for seeing it in some respects as a collision between the Irish mind and the English mind. I take up this matter for speculation because a notion has run in my head for some years that the English are allergic to Christianity, while the Irish readily get hooked on it. There is in Ireland a frank, open religiousness not evident in England. To say that Irish Christians take their religion more seriously than English Christians would be misleading. Some of them, after all, take it more humorously. But no one who has read the literature of the Irish can be insensitive to the way Christianity seems to soak more pervasively into both their seriousness and their humor.

Irish autobiographies abound in records of childhoods dominated by religious practices and religious talk. This often applies to the works of those who have rebelled against the faith as well as of those who have continued in it. It is the same in fiction. There often seems to be a more deeply ingrained awareness of Christianity in novels by Irish unbelievers than there is in novels by English believers. Christianity seems to "take" with the Irish, to get into their bloodstream so that, healthily or pervertedly, gravely or comically, it surfaces in their life and thought. If literature is our guide, it seems that with the Irish Christianity "takes" in such a way that they cannot even shake it off (mentally) when they cease to believe in it.

Are the English, by comparison, Christianity-proof? I ask because the spectacle of unbelievers who seem unable to get Christianity out of their systems is an Irish spectacle, whereas the spectacle of supposed believers, especially theologians, who seem incapable of getting Christianity into their systems is plainly an English spectacle. This, after all, was what Lewis was up against as an apologist.

There are certain aspects of Lewis's work that seem to me to mark him as an Irishman, yet when I try to define them, somehow the concept "Irishness" tends to get lost. For instance, I would point to his mental sharpness, his devastating logic, his pictorial and illustrative abundance, his taste for myth and fantasy, his irony, his humor, his fluency, his rhetoric, his pugnacity, and his symbolism. I would add to these that most central and significant quality of all: the theological clarity and inclusiveness, the all-embracing wholeness of theological articulation that subsumes all experience and all thought within its grasp; the appetite for comprehensiveness and universality.

Obviously writers of various nations could be cited who share many of these qualities; but somehow it is the list that comes to my mind when I try to analyze the recipe behind the overall savor of Lewis's work as an apologist that offended the nostrils of the English establishment and still offends them.

Lewis's rich dialectical combativeness and his taste for inflating the particular to the status of the universal go against the grain of the respectable English preference for niggling at particulars in isolation, for not leaping to conclusions, for avoiding what may lead to head-on intellectual conflict, for discouraging the whipping out of polemical swords, the unfurling of unambiguous credal banners. The English "establishment" prefer blunting sharp edges in controversy and greasing the works of social and intellectual interchange with the oil of noncommitment.

Lewis and Joyce

An Irish writer vastly different from Lewis, and one approved by the establishment that so scorned Lewis, James Joyce has many of the qualities by which I tend to define Lewis's Irishness: mental sharpness, logic, imaginative abundance, humor, rhetoric, and so on.

Interesting comparisons might be detected in the kind of symbolism used by the two writers. Lewis's talking trees in Narnia somehow remind me of the arboreal wedding in the "Cyclops" episode of Joyce's *Ulysses,* and the headlong pursuit in *The Last Battle* reminds me of the chase in Joyce's "Circe" episode. The taste for allusive correspondences and fused layers of meaning is common.

But I have been more interested in the dominant refusal of both writers to see the particular, the prosaic, the apparently trivial except within the context of what is universally significant. For both of them the ordinary person is embryonically heroic, his slightest acts or decisions potentially earth-shaking. Both, in their vastly different idioms and with totally different motives, involve the ephemeral, the pedestrian, and the diurnal with the epic and the cosmic, with archetypes that pattern all our ways.

The universality and comprehensiveness of literary significance cultivated by Joyce and Lewis is vastly different in motivation. The upgrading of the individual to the universal serves in the one case a decisively artistic purpose and in the other case a deeply moral purpose too. When Joyce's advertising agent, Leopold Bloom, strides about the streets of Dublin with a cake of soap clenched in his left hand and a rolled-up newspaper brandished in his right hand, Joyce makes clear that he is equipped with the shield and sword of the epic hero. For soap, the chemical product of modern manufacturing is a sure hygienic defense against all the ills threatening a materialistic civilization, and the newspaper is the weapon with which modern man fights his battles.

The symbolism and the parallels are, in T. S. Eliot's words, "a way of controlling, ordering, of giving a shape and substance to the immense panorama of futility and anarchy which is contemporary history." But of course, to give literary shape and significance to what is futile and anarchic, though of some satisfaction to the aesthetic observer, is not necessarily of much inspiration to the man who would seek to replace futility by purposefulness and anarchy by order in life itself.

It may carry an implicit judgment on modern life, and therefore convey an oblique though vague recommendation to do something about it. In Joyce this is tenuous at best, whereas Lewis never forgets that there is something to be done, and people can do it.

Bloom against Reepicheep

Thus the universality and comprehensiveness of significance cultivated by Lewis is something more than a literary matter. When, in *The Voyage of the "Dawn Treader,"* he upgrades his mouse Reepicheep to the status of the battling hero, he is about something more than Joyce was about in turning Bloom's soap and newspaper into Homeric shield and sword.

In both cases we are meant to smile at the ironic piquancy of the inflation; the plebeian ad-cadger Bloom becomes the epic hero Odysseus; the frail little mouse Reepicheep becomes the swashbuckling warrior. But in Reepicheep's case we are meant also to warm with admiration for courage, and indeed to ask ourselves whether we, in spite of our amusement, could emulate the dauntlessness of this little creature whom we would never have associated with valor.

You see both Joyce and Lewis turn the tables on the reader's initial laughter at the incongruity of humble ad-man or feeble mouse being heroic. But Joyce turns the tables only in the sense that the reader revises his view of the relative status of the anciently heroic and the

currently pedestrian. Lewis turns the tables *qua* moralist. And that gets
to you. Thus Lewis's purpose and technique in inflating the particular
to the level of the universal goes to the root of the fact that he aroused
fervent enthusiasm in some readers and violent antagonism in others;
also to the root of the fact that this enthusiasm and antagonism were
not so much literary and aesthetic as moral and philosophical.

In this respect the issue is precisely Lewis's reading of the human
situation in such terms that the apparently trivial is framed within the
context of what is universally significant. All that man is about from
day to day is embryonically heroic, potentially earth-shaking. The
character of his apologetic and of his fiction alike is determined by
this fact.

For instance, in *The Screwtape Letters,* the powers of Hell and
Heaven bear down on the question whether Wormwood's human
patient is going to overcome his irritation at the way his mother lifts
her eyebrow, or the question whether he will take a country walk
down to an old mill for tea. One day the young man reads a book for
pleasure, instead of for vanity or show, and takes a walk on his own
because he enjoys it, and the senior devil comes down on the junior
devil like a ton of bricks. Two solid but commonplace pleasures have
been disinterestedly enjoyed — without any intrusion of conceit or
self-congratulation — and the diabolical progress to date is all undone.
There is anger in Hell and a hint of joy in Heaven.

The understanding of life in terms such as these plainly overturns
any scale of values based on familiar secular criteria. There is nothing
gimmicky about it. Nor is it simply a device for restoring the status
of myth to pedestrian twentieth-century life — which was what Joyce
was about when he made the smiles and banter of Dublin barmaids
and the sentimental ballads of Dublin ne'er-do-wells lure his hero
into the grip of idle sentiment, and paralleled it with the way Homer's
Sirens tried to charm Odysseus from his duty long ago.

For Lewis was about something more than the task of upgrading
modern man to heroic stature for the purpose of shrouding him in
literary pathos and ironic dignity. Lewis was about the serious business
of putting human souls in the way of salvation. It was, of course, an
imaginary soul that was under assault in the fictional *Screwtape Letters.*
But there was an oblique assault too, a hidden assault, directed — not
by His Abysmal Sublimity from his miserific hideout — but from his

great Enemy's Headquarters, and directed at the soul of the reader himself. For it is not just in fiction that supernatural realities bear down upon the soul of modern man.

Lewis found that he was not safe from them when lifting his eyes from his book in the evening quiet of his study in Magdalen, when riding on a number two bus to Headington, or when being given a lift on a trip to Whipsnade Zoo. As we know from *Surprised by Joy,* there was a divine Chess player at work, watching his every moment of unwariness, and pushing him relentlessly into a corner.[4]

Our Lord's Either/Or

The sense of proportion, the scale of priorities, that the defeated victim of such divine machinations will cherish is not going to be accessible, let alone acceptable, to those who cannot take with deep seriousness the impress of the supernatural upon natural life. Lewis's attitudes, over the various areas of thought and behavior that his wisdom illuminated, so starkly forced into the open our Lord's Either/Or — "He who is not with me is against me" — that the reader is consciously left at a junction.

Cozier theologians leave you at a comfortable resting place. They leave you with a sense that you have temporarily got somewhere, can pause for a breather while you ponder such loose ends as they conveniently leave hanging around you. And there is no great urgency in this pondering, for you have a long way to go before there will be any need for grave concern about whether your route is the right one.

Lewis, on the other hand, leaves you at a sign-posted junction where there can be no possibility of lingering. He prods you in the back so uncomfortably that you have no alternative but to choose your road — if "choose" is the appropriate word when one sign reads "Heaven" and the other reads "Hell."

Lewis's books are *active* books. They work on you. They will not let you be. To that extent they bear the marks of their ultimate Creator. Lewis is a writer who insists on being agreed with or disagreed with. Unless you enter fully into complicity with him against all the lurking

4. *Surprised by Joy* (Harcourt, Brace, and World, 1955), pp. 224-25, 228, and 237.

agents of moral evil and intellectual error that ambush modern man — ambush you in the society that seemed so harmless, so neutral, until he analyzed its hidden operations for you and traced its illusory deceptions back to the Father of all lies — unless you enter fully into complicity with Lewis in this respect, then you are going to have to reject him utterly, or find evasive terms with which to render his method suspect and his message innocuous. You are going to have to find a way to disarm him by patronization (rather dated, I'm afraid, isn't it?) or jump out of the way of his agile weaponry.

In this connection I recall one of the earliest conversations I had with Lewis at the end of a tutorial when I was a young student. The news had just come through that G. K. Chesterton had died (this was 1936). I said how much I had delighted in his work, and Lewis became warmly enthusiastic in his praise. His indebtedness to Chesterton was evident. Like Chesterton, he sensed the larger struggle between Christianity and paganism or secularism implicit in the minor intellectual conflicts of daily life, as he sensed the struggle between angel and devil behind every man's daily moral vacillations.

Chesterton had cultivated a ready knack of imprinting a hint of cosmic conflict between the powers of darkness and the powers of light upon human endeavors, whether they were heroic confrontations on the battlefield or humdrum encounters on a London bus. Chesterton lived mentally in a world lit by tokens of divine order and under threat from the negations of human (and diabolical) rebellion. Lewis inhabited the same world.

A Touchstone of the Christian Mind

This is precisely what cuts a chasm between one reader and another. It could be argued that whether or not a reader responds sympathetically to Lewis's work is a touchstone by which you can measure whether at root he thinks christianly or is infected by secularist criteria. For the Christian mind sees human life and human history held in the hands of God, and there is nothing in daily life and thought, however supposedly trivial, that can be dismissed as being outside the scope of that scrutiny which separates obedience from disobedience, good from evil.

A writer like James Joyce may have focused the telescopic lens of literature on pedestrian minutiae and daily trivia for dramatic and emotive effect. Lewis did it because the close-up on what you and I or anybody else is about from moment to moment reveals nothing less than the fulfilling or negating of God's purposes for us.

A Thoroughly Converted Man:
C. S. Lewis in the Public Square

BRUCE L. EDWARDS

All our merely natural activities will be accepted if they are offered to God, even the humblest, and all of them, even the noblest, will be sinful if they are not.

C. S. Lewis, "Learning in War-Time"

READERS OF C. S. LEWIS'S writing often find themselves reflecting upon an elusive quality they detect in all his works, a feature they grope to label and to explain to amiable agnostics by such terms as wholeness or symmetry, guilelessness or unpretentiousness, winsomeness or personality. They testify that the effect of reading his work is the sensation of entering into a new order of experience or level of insight, whatever the genre — and yet an effect achieved without apparent contrivance or arduous effort on either the writer's or the reader's part.

His work has a winsomeness that draws the reader into a journey with a companion or into a conversation with a gracious host who by turns instructs, delights, and challenges, and always intrigues. His consummate rhetorical skill, intellectual boldness, perspicacious grasp of time and culture, prodigious memory, bracing wit and humor, these are all present in equal doses in every genre of prose and poetry he attempted.

This is the Lewis who created Narnia, Malacandra, Glome, and

27

Belbury, who defended the credibility of the New Testament miracles, articulated the essence of mere Christianity, saw the world from the demons' point of view, and took us on a tour of Hell. But this is also the "other Lewis," the scholar, the writer of learned treatises on medieval and Renaissance literature and the vagaries of literary history, theory, and practice.

By "scholarship" I refer to the academic vocation of marshaling evidence to prove hypotheses or theses and then sharing (for testing and development) the discoveries with peers in the forums of the discipline. Such inquiry assumes the effective use of those tools, verbal or instrumental, available to the scholar; is shaped by the perspectives and values he or she brings (consciously and unconsciously) to the task; and is judged by the cogency of its argument and its impact on both the practitioners of the discipline and the wider commerce of ideas in the culture at large.

By these standards, Lewis is a towering scholarly figure in the world of twentieth-century letters, particularly in the world of literary criticism and history. Between 1931 and 1964 (his last work, *The Discarded Image,* was published after he died), he published an astonishing number of scholarly works, countless articles, and more than five major, seminal works of influence and provocation in literary studies — beginning with the early book that was arguably his magnum opus, *The Allegory of Love,* published in 1936, whose sweeping and meticulous account of the social, cultural, literary, and linguistic milieu of Chaucer's and Spenser's Europe remains today a work of impeccable grace and continuing explanatory power.

The others, all estimable scholarly accomplishments, include his *A Preface to "Paradise Lost"* (1942), which nearly single-handedly rehabilitated Milton's reputation in an era in which his epic poem was either undervalued or valued for the wrong reasons; his massive *English History in the Sixteenth Century, Excluding Drama* (1954), the third volume in the Oxford History of English Literature, which offered with lucidity and grace breathtaking characterizations of and provocative generalizations about scores of texts, authors, and movements, all of which he had read and mastered; *An Experiment in Criticism* (1961); and his last work, *The Discarded Image* (1964), a stunning exposition of the medieval and Renaissance worldview.

He was equally adept at shorter, succinct, and well-aimed rebuttals of critical judgments of works he felt capriciously deprived readers of pleasure and enlightenment, as such collections as *Rehabilitations* (1939), *They Asked for a Paper* (1962), *Studies in Medieval and Renaissance Literature* (1966), and *Selected Literary Essays* (1969) well exemplify.

A Profound Integration

Two men well acquainted with Lewis's life and work, one who knew him intimately all of his adult life, the other immersed in the gritty details of his texts and biography for more than four decades, can help articulate this elusive quality readers find in Lewis, whichever books they read. Owen Barfield, his longtime friend and lifetime intellectual combatant, once declared that "Somehow what Lewis thought about everything was secretly present in what he said about anything." Likewise, Walter Hooper, his principal bibliographer, has referred to him as the "most thoroughly converted man I have ever known."

What might we call this pervasive quality? I would put it this way: in Lewis we find a profound integration: an imagination married to reason and transformed by the revelation of the person of Christ. Lewis's Christian witness is not a "value-added" aspect of his scholarly work. It is not ladled on artificially like thick gravy on cake, nor is it an isolatable "component" of his work. It is something integral to every text he crafted. This thoroughly converted man offered the academic and the Christian world a scholarship that incarnates the ancient faith, and does so in the most disarming yet natural ways.

Between "the Christian World of C. S. Lewis" and "the Scholarly World of C. S. Lewis," there is no final distinction. He had discovered that revealed truth is central to fruitful scholarly inquiry, and as a Christian scholar he wrote all his works as a confident but unassuming man who, in Archimedean terms, has found a place to stand, a man who is ready, albeit with all due deference to his readers' own aspirations and circumstances, to move the world closer to the truth.

For Lewis knew that what is true can never be essentially or only the product of private contemplation, and certainly can never be relegated to the realm of the merely personal, as a taste or opinion. "Under Pontius Pilate he suffered . . . and on the third day he rose again": even the heart of the gospel, the death and Resurrection of Jesus Christ, is a public, historical event, and the reports of it must be believed or doubted on rational, historical grounds. Truth is derived as conviction specifically from participation in the public square, in the dynamism of a public world where men and women meet and share, debate, and apprehend the truth.

Lewis could not conscientiously conduct his scholarly work on a different basis from that of his fiction or his apologetics. Truth is one, and his preparation, conviction, and determination equipped him to speak authoritatively and faithfully whether he was writing literary history, commenting on trends in British education, or championing the virtues of a pagan poet. The epigraph to this essay well exemplifies his personal view of the scholarly vocation and its role in the discipleship of a believer. Drawn from "Learning in War Time," a sermon he preached in October 1939 in the dark, earliest days of World War II, these remarks address the question, "With the world falling down about me, why should I even think about engaging further in an education or any scholarly pursuit?"

In effect, Lewis's answer is an extended meditation on St. Paul's exhortation to the Corinthians, "Whether ye eat or drink, or what-soever ye do, do all to the glory of God" (1 Corinthians 10:31). Whatever one has been gifted to do, even if it is to skulk about old libraries and illuminate the forgotten worldviews of Anglo-Saxons and their kin, can bring glory to God — if offered to God and done with proper humility and full-hearted effort. For God is the Author of the world's story, and in it there are no irrelevant facts, minor characters, or unresolved plot lines. The Anglo-Saxons are part of his story, and worth studying for that reason.

The war, he pointed out, only made obvious the constant condition of human life. Culture is always subordinated to "something infinitely more important than itself." The Christian has always to answer the particular question "How can you be so frivolous and selfish as to think about anything but the salvation of human souls?"[1] The answer Lewis gave is that some people are called to scholarly work as their way of helping themselves and others "advance to the

---

1. "Learning in War-Time," in *The Weight of Glory,* ed. Walter Hooper (Macmillan, 1965), p. 47.

vision of God," and they are humbly to leave alone the question of the relevance of their work.

The life of the Christian scholar can and should unfold as an act of discipleship to Christ. The scholar cannot "compromise between the claims of God and the claims of culture, or politics, or anything else. God's claim is infinite and inexorable," yet his claim "does not exclude any of the ordinary human activities," and among these activities scholarship may take its proper place. "An appetite for these things exists in the human mind, and God makes no appetite in vain," and Christians "are members of one body, but differentiated members, each with his own vocation."

Christian scholars have two other reasons for pursuing their work, which Lewis called the "indirect values" of scholarship. First, scholarly work is needed to protect others — those who have other gifts and callings — from the errors of scholars. "To be ignorant and simple now — not to be able to meet the enemies on their own ground — would be to throw down our weapons, and to betray our uneducated brethren who have, under God, no defense but us against the intellectual attacks of the heathen," he said. "Good philosophy must exist, if for no other reason, because bad philosophy needs to be answered."[2]

Second, they need to know the past — not just know about the past. They need to know it not because it "has any magic about it" (Lewis was not a reactionary),

> but because we cannot study the future, and yet need something to set against the present, to remind us that the basic assumptions have been quite different in different periods and that much which seems certain to the uneducated is merely temporary fashion. A man who has lived in many places is not likely to be deceived by the local errors of his native village; the scholar has lived in many times, and is therefore in some degree immune from the great cataract of nonsense that pours from the press and the microphone of his own age.[3]

2. Ibid., p. 50.

3. Ibid., pp. 50-51. See also Lewis's comments on the way the "literary" and "unliterary" man read books in *An Experiment in Criticism* (Cambridge University Press/Canto Books, 1992), esp. pp. 27-39 and 130-41.

Order, Opposition, and History

As one may discern from these remarks, Lewis found nothing in his
Christian commitment that limited or inhibited his work as a literary
scholar. In them he articulated three characteristic features of his
scholarship. First, he expressed his allegiance to a transcendent order
that shapes our witness to the discovery of truth: God alone, an infinite
yet personal God, will himself define what reality is, and what constitutes its accurate portrayal. Second, he recognized the necessity of
addressing opposing propositions, to engage the contemporary paradigms not only with a firm grasp of the field but with an informed
grasp of the issues and the current vocabulary of the debate.

And, third, he championed the necessity of having a wide historical perspective, whose panoptic vistas save one from local errors. We
cannot afford to be "chronological snobs," as his friend Barfield put
it, who use the calendar to decide whether something is valid or true.
And it needs to be said as well that this perspective is available only
to those willing to leave the safe confines of their own period and its
thought patterns and make the effort to see with the eyes of others in
other ages.

Lewis the well-prepared *public* scholar was thus equipped by Lewis
the well-converted *Christian* scholar to face, and face down, the skeptical movements in literary study — and not only in literary study but
in the wider intellectual world. His public approach to scholarship,
assisted by his vast historical perspective, his intimate acquaintance
with the thought and vocabulary of the present, and his knowledge
of eternity, allowed him to speak about the faith and about the issues
of his day as a scholar who "knew his stuff." Who can forget the great
lines in his 1959 address on "Modern Theology and Biblical Criticism," wherein, defending the historicity of the New Testament accounts of Christ's miracles, he critiqued the typical skeptical biblical
scholar

> who has spent his youth and manhood in the minute study of NT
> texts and of other people's studies of them, whose literary experiences
> of those texts lacks any standard of comparison such as can only grow
> from a wide and deep and genial experience of literature in general.
> [Such a man] is, I should think, very likely to miss the obvious things

about them. If he tells me that something in a gospel is legend or romance, I want to know how many legends and romances he has read, how well his palate is trained in detecting them by the flavour; not how many years he has spent on that gospel.[4]

This is the declaration of a man whose learning gives him both the courage and the freedom to speak directly, unapologetically, and authoritatively on a topic outside his professional discipline. As a lover of the truth, he could have no qualms about letting the integration of heart and mind, soul and spirit, work and faith manifest itself on this, and indeed any occasion.

How far we are from sharing Lewis's notions or motives — or St. Paul's for that matter — is revealed in the punch line of a recent political joke. It captures well the challenge, and perhaps ambivalence, most of us face of living out our Christian convictions in the public square: Have you heard about the politician whose morals were so private he did not even impose them on himself?

Yes, that embodies it: in *fin de siècle* Western culture, convictions of any sort, especially convictions about religion, may be held but not openly practiced, alluded to but not nakedly declared; for any hint of actual commitment to real principle implies some sort of standard, and where standards are, expectations — and measuring rods — follow. The private world of "values" must not impinge upon the public world of "facts." It is better to keep one's faith meek and mild and private than to publicly champion one's belief and risk the inevitable charges of hypocrisy, bias, or (the worst charge in today's academic culture) imposing one's values on others.

The Impotent West

In *The Abolition of Man* Lewis predicted the coming impotence of the West to speak meaningfully of universal truths. He saw the chief casualty of the destruction of universal, objective, historically and culturally transcendent truth as the death of the public realm, that

4. "Modern Theology and Biblical Criticism," in *Christian Reflections,* ed. Walter Hooper (Eerdmans, 1967), p. 154.

realm in which men and women of goodwill though different beliefs might indeed investigate, probe, and debate the foundations of what was once called the good life or "civilization."

He would not be surprised that Christianity is increasingly relegated to the sphere of the private and the personal, a sphere that seems to shrink daily. He knew that when religion is privatized, any public, meaningful expression of faith, especially in one's vocational setting, is by default prohibited as bad taste, presumption, or arrogance, if not actually endangering the peace of the public square.

Many North Americans, Christians and non-Christians alike, are made quite nervous by any sort of publicly held faith, by any open alignment of scholarship with conviction and purpose. Pulled, pushed, and pressured on all sides, we learn too well that we are expected to hide, disguise, or confine our faith to more and more private settings. And even then the church itself is expected to tone down its voice and remain placid and tranquil in the midst of attack and disenfranchisement. In short, we become accustomed to accommodation, to seeking a place where our faith may rest or fit comfortably — where it will neither disturb others nor risk embarrassing questions being asked of ourselves.

What Lewis thought most indispensable about the Western tradition was its creation of such a public ground for the training of the young and the managing of responsible cultural change in a society of equals. Through its invention and promotion of alphabetic literacy, the West had given birth to a public world where texts served as the place people of different views could wrestle with and resolve matters of mutual importance. The public world, a world available, present, and negotiable by human beings, is assumed in the literature Lewis loved best.

Therefore, for him the most helpful critic is one who promotes just such a "public text" — who examines "the poem the author really wrote" instead of one he effectively made up himself. To do otherwise is the obverse of true reading, which for Lewis always lifts up the reader "out of his provincialism by making him 'the spectator' if not of all, yet of much, 'time and existence'" and brings him "into a more public world."

Such a public world allows the text to speak out of its own time and culture to the present and to give a perspective on one's own age as a "period" that needs to be corrected by the past. In Lewis's estimation, the critic should not be too intrusive in directing the reader, and should as much as possible allow the text to work its own magic on a modern reader.

Still, especially in reading ancient works, one may need "a tolerable map" of the work's original milieu for the text to work its magic at all, and thus a critic may need to guide a reader outside the work "in order that we may presently come inside it again, better equipped." As he wrote in *A Preface to "Paradise Lost"* (with prophetic relevance to postmodern criticism, in which "the text" has no "determinate meaning"), to judge anything you must "know *what* it is. . . . [A]s long as you think the corkscrew was meant for opening tins or the cathedral for entertaining tourists you can say nothing to the purpose about them."5

This indeed is one of Lewis's greatest strengths as a literary critic: his ability to help the reader to know what a text is and to confront it "in public," that is, better understand the conceptual framework and commitments that undergird it or, indeed, the entire period in which it was written. In reading his criticism, one thus encounters an uncommon enthusiasm for reading itself and a contagious delight in inhabiting the fictional landscapes of other authors — for the experience of the "other," and not for a mirror of our own tastes and predilections.

The Christian Scholar

Two particular features of Lewis's public work need further attention. First, his example teaches us that Christian scholarship must be both relevant *and* anachronistic. It must speak to the issues of our time in ways that respect and engage the language and thought of the culture, and yet be anchored in a transcendent order that permits the conventional wisdom or radical new program to be critiqued and gauged by their fidelity to it.

5. *A Preface to "Paradise Lost"* (Oxford University Press/Galaxy Book, 1961), p. 1. The second chapter, "Is Criticism Possible?", criticizes the critical theory of T. S. Eliot, which Lewis thought removed the poem from the public realm.

In an essay delivered at the invitation of a religious society in Oxford and published first in *Rehabilitations* (1939), Lewis considered whether there can be a distinctively *Christian* form of literature and whether Christian piety is required for literary artistry.[6] To answer "yes" to either question would isolate the Christian experience from the public world, would in other words privatize the creation and reading of literature in such a way as to make of it a special kind of genre that only an elite few, educated in a particular secret code, could rightly understand. That answer would confirm the world's suspicions that Christianity was at best a nonhistorical and at worst an ahistorical faith, cultic and nothing more, and of no relevance to the "real world."

What Lewis did in fact answer was that "Christian literature can exist only in the same sense in which Christian cookery might exist," its success depending on "the same qualities of structure, suspense, variety, diction, and the like which secure success in secular literature." However, a Christian (writer or reader) will approach and value the work differently than a secular reader. This "difference of temper" depends not upon the Christian's unique use of language or private spiritual experience, but upon his reception of the revelation that God himself is, so to speak, the ultimate critic.

Modern criticism prizes above all creativity, spontaneity, and freedom, and pejoratively juxtaposes them with the derivative, conventional, and rule-keeping. To write sonnets greater than Shakespeare's would not win a poet renown from modern critics or academics, and to try to reflect the moral order would prove less acceptable to them than intentionally "transgressive" or "playful" postmodern works that set out to shatter any idea of order. For the Christian, the Incarnation teaches us not to despise but to honor imitation, order, and reflected glory — or rather, to find within them true creativity, spontaneity, and freedom. The New Testament, Lewis wryly pointed out, is not interested in genius but in goodness, and the central concern of the Christian critic is not originality or novelty but that which is eternal. One

> with the mind of the New Testament would not, and indeed could not, fall into the language which most critics now adopt. In the New Testament the art of life itself is an art of imitation: can we, believing

6. "Christianity and Literature," republished in *Christian Reflections,* pp. 1-11.

this, believe that literature, which must derive from real life, is to aim at being "creative," "original," and "spontaneous." . . . Our whole destiny seems to lie in the opposite direction, in being as little as possible ourselves, in acquiring a fragrance that is not our own but borrowed, in becoming clean mirrors filled with the image of a face that is not ours.

Thus, for the Christian, "the basis of all critical theory [is] the maxim that an author should never conceive of himself as bringing into existence beauty or wisdom which did not exist before, but simply and solely as trying to embody in terms of his own art some reflection of eternal Beauty and Wisdom." The Christian writer will see his own experiences and feelings only as "the medium through which, or the position from which, something universally profitable appeared to him."

Such a writer or reader will never "make literature a self-existent thing to be valued for its own sake," but will see this view as an idolatry that must give way to the recognition that "the salvation of a single soul is more important than the production or preservation of all the epics and tragedies in the world." Thus, Lewis was able to demonstrate the coherence of Christian critical practice by reference to the principles of poetics available to all, while also distinguishing its mode of operation and humane effects from modern criticism that uncritically exalts the conventional wisdom and the radical new program and values "art" more than the good of individual men and women.

An important irony should be noted. Against the assumptions of the modern critic, the poet who submits to the conventions and rules is often the most truly original. It is "the greatest error," Lewis noted in *A Preface to "Paradise Lost,"* to assume that imposition of a form like the sonnet or the epic on the poet's "internal matter" (by which he meant the poet's thoughts, feelings, and experiences) kept him from being original. "The matter inside the poet *wants* the Form: in submitting to the Form it becomes really original, the origin of great work." In contrast,

the attempt to be oneself often brings out only the more conscious and superficial parts of a man's mind; working to produce a given kind of poem which will present a given theme as justly, delightfully, and lucidly as possible, he is more likely to bring out all that was really in him, and much of what he himself had no suspicion.[7]

The second feature of Lewis's scholarship needing attention is that it teaches us to be wary of using other minds prosthetically, in lieu of our own development as scholars and our own personal encounter with ideas and experience; we must not allow our present colleagues, or our ancient ones, for that matter, to deprive of us of the joy of wrestling with and coming to understand the Great Ideas. Lewis was a profound proponent of the primary experience of texts — and of ignoring the "stilts" of secondary sources and endless footnotes that draw us aside from the texts themselves. In a memorable phrase, Lewis noted that "we don't need the critics to enjoy Chaucer, but need Chaucer to enjoy the critics."[8]

Our own calling, in other words, is not to be servants of those worthy thinkers who have come before us, but to build upon their insights and to provide a bridge from them to our own period. Another way of saying this is that we must emulate the dedication and discipline of Lewis's scholarship, and not think that piety alone replaces or repairs one's lack of preparation in the field of study. To represent the mind of Christ in the public arenas of academic scholarship demands that we pay the cost of honest, perspicacious engagement with our subjects and those spokespersons who have center stage in our own times.

The Role of Civilization

We may see, then, that in his scholarship, as in his fiction and apologetics, Lewis vehemently denied that facts and values could rest on a personal epistemology, on an autistic world of personal religious conviction or ethnogender-specific truths, on commitments and knowledge inaccessible to the outsider. The role of civilization in general, and Christian civilization in particular, is to help make public persons

---

7. *A Preface to "Paradise Lost,"* p. 3.
8. *An Experiment in Criticism,* pp. 123-24.

of private persons. It is to lift men and women out of their provinciality and narrowness into a more expansive realm of transchronological persons, ideas, and ideals, into an arena in which character is built, affirmed, and celebrated as a public good that promotes the health of the society at large.

Lewis abhorred the inner ring and the occultic creed and the coercive ideologies they create — the making private of the public and the imposing of the private upon the public while disguising it as a salutary corrective. Thus, one of the greatest things Lewis has to teach us as we enter a new millennium is this credo: To know the truth I need not be part of an elite or intelligentsia, I need only be human. The foundation of all free thought and inquiry is the unique person-hood and humanity of man: I am human, therefore I may know the truth.

Access to truth, to the real world, is the birthright of all. To resist this dilemma, we must follow Lewis in refusing to divorce our per-sonal faith from our public behavior. We must live the faith in and out of our cloisters. We must not retreat from the public square.

Thus Lewis would see our century's new challenges to biblical orthodoxy as an opportunity for Christians to serve as both "speci-mens" of a true engagement with the issues of the day and as antidotes to the intellectual and moral chaos that these times provide. His life and career exemplify the virtue of rejecting the split between the sacred and the secular, the public and the private that haunts and inhibits so many of us, of obedience to St. Paul's admonition to "be not conformed to this age, but be ye transformed by the renewing of your mind" (Romans 12:1-2). He pointed his listeners and his readers, his students and his friends, to a stance that integrates faith and life, vocation and confession.

Life before Pilate

If I were to describe Lewis in a single phrase, it would be this: C. S. Lewis was a man who lived his life before Pilate. That is to say, he carried out his daily tasks as teacher, citizen, and believer as one who knew he was always standing before a skeptical inquisitor, an inquisitor who too often hides from the truth and masks his fear of knowing the truth behind indifference, agnosticism, or the pretense of being on the search — as Pilate did in the presence of Our Lord (John 18:37). He knew that faced with a troublesome truth, the skeptical inquisitor will if he can send it out to be killed.

This being the case, Lewis is a model for Christians in any walk of life who must integrate and apply their faith in their fields. He tried neither to hide nor foreground his faith in his work, but simply to speak from Christian conviction in the ways appropriate to his discipline. Whatever else he was, he was a man of faith willing to pay the price for his public confession that Jesus Christ was God in the flesh. Deplored and despised by colleagues jealous of his scholarly prowess and shamed or angered by his open association with popular literature and "mere" Christianity, Lewis was denied a professorship at Oxford at the peak of his scholarly accomplishment.

As Christopher Derrick, Lewis's pupil and friend, has judiciously observed, Lewis was a man willing to "challenge the entrenched priesthood of the intelligentsia." And he did so from within the cloister, at the cost of being thought a traitor by many of his peers. One finds in him an uncommonly valiant and articulate skeptic of the modern era, one forthrightly opposed to the "chronological snobbery" of our times that assumes truth is a function of the calendar and that the latest word is the truest one.

Those who read through the entire Lewis corpus receive an education in history, philology, sociology, philosophy, and theology so extensive and exhilarating that most others seem thin and frivolous in comparison. While Lewis caricatured himself as a dinosaur, the last of the Old Western Men,[9] many today see him as a forerunner of what may still be the triumph of men and women of biblical faith in an age that derides the pursuit of truth and righteousness.

In the year of his centennial, we can offer him no better tribute than to try to walk in the steps of one who earnestly followed the steps of his Lord.

---

9. *"De Descriptione Temporum,"* in *They Asked for a Paper* (Bles, 1962), pp. 9-25.

The Work of a Witness

Saving Sinners and Reconciling Churches: An Ecumenical Meditation on *Mere Christianity*

MICHAEL H. MACDONALD AND MARK P. SHEA

WE WILL SAY IT up front. One of us is Presbyterian and the other a Roman Catholic, and we both love C. S. Lewis. Several years ago at a C. S. Lewis Institute banquet at which I (Michael) was host, Walter Hooper, who knew of my love for the book *Mere Christianity,* joked that if Michael Macdonald were able to take only three books to a desert island, he would take three copies of *Mere Christianity*.

The book has been enormously influential, not only in our own lives and thought, but in the lives of countless others. In this reflection on Lewis's apologetics, we intend to meditate on some of the ways in which his defense of Christianity (articulated over fifty years ago) can still speak to a generation about to embark on the Third Millennium.

The Genesis of *Mere Christianity*

Many evangelists in the modern world begin, thought Lewis, in the wrong place. They begin with the offer of grace and forgiveness in Christ. However, this call to repentance and forgiveness necessarily presupposes that their hearers have a consciousness of sin, the very thing to which countless English people in his day and even more Americans in our day are oblivious. Thus he believed that it was, as

43

it were, essential to address the problem, "If Jesus is the Answer, what is the Question?" He saw that the Question was threefold:

1. Is there such a thing as a Law of Human Nature imposed on us by God and recognized by our conscience which demands we do justice, love mercy, tell the truth, not kill, and so forth? (Yes)
2. Does any of us obey this Law? (No)
3. *Now* what do we do?

It was, Lewis believed, essential to make clear this Bad News of sin before one could really begin to talk about the Good News of Christ, and to make it clear to people not able easily or naturally to hear it.

Thus, rather than making an immediate appeal to "come to Jesus" or explaining Christ's ministry or introducing the church, Lewis begins right where we live. "Everyone has heard people quarreling," he wrote, and every quarrel is an appeal to some objective standard of justice ("Be fair!" "You promised!" "How would you like it if somebody did that to you?"). Few people reply "To hell with your standard."[1] Instead they try to show that they did not really violate justice because they have some special exception to its rules. They accept that there is an eternal standard to which they may appeal.

Lewis rejected the idea (so popular today) that this standard, which he called the Law of Human Nature, was simply an invention of Western culture or only "what's true for me" or something relative that varied with the person and the situation. He insisted instead that it was distinct, objective, and common to all human cultures at all times, though each culture misperceived and suppressed some aspects. "Think of a country where people were admired for running away in battle, or where a man felt proud of double-crossing all the people who had been kindest to him," he wrote.

> You might just as well try to imagine a country where two and two made five. Men have differed as regards what people you ought to be unselfish to — whether it was only your own family, or your fellow countrymen, or everyone. But they have always agreed that

1. *Mere Christianity* (Macmillan, 1976), p. 17.

you ought not to put yourself first. Selfishness has never been admired. Men have differed as to whether you should have one wife
or four. But they have always agreed that you must not simply have
any woman you liked.[2]

Thus, the conclusion is that (1) there is an objective Reality behind right and wrong, and (2) we often don't obey this Reality and
do what is right. "These two facts," said Lewis, "are the foundation
of all clear thinking about ourselves and the universe we live in."[3]
They constitute the human predicament, the Question to which Jesus
is the Answer.

Lewis's Way Out

The existence of a Moral *Law,* Lewis argued, strongly implies the
existence of a Moral *Lawgiver.* What is behind the universe is probably
"more like a mind than it is like anything else we know."[4] In varying
degrees, this has been the conclusion of all the great civilizations of
the world, Roman, Greek, Egyptian, Hindu, Platonist, Stoic, and
Muslim. Theism, in one form or another, is clearly the view of the
majority of the human race.

The modern Western European materialist is in a very small
minority. In defense of his rejection of the near consensus of humanity
through history, the materialist often objects that the existence of evil
proves there is no God. Lewis turned this objection on its head and
replied that the very recognition of real evil depends on the reality
that there is an objective Law being violated and therefore an objective
Lawgiver behind the universe. As an analysis of human life, atheism
is "too simple."[5] Evil, Lewis asserted, is therefore ultimately a corruption of our will, a turning away from this real God. Of this both
humans and fallen angels are guilty.

This mysterious, unseen Lawgiver revealed himself gradually to
the human race, as he prepared the answer to the Question of the

2. Ibid., p. 19.
3. Ibid., p. 21.
4. Ibid., p. 32.
5. Ibid., p. 46.

human predicament. He gave us not only conscience but a hint, those "good dreams . . . queer stories scattered all through the heathen religions about a god who dies and comes to life again and, by his death, has somehow given new life to men." And he prepared a people, the Jews, to carry the message, "and spent several centuries hammering into their heads the sort of God He was."[6]

And finally, in the fullness of time, God presents us with the great shock, the announcement of which is at the heart of Lewis's apologetics:

> Among these Jews there suddenly turns up a man who goes about talking as if He was God. He claims to forgive sins. He says He has always existed. He says He is coming to judge the world at the end of time. Now let us get this clear. Among Pantheists, like the Indians, anyone might say that he was a part of God, or one with God: there would be nothing very odd about it. But this man, since He was a Jew, could not mean that kind of God. God, in their language, meant the Being outside the world Who had made it and was infinitely different from anything else. And when you have grasped that, you will see that what this man said was, quite simply, the most shocking thing that has ever been uttered by human lips.[7]

Lewis noted how not only Jesus' words but his actions all show him claiming to be God. He claims to forgive sins — any and all sins. Unless he really is God, his claim to forgive sins is preposterous and comic. What should we make of a person who announces that he forgives you for offending someone else? He can do so only if he really is the God whose laws are broken and whose love is wounded in every offense. And so Lewis concluded his argument for the deity of Christ with these powerful, memorable words:

> I am trying here to prevent anyone saying the really foolish thing that people often say about Him: "I'm ready to accept Jesus as a great moral teacher, but I don't accept his claim to be God." That is the one thing we must not say. A man who was merely a man and said

---

6. Ibid., p. 54. See also his comments in "Religion without Dogma?" in *God in the Dock,* ed. Walter Hooper (Eerdmans, 1970), pp. 129-46.

7. *Mere Christianity,* pp. 54-55.

the sort of things Jesus said would not be a great moral teacher. He would either be a lunatic — on the level of a man who says he is a poached egg — or else he would be the Devil of Hell.

Thus we must choose, Lewis declared.

Either this man was, and is, the Son of God: or else a madman or something worse. You can shut Him up for a fool, you can spit at Him and kill him as a demon; or you can fall at His feet and call him Lord and God. But let us not come with any patronizing nonsense about His being a great human teacher. He has not left that open to us. He did not intend to.[8]

Lewis and the Secular West

Thus Lewis's apologetic approach to the average secular man and woman in the West. But he had in *Mere Christianity* another message for us. We are living in a time when Western culture has become largely post-Christian and is characterized by a loss both of intellectual cohesiveness and of a moral center. Abandoning even an implicit adherence to Christian assumptions, it has turned instead to a resurgent neopaganism (expressed mainly in New Age movements) and committed skepticism and even nihilism (expressed mainly in "postmodernism"), for both of which the moral and doctrinal tradition of Christianity is the enemy. But perhaps providentially, we are also living in a time when many (but not all) of the barriers between the various Christian traditions are falling down.

Christians are recognizing as never before that the great fault lines in our culture are no longer "Catholic vs. Protestant," as was the case for centuries. The real fault line is now "Ethical Monotheism vs. Secular Relativism/Hedonism/Materialism." The need to combat this new religion makes unity among all Christians even more imperative. Thus, on the one side we find (in an alliance our great-grandfathers would have been stunned by) orthodox Catholics, orthodox Protestants, Orthodox, and even conservative Jews and Muslims against what Pope John Paul II has aptly described as the "culture of death":

8. Ibid., pp. 55-56.

the broad and cancerous popular notion that truth is whatever we think it is, that human life is valued by what it can produce by those who have the power to decide, and that the Imperial Autonomous Self is ultimately the true and only God worthy of our obedience.

Fifty years ago Lewis saw the need for such an alliance among Ethical Monotheists (and particularly among the followers of the incarnate God) and therefore aimed to make his apologetics a defense, not of Anglicanism vs. Papism or of Catholic vs. Evangelical, but of Christianity vs. Unbelief. Lewis stressed that the only unity we should seek is unity in the truth. Truth will prevail in the end. He called the division of the churches a "sin and a scandal" and recognized that unity is not really an option; it is an order. Now, fifty years later, Lewis's vision is beginning to bear fruit.

Recently, evangelical Protestants and Roman Catholics have been led through prayer, study, and discussion to common convictions about faith and mission, expressed in the statement *Evangelicals and Catholics Together (ECT)*, released in March of 1994 by fifteen prominent Roman Catholics and evangelical Protestants.

According to Charles Colson, one of the participants, *ECT* seeks to continue Lewis's legacy by focusing on mere Christianity so that adherents of both traditions can work together in the common task of evangelizing the nonbelieving world. Colson is very clear about Lewis's influence in this new ecumenism. Indeed, for many believers among both Protestant and Catholics — including Colson himself — it was Lewis's concise explanations of the Trinity and the Incarnation, the Fall and redemption, the Moral Law, and the disciplines of the Christian life that enabled them to understand, and to believe, the truth of Christianity.[9]

This new Lewisian ecumenism therefore rejects lowest-common-denominator liberal ecumenism, which seeks unity by disregarding important doctrinal differences. It holds rather that a genuine alliance allows, and even encourages, its participants to embrace the convictions of their distinctive traditions. "Hostility has come more from the borderline people . . . men not exactly obedient to any communion," Lewis noted of his own experience of interdenominational squabbles.

9. Charles Colson, "The Common Cultural Task: The Culture War from a Protestant Perspective," in *Evangelicals and Catholics Together* (Word, 1995), p. 34.

This I find curiously consoling. It is at her centre, where her truest children dwell, that each communion is really closest to every other in spirit, if not in doctrine. And this suggests at the centre of each there is something, or Someone, who against all divergences of belief, all differences of temperament, all memories of mutual persecution, speaks with the same voice.[10]

Therefore Lewis and we firmly believe that we can be resolved in the truths expressed in the great Apostles' Creed. In fact, this may well be our high calling, our mission, that which can give our civilization its greatest hope as we at last begin to challenge and learn from one another, always speaking the truth in love, building up, not tearing down, the whole body of Christ.

Rediscovering the Body

Seen in this light, the members of the various Christian communions can return again to St. Paul's theology of the Body and begin to discover anew the gifts and graces God has poured out on all the baptized. And this is already happening in a curious "grass-roots" way.

Evangelicals, who have tended to rely on the principle of *sola scriptura,* are increasingly exploring the excellent metaphysicians and moral philosophers produced by the Catholic tradition. Similarly, many lay Catholics are learning from evangelicals the value of intense Bible study and small group meetings. In addition, Catholics are edified to see how evangelicals energetically carry the Faith into the public square in evangelization and pro-life social action. Conversely, evangelicals are surprised to find themselves appreciating how Catholics are confirmed in relationship with Christ when they engage in the invocation of saints, make use of icons in prayer, or pursue other forms of prayer that evangelicals find difficult.

Catholics have much to learn from evangelicals who display a contagious and well-articulated enthusiasm for the gospel. Evangeli-

10. *Mere Christianity,* p. 9. By wide reading through history, Lewis noted, one would find that there really was a recognized and unified "mere Christianity," and not the diversity and contradiction many people assumed there was. "On the Reading of Old Books," in *God in the Dock,* pp. 203-4.

cals have much to learn from the sacramental/liturgical ways pioneered by so many Catholics, ways that have enormous power to mediate a living communion with God. Evangelicals are beginning to awaken to the role of tradition, to which they adhere without being fully conscious of doing so.

Similarly, many Lutherans (some say most) seriously hope for eventual reunion with Rome. The single major obstacle, which justified Luther in his own mind for the terrible act of tearing apart the visible fabric of the church of Christ, was the doctrine of justification by faith. Yet over ten years ago the Vatican and the German Lutheran bishops announced that they are no longer divided on that issue, that both churches agree in substance, though they use different terms.

Likewise, reconciliation and healing have taken place between Roman Catholics and Orthodox Christians. Official steps were begun on December 7, 1965, when Pope Paul VI and Athenagoras revoked the mutual excommunication decrees that had been blocking reunification efforts between the two churches for almost a thousand years. Subsequently, the work of unity between the Eastern Church and the Roman Catholic Church has been moving forward. Pope John Paul II has made reunion with the East one of the principal objectives of his pontificate.

All this is very much in the spirit of Lewis. For he clearly recognized that the distance between the various stripes of Christendom, even between the various types of Western religious traditions, were insignificant compared to the vast gulf between belief in a transcendent God of love and justice, and the materialist, hedonist, relativist ideologies that were germinating in his day and that are coming to fruition in our own.

He believed that the key for each Christian was to go to the heart of his own communion while simultaneously locking arms with other Christians to fight the real enemy of unbelief. Analogously, during World War II, the various Allies united to fight a common enemy. Yet the French remained French and the English remained English. Their common alliance did not submerge their unique gifts.

Many point today to a new war, a war for the soul of Western civilization, with an enemy as insidious as the enemy in World War II: the culture of death. This enemy does not do *public* violence with guns and bombs. Rather, it seeks to *privatize* (and hide) violence with abortion in clinics and euthanasia in hospital rooms.

It aims, in the classroom, to sell our children the idea that the core of the human condition is not the love of God and neighbor, but the struggle for power and the eternal war of race, class, and sex. It aims, via consumer culture, to indoctrinate each one of us into a deep faith in instant gratification, violence to attain that gratification, and a profound distrust of anything beyond our own appetites and feelings.

Such a culture can only cause the dissolution of the family, the destruction of childhood, and the decomposition of human society into millions of atomized individuals who regard each other as competitors, not brothers and sisters.

And, if Christians do not fight it, this ideology will dissolve and debunk our faith in conscience, the Moral Law, and the Moral Lawgiver and replace them with faith in appetite, feeling, and, ultimately, power. After this will surely come the deluge. For as Lewis warned in his prophetic little book, *The Abolition of Man:* "The impulse to scratch when I itch or to pull to pieces when I am inquisitive is immune from the solvent [of skeptical relativism] which is fatal to my justice, or honour, or care for posterity. When all that says 'it is good' has been debunked, what says 'I want' remains."[11]

A civilization that despairs of faith in the love of God can only fall back on faith in Power, for power cannot be debunked. Already in our century we have seen numerous examples of cultures that have done just this as they abandoned the Moral Law and the Moral Lawgiver. They have not believed in nothing, but in anything from the Power of Adolf Hitler to the Power of Joseph Stalin to the Power of Mao to the Power of Pol Pot.

All such cultures sooner or later discover that the state seizes the absolute sovereignty the Imperial Autonomous Self sinfully denies to God. The body count on the altar of Power is at least 100,000,000 as the century comes to close (with about 1.5 million being added by abortion each year in our country alone).

---

11. *The Abolition of Man* (Macmillan, 1978), pp. 77-78.

The Culture of Death

It is, then, this culture of death, the great and true nemesis in the culture war today (as in Lewis's day), that involves all who name the name of Christ in a conflict vastly greater than the relatively minor differences that divide the various Christian communions. The fundamental differences about truth and ultimate reality, the nature of God, the moral law, and the human condition which all Christians (and indeed all ethical monotheists) have with postmodern relativist culture made a return to Lewis's thought essential.

For today, even more than in his day, people have not only forgotten that Christ is the Answer, they have forgotten what the Question was. We also need to hear the Bad News of sin. But we need to do so only that we might hear the Good News, News Lewis can speak more powerfully than almost any writer in this century, News of such intense beauty that the evils of the world pale before it, News at the core of mere Christianity.

As Christians entering the Third Millennium, we do well then to emulate Lewis by fighting the good fight, not against each other, but "against the principalities, against the powers, against the spiritual hosts of wickedness in the heavenly places" (Ephesians 6:12). But even more, we do well to remember the enormity of the hope of Christ Lewis so beautifully proclaims.

For Lewis was always clear-headed enough to recognize that the battle is ultimately not for "civilization" or "culture" or any other such abstraction. It is for every human person. As he wrote in his sermon "The Weight of Glory":

> Nations, cultures, arts, civilization — these are mortal, and their life is to ours as the life of a gnat. But it is immortals whom we joke with, work with, marry, snub, and exploit — immortal horrors or everlasting splendours. . . . Next to the Blessed Sacrament itself, your neighbour is the holiest object presented to your senses. If he is your Christian neighbour, he is holy in almost the same way, for in him also Christ *vere latitat* — the glorifier and glorified, Glory Himself, is truly hidden.[12]

12. "The Weight of Glory," in *The Weight of Glory and Other Addresses* (Eerdmans, 1965), p. 15.

God of the Fathers:
C. S. Lewis and Eastern Christianity

KALLISTOS WARE

TO JUDGE FROM C. S. LEWIS'S autobiography *Surprised by Joy*, the church fathers seem to have played no part in his intellectual formation or in his conversion, although St. Augustine is mentioned twice in passing.[1]

Occasionally he appealed in general terms to the patristic tradition, as when he stated in his essay "Christian Apologetics" that "We are to defend Christianity itself — the faith preached by the Apostles, attested by the Martyrs, embodied in the Creeds, expounded by the Fathers," and in another essay referred to the Nicene Creed as a document "I wholly accept."[2] But in fact references to the fathers are very sparse in his writings, and when he did cite them it is usually the Latin fathers to whom he appealed, most notably Augustine.[3]

A Greek patristic work, the fifth-century writings of pseudo-Dionysius, is discussed at some length (five pages) in *The Discarded Image*,[4] but the reason for this is the cardinal importance of the Dionysian corpus for the medieval Latin West. In *Miracles* there are three

1. *Surprised by Joy* (Harcourt, Brace & World, 1955), pp. 7, 217.
2. "Christian Apologetics," in *God in the Dock* (Eerdmans, 1970), p. 90, and "Christianity and Literature," in *Christian Reflections* (Eerdmans, 1967), p. 5. In the latter he included the Athanasian Creed with the Nicene as documents he completely believed.
3. Augustine is discussed on pp. 64-66 of *The Allegory of Love* (Oxford University Press, 1958) and cited in *The Discarded Image: An Introduction to Medieval and Renaissance Literature* (Cambridge University Press, 1964) on pp. 49, 50, 107n., 121n., and 175.
4. *The Discarded Image*, pp. 70-75.

isolated references to patristic authors, but all appear on a single page and two are taken secondhand from modern Western writers.[5]

Lewis wrote an introduction to the English translation of St. Athanasius's *The Incarnation of the Word of God* not because he was especially interested in Athanasius, but because the translator, Sister Penelope, CSMV, was his personal friend. Less than a quarter of the introduction is devoted to Athanasius himself, the rest to a defense of reading old books rather than new. Indeed, when he lists the old books from which the "standard of plain, central Christianity" is to be derived, he mentions the Apostles Luke and Paul and four Western theologians: St. Augustine, Thomas Aquinas, and the Anglican theologians Richard Hooker and Joseph Butler.[6]

Some have tried to find in his stories ideas taken from the fathers, but the connections seem generally doubtful. It has been suggested that the "deep magic" of Narnia invoked by the White Witch in *The Lion, the Witch and the Wardrobe* is based on the "ransom" theory of the atonement found in St. Gregory of Nyssa.[7] But the parallels with Gregory are not in fact particularly close; Augustine is at least as probable a source, and Lewis may well have derived his knowledge of the "ransom" theory from books by modern writers.

All this leads me to agree with the conclusion reached by Lewis's friend and pupil Dom Bede Griffiths (to whom Lewis dedicated *Surprised by Joy*):

> It is remarkable also that Lewis showed very little interest in the Fathers of the Church. With his wide classical culture one would have expected him to be naturally attracted to the Greek and Latin Fathers, but apart from mention of St. Augustine's *Confessions* I don't remember his ever referring to one of the Fathers.[8]

With a few exceptions Lewis's theological sources are Western,

---

5. *Miracles: A Preliminary Study* (Macmillan, 1960), p. 76.

6. Reprinted under the title "On the Reading of Old Books," in *God in the Dock,* pp. 200-207; cf. Andrew Walker's "Under the Russian Cross," in *A Christian for All Christians,* ed. Andrew Walker and James Patrick (Regnery Gateway, 1992), pp. 63-67.

7. Walker, "Under the Russian Cross," p. 64.

8. Alan Bede Griffiths, "The Adventure of Faith," in *C. S. Lewis at the Breakfast Table,* ed. James Como (Collier Books, 1979), p. 21.

not Eastern; and they are medieval and modern rather than patristic. His mentors, apart from Plato, Augustine, and Boethius, are such writers as Dante, Hooker, Spenser, Milton, Samuel Johnson, George Macdonald, G. K. Chesterton, and — last but not least — Charles Williams. It is a mixed bag, Roman Catholic, Anglican, and Protestant, but there is no Eastern Christian in the list. As Andrew Walker rightly noted, "Lewis was a thoroughly Western man."[9]

A Patristic Theology

That, however, is not the whole story. Even though Lewis's writings contain little that is taken immediately from the Christian East, and his personal contacts with the Orthodox Church were not extensive, yet at the same time his thinking is often profoundly in harmony with the patristic and Orthodox standpoint. Starting from Western premises, he reached conclusions that an Eastern Christian can wholeheartedly endorse.

The fact that the similarities are not due to any direct influence makes them all the more impressive. For evidence of Lewis's implicit Orthodoxy, I shall appeal mainly to his imaginative rather than to his apologetic works, for it is primarily in the imaginative writings that his theological vision can be found expressed with the greatest depth and originality.

First of all, however, I cannot avoid mentioning a feature in Lewis's outlook that, at any rate in the eyes of an Orthodox Christian, appears as a shortcoming. In 1962, a year before his death, he wrote to Bede Griffiths, "I cannot take an interest in liturgiology." Commenting on this, Griffiths said that toward the end of his life, "Lewis was . . . to acquire a deep reverence for and understanding of the mystery of the Eucharist," but an appreciation "of the Church as a worshipping community and of cult as something 'sacred,' a reflection on earth of a heavenly reality, remained hidden from him."[10]

The Orthodox approach to the Christian faith, on the other hand, is fundamentally liturgical. Theology is above all else an articulation

9. Walker, "Under the Russian Cross," p. 63.
10. Griffiths, "The Adventure of Faith," p. 20.

of the church's self-awareness as a worshiping community, an ordered and coherent expression of the experience of "Heaven on earth" which is revealed in the Divine Liturgy. Here Lewis's theological approach, in its neglect of the liturgical dimension, does indeed set him apart from the Orthodox tradition.

This point of divergence, however, is more than counterbalanced by four significant points of convergence between Lewis and Orthodoxy.

In the first place, in common with the Orthodox tradition, Lewis was acutely conscious of the hiddenness of God, of the inexhaustible mystery of the Divine. It is true that much of his apologetic writing, with its seemingly overconfident appeal to reason and to universal moral law, suggests a theological stance that is affirmative rather than negative: in Andrew Walker's words, "his cast of mind . . . was clearly of a more *cataphatic* mould than the *apophatic* die of the Eastern church."[11]

But there is also an apophatic side to Lewis, which came to the fore particularly in his imaginative writing. Despite his appeal to reason, he accepted that human language and the concepts used in discursive argumentation can never adequately express the transcendent truth.

He realized that the rational discourse of philosophical theology can do no more than hint at the unsayable. Often, so he recognized, we come closest to the divine realm through the use of poetry, myth, and symbol; and that is why he himself expressed many of his deepest theological insights through the medium of imaginative writing and of fantasy.

Lewis's apophaticism comes out unmistakably in the book that he wrote at the end of his life, which constitutes in a sense his "last will and testament": *Letters to Malcolm: Chiefly on Prayer.* In our relationship with God, he insisted in this work, "we are approaching — well I won't say 'the Wholly Other,' for I suspect that is meaningless, but the Unimaginably and Insupportably Other. We ought to be — sometimes I hope one is — simultaneously aware of closest proximity and infinite distance."

The fact of this "infinite distance" means that every visual image, and still more every abstract concept, has to be negated: "Not thus,

11. Walker, "Under the Russian Cross," p. 64.

not thus, neither is this Thou." If our images should not be taken literally, far less should our theological abstractions. "All creatures, from the angel to the atom, are other than God; with an otherness to which there is no parallel: incommensurable. The very word 'to be' cannot be applied to Him and to them in exactly the same sense." Because of this incommensurability between God and creation, "He must constantly work as the iconoclast. Every idea of Him we form, He must in mercy shatter."[12]

All of this, and especially the last notion of God as the iconoclast, recalls St. Gregory of Nyssa's point of view in *The Life of Moses*. Every religious concept, if taken literally, becomes an "idol of God," said Gregory; when Moses is told in the Ten Commandments to destroy all graven images and idols (Exodus 20:4), the ordinance is to be given a symbolical interpretation.[13]

An Existential Understanding

Lewis's apophaticism led him to adopt an existential rather than a strictly rational understanding of religious belief. Despite his appeal to reason in his apologetic writings, in the last resort he agreed with the dictum of his friend Charles Williams that no one can possibly do more than *decide* what to believe. Belief, that is to say, consists not so much in being convinced by arguments as in making a choice; and, by the same token, if a person chooses *not* to believe, no amount of logical argument will force him into belief.

This is a recurrent theme in the Chronicles of Narnia. "How are we to know that you're a friend?" says Edmund to Ramandu's daughter in *The Voyage of the "Dawn Treader,"* and she replies, "You can't know. . . . You can only believe — or not."[14] Out of willful stupidity, Uncle Andrew in *The Magician's Nephew* convinces himself that Aslan's song is nothing but a series of roars, and even Aslan

12. *Letters to Malcolm: Chiefly on Prayer* (Harcourt Brace Jovanovich/Harvest Books, 1964), pp. 23, 34, 98-99, 109.

13. *The Life of Moses* ii.165, tr. Abraham J. Malherbe and Everett Ferguson, in *Gregory of Nyssa* (New York, 1978), p. 96.

14. *The Voyage of the "Dawn Treader"* (Macmillan, 1952), pp. 182-83.

himself cannot persuade the old man to think otherwise: "He has made himself unable to hear my voice."[15]

It is the same with the dwarfs in *The Last Battle*. When they pass through the door into Aslan's new country, all that they find is a dark and smelly stable; to them the flowers are dung, and the splendid feast that Aslan provides is nothing but hay, old turnips, and dirty water. They *cannot* see because they *will not* see. As Aslan remarks, "Their prison is only in their own minds, yet they are in that prison; and so afraid of being taken in that they cannot be taken out."[16]

Lewis's apophatic standpoint is particularly apparent in what is for me by far the most moving of all his books: the "myth retold" he entitled *Till We Have Faces*. This was Lewis's favorite among his imaginative writings, and it is mine too.

The elusive nature of religious belief is emphasized in the incident in which Orual cannot see Psyche's palace (except for a brief and tantalizing moment). "It's no use, Maia," says Psyche to Orual. "I see it and you don't. Who's to judge between us?"[17] The *leitmotif* of the whole work is the hiddenness of the Divine. That is exactly Orual's complaint: "Why does the god not show his face?" She pleads for a sign, and none is given:

> Then I did a thing which I think few have done. I spoke to the gods; myself, alone, in such words as came to me, not in a temple, without a sacrifice. I stretched myself face downward on the floor and called upon them with my whole heart. I took back every word I had said against them. I promised anything they might ask of me, if only they would send me a sign. They gave me none. . . . I was left utterly to myself.[18]

The gods set us riddles, Orual protests, but they give us no answers: "Why must holy places be dark places?"[19]

Yet *Till We Have Faces* does not conclude on this despairingly negative note. What the gods offer, as Orual discovers at the end of the story, is not a verbal answer expressed in logically articulated

15. *The Magician's Nephew* (Macmillan, 1955), p. 168.
16. *The Last Battle* (Macmillan, 1956), p. 150.
17. *Till We Have Faces* (Harcourt, Brace, 1985), p. 136.
18. Ibid., p. 159; cf. p. 168.
19. Ibid., p. 259.

sentences, but a personal encounter — not, it is true, a personal encounter in the form of an open vision, but an encounter nonetheless sufficiently direct to carry total conviction. "I ended my first book with the words *No answer*," says Orual. "I know now, Lord, why you utter no answer. Before your face questions die away."[20]

This calls to mind the *Gnostic Chapters* of the fourth-century desert father Evagrius of Pontus (which Lewis almost certainly had never read). Asked what is the nature of the "naked" intellect, Evagrius replied: "To this question there is at the present moment no answer, but at the end there will not even be a question."[21]

All of this indicates how close Lewis was to the apophatic approach of the Christian East. His Aslan is a profoundly apophatic lion. "But who is Aslan? Do you know him?" asks Eustace. Edmund can do no more than reply, "Well — he knows me."[22] As Lucy is told, first by Mr. Beaver and then by the Magician, Aslan is not a "safe" or "tame" lion.[23] He is never under the control of our human will or of our human logic; he remains always "the Unimaginably and Insupportably Other," who is yet uniquely close to us.

Lewis on the Trinity

The first point of convergence that we have been exploring — the apophatic dimension of Lewis's thought — concerns the basic approach and method to be employed in all theology, the spirit permeating religious inquiry as a whole. Turning now to three areas of Christian doctrine — the Incarnation and the Trinity; the sacramental character of creation; and the vocation of the human person — let us try to discover how far there is also a convergence here between Lewis's thought and the patristic standpoint of Orthodoxy.

When in the mid-1920s the young Derwas Chitty was a theological student at Cuddesdon, a theological college near Oxford, he was

20. Ibid., p. 319.
21. *Kephalaia gnostika* iii.70.
22. *The Voyage of the "Dawn Treader,"* p. 104.
23. *The Lion, the Witch and the Wardrobe* (Macmillan, 1950), p. 77; *The Voyage of the "Dawn Treader,"* p. 149.

asked by a visiting Russian layman what were the most important things that the English needed to learn from the Russian Orthodox. Without hesitation Derwas replied: "A revitalized belief in the dogmas of the Trinity and of the Incarnation." Initially the Russian was somewhat disappointed — he was hoping for something more "practical" — but he later agreed that Derwas was perfectly right.[24]

Seventy years later, most Orthodox would certainly endorse Fr. Chitty's order of priorities. At a time when large numbers of Christians find it impossible to believe any longer in Christ's godhead, and when all too many of them see the doctrine of the Trinity as an unnecessary complication, Orthodox Christianity insists on adopting a "maximalist" position: Christ is fully and completely divine and at the same time fully and completely human; and God is irreducibly both one and three.

What of Lewis? In a work such as *Mere Christianity* he was entirely uncompromising on both points. About Christ's Incarnation, he wrote: "He was and is God. God has landed on this enemy-occupied world in human form."[25] He devoted a major section to the doctrine of the Trinity, a section appropriately entitled "Beyond Personality." In particular he emphasized the trinitarian depth of Christian prayer: when we pray we are "caught up" and "actually drawn into" what Lewis calls "the whole threefold life of the three-personal Being."[26]

This is exactly the sort of language that a Christian in the Orthodox tradition would employ (although he or she might not choose the term "enemy-occupied," which reflects the wartime situation in which Lewis was writing). Indeed, the main reason why Lewis is so popular in Orthodox circles today is precisely his firm and clear defense of the two doctrines of the Incarnation and the Trinity.

Lewis's Christomonism

While, however, there can be no doubt about the centrality of these two doctrines in Lewis's apologetic works, how far is this also the case with his imaginative writings? Certainly these writings are strongly

24. *Eastern Churches Review* 6.1 (1974): 9.
25. *Mere Christianity* (Macmillan, 1976), p. 53.
26. Ibid., p. 139.

Christocentric, and this is true especially of the Narnia books. But how effectively is the doctrine of the Trinity woven into his tales of imagination and fantasy? Here I share the reservations of Dr. Paul Fiddes in his perceptive essay "C. S. Lewis the Myth-Maker."[27]

In *Out of the Silent Planet,* the first volume of his science fiction trilogy, Lewis spoke about Maleldil the Young, who "lives with the Old One,"[28] but the "Old One" himself remains a remote and shadowy figure, scarcely ever mentioned, while there is no reference to the Holy Spirit. The Spirit is in fact mentioned once in passing at the end of *Perelandra,* when it is said that, while in the land of Lur, Tor the King has learned "new things about Maleldil and about His Father and the Third One."[29] This is the sole trinitarian allusion at any point in *Perelandra;* nothing further is said about Maleldil's Father, while the designation of the Holy Spirit as "the Third One" remains curiously imprecise.

How far, I wonder, did Lewis in fact have a developed doctrine of the Spirit? The conclusion of Dr. Fiddes seems inescapable: "During the course of these science fiction novels, the only dimension of divinity actually encountered is Maleldil, who is 'the one God'; this is a virtual modalism, and hints at nothing of participation in the three-fold life of God."[30]

The same problem arises in the Narnia books. Their perspective is christomonist rather than trinitarian; attention is concentrated almost exclusively on the Christ-figure of Aslan. Admittedly, he is styled "the son of the great Emperor-beyond-the-sea,"[31] but this "great Emperor" plays no part in the stories; and once more we cannot avoid asking, "Where is the Holy Spirit?"

It might be answered that we are not to expect too much from what are fairy tales and works of fantasy, not exhaustive manuals of Christian doctrine. But since the Christian "myth" is specifically and distinctively trinitarian, we have a right to expect this threefoldness to

---

27. Paul S. Fiddes, "C. S. Lewis the Myth-Maker," in *A Christian for All Christians,* pp. 132-55.

28. *Out of the Silent Planet* (London, 1938), p. 77.

29. *Perelandra* (London, 1943), p. 241.

30. Fiddes, "C. S. Lewis the Myth-Maker," pp. 142-43.

31. *The Lion, the Witch and the Wardrobe,* p. 77.

be reflected more dynamically in the "myths retold" that Lewis offers to his readers old and young.

There is, however, one definitely trinitarian moment in the Narnia books, and this comes during the incident of the "unwelcome Fellow Traveler" in *The Horse and His Boy*. Shasta questions the mysterious companion, invisible in the mist, who walks beside him through the mountain pass:

> "Who are you?" asked Shasta. "Myself," said the Voice, very deep and low so that the earth shook: and again "Myself," loud and clear and gay: and then the third time "Myself," whispered so softly you could hardly hear it, and yet it seemed to come from all round you as if the leaves rustled with it.[32]

Lewis explains in one of his letters that these three replies are intended to "suggest the Trinity."[33] What a pity that there are not more "suggestions" of this kind elsewhere in his imaginative writings!

Before we leave the subject of the Incarnation, let us note an omission that Orthodox Christians find disappointing. Alike in his apologetic and in his imaginative writings, Lewis ignored the Blessed Virgin Mary. He accepted the doctrine of Christ's Virgin Birth, just as he accepted all the other doctrines affirmed in the Creed, but otherwise he has little to say about the Mother of God.

In *Mere Christianity* he stated in self-defense that he did not wish to venture into such "highly controversial regions,"[34] but limited himself to what all mainstream Christians hold in common. Christians of the Orthodox (as well as the Roman) tradition, however, for whom devotion to the Holy Virgin is not an optional extra but an integral part of their daily religious life, are bound to regret his silence at this point.

The World a Very Thin Place

What of the theology of creation? How far is there a correspondence here between Lewis and the Orthodox Church? In one of her

---

32. *The Horse and His Boy* (Macmillan, 1954), p. 147.
33. *Letters of C. S. Lewis,* ed. W. H. Lewis (Harcourt, Brace and World, 1966), p. 486.
34. *Mere Christianity,* p. 7.

addresses the Anglican writer Evelyn Underhill recalled the words of a Scottish gardener who, on meeting someone newly returned from the island of Iona, remarked, "Ah! Iona is a very thin place." When asked what he meant, he answered, "There's very little between Iona and the Lord."[35]

This is the Orthodox approach to the realm of nature. Creation is seen as a sacrament of the divine presence; the cosmos is a vast and all-embracing Burning Bush, permeated with the fire of God's eternal glory. Such is the master theme that dominates the writings of St. Maximus the Confessor: within each created thing the Creator Logos has implanted an indwelling *logos* or uncreated inner principle, which holds that thing in being and makes it distinctively what it is, while at the same time drawing it upward toward God. St. Gregory Palamas looked on the universe from the same point of view: for those with eyes of faith to see, all created things are alive with the dynamic presence of God's uncreated energies.

Lewis thought in a closely similar fashion. For him also the world is "a very thin place." One of the themes in the Narnia stories is the manner in which the "other world" — the world of Narnia — impinges upon the world of our daily experience. In unexpected ways, unnoticed by the great majority of those who pass by, a familiar object or place may serve as a means of access into the other world. Perhaps, as in *The Lion, the Witch and the Wardrobe,* the entrance will be through a wardrobe in a disused room at the top of an old house, or else as in *Prince Caspian* through a cave high on a mountain, "one of the magical places of the world, one of the chinks or chasms between that world and this."[36]

Like Charles Williams, Lewis was fascinated by the interaction of other worlds with our own, by the interpenetration between the natural and the supranatural, between earth and Heaven, and equally between earth and Hell. Lewis saw nature in strongly sacramental terms. He was attracted to the teaching of seventeenth-century Cambridge platonist Henry More, who — in a manner that recalls Maxi-

35. *Collected Papers of Evelyn Underhill,* ed. Lucy Menzies (Longmans, Green and Company, 1946), p. 196.
36. *Prince Caspian* (Macmillan, 1951), p. 190.

mus the Confessor — looked on reason, *logos,* as a vital and energizing principle active throughout the universe.

Lewis recalled with a certain nostalgia the period in the distant past when trees and plants, springs and rivers, were all regarded as living beings. Underlying this seemingly outdated mythology, so Lewis believed, there is to be discerned an all-important truth: that nature is not dead matter but living energy, vibrant with the immanence of God. As he put it in his preface to D. E. Harding's *The Hierarchy of Heaven and Earth:*

> The process whereby man has come to know the universe is from one point of view extremely complicated; from another it is alarmingly simple. We observe a single one-way progression. At the outset the universe appears packed with will, intelligence, life and positive qualities; every tree is a nymph and every planet a god. Man himself is akin to the gods. The advance of knowledge gradually empties this rich and genial universe: first of its gods, then of its colours, smells, sounds and tastes, finally of solidity itself.[37]

In his imaginative writing Lewis sought to reverse this "one-way progression" and to reaffirm the personal, sacramental, "elf-patterned" character of the world. The talking animals and talking trees of Narnia are much more than an idle conceit to amuse young children; they have a theological purpose, and this purpose brings Lewis close to the Orthodox tradition. Although he never referred to Maximus or Palamas, he was one with them in his vision of the created order.

Why So Much Violence?

How far, finally, does Lewis's "image of man" concur with the Orthodox understanding of what it is to be a human person?[38] Let me begin by expressing a personal reservation about his books. I am conscious that many Orthodox and many admirers of Lewis will not

37. "The Empty Universe," in *Present Concerns,* ed. Walter Hooper (Harcourt, Brace, 1987), p. 81.

38. I take the phrase "image of man" from the excellent book of William Luther White, *The Image of Man in C. S. Lewis* (Abingdon Press, 1970). After a quarter of a century, this remains one of the best studies written about Lewis.

agree with me, but I have always felt uneasy about the amount of physical violence that occurs in his imaginative works. Now Lewis was indeed no pacifist, and he offered a carefully reasoned defense of his position.[39] On this matter he was of course in agreement with the mainstream Christian tradition, both Western and Eastern, at any rate since the conversion of the emperor Constantine in the early fourth century. That, however, is not my present difficulty. What troubles me is the undue emphasis (as I see it) that is placed in his writings upon brute force, upon ferocious fighting and bloodshed.

The element of violence is particularly evident in the savage denouement of *That Hideous Strength,* which among all Lewis's imaginative writings is the one that appeals to me the least. But even in *Perelandra* — which, along with *Till We Have Faces,* is my favorite book in the Lewis canon — it seems to me a blemish that the subtle three-cornered discussion between the Lady, Ransom, and Weston the "Un-Man" eventually degenerates into a crude physical combat between Ransom and Weston: into punching, biting, and mangling.

Doubtless Lewis would reply that evil has to be combated on a physical as well as an intellectual level; but is that a sufficient answer? It is true that the "heroic" era envisaged in the Narnia books makes it inevitable that there should be a large amount of fighting. But is there not something little short of sadistic about the way in which Aslan claws open Aravis's back in *The Horse and His Boy?*

"Never Did He Utter One Word Twice"

Let us turn to more positive themes. In Lewis's depiction of the human vocation there are at least four points that appeal particularly to an Orthodox reader. First, he underlined the *uniqueness* of each human person: as the eldil says in *Perelandra* at the beginning of the Great Dance, "Never did He make two things the same; never did He utter one word twice."[40]

In his book *George MacDonald: An Anthology,* Lewis quoted several

---

39. "Why I Am Not a Pacifist," in *Timeless at Heart,* ed. Walter Hooper (Collins/Fount Paperbacks, 1987), pp. 48-65.

40. *Perelandra,* p. 246.

passages from MacDonald's *Unspoken Sermons,* in which this uniqueness is linked in particular with the giving of the new name written
on the "white stone" (Revelation 2:17):

> The name is one "which no man knoweth saving he that receiveth
> it." Not only then has each man his individual relation to God, but
> each man has his peculiar relation to God. He is to God a peculiar
> being, made after his own fashion, and that of no one else. Hence
> he can worship God as no man else can worship Him. For each, God
> has a different response. With every man He has a secret — the secret
> of a new name.[41]

This is reflected in the ending to his famous sermon "The Weight
of Glory" and perhaps also in Aslan's refusal to tell anyone another's
story.

Second, and closely linked with the first point, there is the significance Lewis attached to *the face.* This at once calls to my mind the
use of the Greek term for the person, *prosopon,* by contemporary
Orthodox theologians such as Christos Yannaras or Metropolitan John
(Zizioulas) of Pergamos.[42] *Prosopon* has precisely the literal sense of
"face" or "countenance" (or more exactly, "facing toward": that is,
pros, "toward," and *ops,* "face"). To be a person, that is to say, is to
face another, to look toward and to enter into relationship with the
other; there is no true personhood without relationship.

The meaning of the face is the central theme in that most
fascinating and enigmatic of all Lewis's works, *Till We Have Faces.*
Orual's chief argument when she confronts Psyche in the mountain
valley is that Psyche's lover does not reveal his face: "What sort of
god would he be who dares not show his face? . . . Nothing that's
beautiful hides its face."[43] At a later point in the story, Orual herself
(who is far from beautiful) veils her own face, with the result that
people come to imagine that she has no face at all.[44] The statue of

---

41. *George MacDonald: An Anthology* (Touchstone Books, 1966), p. 28.
42. See Christos Yannaras, *The Freedom of Morality* (St. Vladimir Press, 1984), pp.
20-22; John D. Zizioulas, *Being as Communion: Studies in Personhood and the Church*
(St. Vladimir Press, 1985), pp. 27-49.
43. *Till We Have Faces,* p. 168.
44. Ibid., p. 237.

the dark goddess Ungit has no face; likewise the statue of Psyche in the little forest temple has a scarf wrapped around it so that the face is concealed.[45]

The importance of the face is also apparent in the final conclusion of the story. "I saw well," says Orual, "why the gods do not speak to us openly, nor let us answer. . . . How can they meet us face to face till we have faces?"[46] That is to say, there cannot be a relationship between two subjects unless both have a face, a sense of identity; and so we cannot begin to understand the Divine until we have in some measure confronted and come to terms with our own inwardness, with the complexities and darkness in ourselves.

The Divinized Person

Lewis's convergence with Orthodox anthropology extends beyond these two issues of our personal uniqueness and the meaning of the face to two further points, both of fundamental significance for Orthodoxy.

In the third place, in the understanding of the Christian East salvation involves nothing less than *theosis,* "deification" or "divinisation." We humans are called to be "partakers of the divine nature" (2 Peter 1:4), to share by grace — in a direct and unmediated manner — in the transforming life and glory of God. Such is likewise Lewis's understanding of salvation: "Century by century God has guided nature up to the point of producing creatures which can (if they will) be taken right out of nature, turned into 'gods'."[47] Lewis would have come across the idea of *theosis* in the work of St. Athanasius, *The Incarnation of the Word of God,* to which he wrote an introduction; as St. Athanasius says of Christ the Logos, "He became man that we might be made god."[48]

Fourthly and finally, many of the Greek fathers — most notably

45. Ibid., pp. 281, 250.
46. Ibid., p. 305.
47. *Mere Christianity*, p. 185. Lewis has in mind Psalm 82 [81]:6, cited in John 10:34: "I said, 'You are gods.'"
48. *On the Incarnation* 54.

St. Irenaeus, St. Gregory of Nyssa, and St. Maximus the Confessor
— envisage eternal life (insofar as it can be envisaged at all) in terms
of *epektasis*, of infinite progress and unending advance. The perfection
and blessedness of Heaven are not static but dynamic, not fixed but
inexhaustibly creative. As St. Gregory of Nyssa states in a fine paradox,
the very essence of perfection consists in the fact that we never become
totally perfect, but unceasingly press onward "from glory to glory"
(2 Corinthians 3:18).

Such is exactly the picture of eternal life that Lewis presents at
the end of *The Last Battle,* in the chapter "Farther Up and Farther In."
Heaven is "like an onion: except that as you go in and in, each circle
is larger than the last."[49] Lewis implies that, to this sequence of ever-
enlarging onion skins, there is no ultimate limit. Our continuing
exploration "farther up and farther in" extends uninterrupted into the
"ages of ages":

> And as He spoke He no longer looked to them like a lion; but the
> things that began to happen after that were so great and beautiful that
> I cannot write them. And for us this is the end of all the stories, and
> we can most truly say that they all lived happily ever after. But for
> them it was only the beginning of the real story. All their life in this
> world and all their adventures in Narnia had only been the cover and
> the title page: now at last they were beginning Chapter One of the
> Great Story which no one on earth has read: which goes on for ever:
> in which every chapter is better than the one before.[50]

Whenever I read that passage, my heart is "strangely warmed."

An Anonymous Orthodox

Again and again we have found that C. S. Lewis articulates a vision
of Christian truth that a member of the Orthodox Church can wholeheartedly endorse.

His starting point may be that of a Western Christian, but repeatedly his conclusions are Orthodox, with a large as well as a small

49. *The Last Battle,* p. 181.
50. Ibid., pp. 183-84.

"o." His apophatic sense of God's hiddenness, his teaching on Christ and the Trinity, his understanding of creation and of personhood, were all expressed in terms that appeal to Orthodox Christendom. Surely he has a strong claim to be considered an "anonymous Orthodox."

The Heart's Desire
and the Landlord's Rules:
C. S. Lewis as a Moral Philosopher

JAMES PATRICK

C. S. LEWIS is usually remembered in the scholarly world first as a critic, author of *The Allegory of Love* and the history of sixteenth-century English literature; then as a poet, author of the *Poems* and *Till We Have Faces*. Among Christians, he is remembered as a great apologist, the author of *Mere Christianity;* then as a moral theologian, the author of *The Screwtape Letters* and *The Great Divorce*. But before Lewis was a critic, poet, apologist, or moral theologian, he was an Oxford graduate looking for a fellowship not in literature or theology but in philosophy. When he began to teach and write, the philosophic lines were never far beneath the surface, and they remained close to the surface even in his later popular religious works.

When in 1922 he tried, unsuccessfully, for a fellowship at Magdalen College, the essay he submitted was titled "The Hegemony of Moral Value," and posed the existence of natural law as the resolution of the argument between utilitarians and idealists. Titled "The Practical Hegemony of the Moral Value," it became the penultimate lecture in the course in moral philosophy Lewis taught as substitute for E. F. Carritt in 1924.

His first prose work, *The Pilgrim's Regress* (1933), was constructed around the problem of the relation between what we desire and imagine on one hand and the rules we are to follow on the other, and is (as far as the middle of its ninth book) essentially moral philosophy.

So in its entirety is *The Abolition of Man* (1943), which begins with an analysis of the inherent morality of language and a defense of the objectivity of value — represented by the great moral platitudes shared by all cultures and religions — and ends with a historical argument that values are objective and transcultural. The space trilogy, especially the third volume, *That Hideous Strength,* is full of moral philosophy and, like *Abolition,* is especially concerned with the relation between man and nature.

The Meaning of Moral Philosophy

To use the title "moral philosophy" is to invoke a particularly nineteenth-century understanding of a science, a part of philosophy that would now be called ethics, which included the consideration of the good, of duty, of the grounds of our knowledge of what we ought to do. Moral philosophy is distinguished within the larger field of philosophy, in which reason investigates subjects like existence and truth, by its interest in the great moral questions: "What is good?" and "What is my duty?" It is distinguished from moral theology, which assumes that holiness and the theological virtues are the end of human life, by its method, which is an appeal to reason alone. Anyone can and should pursue duty and the good, a fact that makes moral philosophy a great, if imperfect, unifier of mankind.

When Lewis came up to Oxford in January 1919, most moral philosophers would not have been as frightened of God as their late twentieth-century successors (our contemporaries). They would have recognized that their warrant was primarily natural and philosophic, that their discipline had to do with that kind of knowledge of the good and of our duties which any thoughtful person, Christian or not, might gain.

Unlike the ethical theories that dominated academic discourse after 1945, the moral philosophy of the 1920s was not (generally) relativistic. Appeals to history, to the great tradition represented by the Ten Commandments and the twelve tables of Roman law, were not yet ruled out by insistence that nobody could really tell what goodness and virtue might be or by the warning that virtue might mean something different to Estonians and Eskimos. No alarm was sounded when the reader was led by moral philosophy across its own natural terrain into the borderlands of moral theology and Christian behavior.

But as Lewis came to intellectual maturity, the philosophic wars, rooted in the skepticism and utilitarianism of the late Victorian era and occasioned by the "intuitionism" of G. E. Moore and his Cambridge mentor Henry Sidgwick, were quietly heating up. Moore's new moral philosophy, presented to the world in his *Principia Ethica* in the last year of Victoria's reign (1900), though harbinger of theories yet to come, was only one contender in a disorderly and rambunctious field of moral ideas that contained as well the lively Kantianism of the school of the Oxford philosopher T. H. Green, the still-influential, native British utilitarianism of David Hume and John Stuart Mill, and a classical school that, while taking Kant (and even Moore) into account, harked back to Plato, Aristotle, and the sixteenth-century Anglican theologian Richard Hooker.

To understand Lewis as a moral philosopher, the hard exercise of understanding something of each of these schools, to which he was always reacting and to which he referred in many of his works, must be undertaken.

Native Utilitarianism and Kantian Idealism

Utilitarianism was a native English school, rooted in the thought of the eighteenth-century philosopher and historian David Hume and always tempting because its first principle is very obvious. Happiness is the great good. As John Stuart Mill wrote in the nineteenth century: "actions are right in proportion as they tend to produce happiness, wrong as they tend to produce the reverse of happiness." Aristotle said happiness was the one thing we were likely to pursue for its own sake and argued that it was impossible to be happy without being virtuous. Our Lord told us that practicing the beatitudes would make us blessed or, as the modern translation goes, happy. It was an idea so often thought that when the utilitarians wrote that the highest good was the greatest happiness for the greatest number, they had an instant audience, and one that has, if anything, grown steadily greater.

But there are difficulties. As a moral category, happiness is temptingly subjective and at least potentially self-serving. What does it mean? Does happiness mean the satisfying of one's desires, or does it mean the contentment that comes from respect for law? Or does it mean what Christians call blessedness, which is attained in circumstances far from "happy," including poverty and persecution? We seldom do anything that we believe will not make us happy. The imitation of the beatific vision in the faces of the crowd at Nazi rallies betokens happiness, as do the sweet smiles of frescoed thirteenth-century saints.

Faced with the difficulty of defining a universally recognized happiness, utilitarians tend, quite understandably, to locate happiness at the obvious, animal end of existence. Happiness is sufficient food, drink, and sex, a practical conclusion so obvious within the narrow meaning of happiness that one would hardly wish to refute it, but a definition that at the same time makes duty unintelligible and makes nonsense of St. Paul's famous reflection that he wanted to do that which he ought not, presumably because at least sometimes whatever it was that St. Paul wanted to do would have in some sense made him happy. But it would not have made him St. Paul.

Lewis wrote "We Have 'No Right to Happiness,'" his last essay written for publication, because he saw that in modern culture the classical Aristotelian proposition that all men seek happiness, which happiness could never be achieved apart from virtue, had degenerated into a headlong rush for pleasure, the most obvious of human purposes.[1] The nineteenth-century utilitarians, Newman wrote, aimed low but fulfilled their aim.

Beginning about 1870 another, very different kind of moral philosophy, imported from Germany long after it had become popular on its native ground, overlaid this British utilitarianism. Its main exponent in England was Thomas Hill Green, who made a moral theory based on the gentle seasoning of the philosophy of Kant with light Hegelian sauce famous at Oxford, first as a don at Balliol College and then as Whyte Professor of Moral Philosophy from 1878 until his death in 1882.

The eighteenth-century German philosopher Immanuel Kant had argued in his lectures and books on moral philosophy that "I ought,"

---

1. "We Have No 'Right to Happiness,'" in *God in the Dock* (Eerdmans, 1970), pp. 317-22. It was published first in *Life* magazine.

the universal awareness of obligation, was the heart of human goodness. Morality could not be the consequence of inclination or interest
or feelings, but must somehow be the result of a reflection of a more
universal kind that implies our willingness that the rules we make for
ourselves should be made the law under which we and all mankind
must live.

Despite a good deal of high-sounding talk about the starry heavens
above and the moral law within, Kant never encouraged the conclusion that morality was anything more than one's legislation for oneself
writ large. This kind of thought was a sort of moral idealism, idealistic
because reality was a set of moral ideas, not some utilitarian object;
but subjective because the idea of the good, the moral imperative, was
simply discovered within us, nowhere else.

This kind of idealism was a relief or escape from the world of the
utilitarians. It was welcomed in the universities, if not always in the
larger world, and influenced the late Victorian and Edwardian genera-
tions of teachers, politicians, and imperial administrators. "Oxford lay
abjectly imprisoned within the rigid limits of Mill's logic," wrote
Henry Scott Holland, the great dean of St. Paul's cathedral in London.
"Individualistic sensationalism held the field. There was a dryness in
the Oxford air. . . . Out there in the huge and hideous cities, the awful
problem of industry lay like a bad dream." By challenging utilitarianism, Green's teaching "broke for us the sway of sensationalism,"
and "gave us back the language of self-sacrifice, and taught us how
we belonged to one another."

Green defeated the utilitarianism of Mill as Kant had turned the
materialistic arguments of David Hume by arguing that consciousness
of nature is something nature cannot explain, that the world we
experience is rather obviously not a collection of things but an organic
whole, a system of relations known. It followed that morality was not
some consequence in the world, but, first and most importantly, a
matter of conscience and duty; that, as Green wrote in his *Prolegomena
to Ethics* (published in 1883), "in all conduct to which moral predicates
are applicable a man is an object to himself." The motive for good
conduct, then, is "an idea of personal good which the man seeks to
realize by action." Thus character depends upon the nature of the
objects we see, "ranging from sensual pleasure to the fulfillment of a
vocation conceived as given by God."

Green's argument against the materialism of the utilitarians was Kant pure and simple, but in other respects Green was an unremarkable disciple of Aristotle. Doing good depended upon our having an idea about the good we would do, and for Green sensuality and fulfilling a God-given vocation were not morally equivalent ideas. Kant was surely right in arguing that doing good for the sake of some base reward was hardly moral goodness at all, but was it true that *any* desire, even the desire for knowledge of God or the desire to hear "Well done, faithful servant," was morally flawed?

Green thought not, and Lewis would follow both Green's argument that virtue cannot consist in some utilitarian object but rather describes the character of our soul and his argument that *what* the soul desires is not only important but knowable. For the morally serious person that desirable good, Lewis would argue in *The Pilgrim's Regress,* is not pleasure, power, or sex, but something or someone who is not to be found among the objects of this worldly desire, not even in the distant mountains of romantic longing, but in a face and a voice that lie beyond even the beauty of Ulster's Castelreagh hills.

The school of Green, Lewis once wrote, seemingly in secure possession of the philosophic field in 1919, went down like the Bastille. But it did not fall before important principles had been passed along to a young Magdalen College don who at the beginning of his Oxford career thought he would be a philosopher. It was from this school that at least two Lewisian moral themes derive: his argument that the rules must be rooted in something more than human conscience or personality, in God or in nature; and his persistent interest in the difficulty posed by the Kantian doctrine that we should pursue goodness without any inclination or interest or desire or feeling.

The Classical School and Moore's Intuitionism

Related at least obliquely to the Kantian school was a loosely organized body of opinion that might be called either eclectic or classical. This school would have been represented in the decade of Lewis's conversion by A. E. Taylor of Edinburgh University, whose Gifford Lectures of 1928-29, published as *The Faith of a Moralist,* were characteristic of the school; by Charles Gore, an Anglican bishop whose *Philosophy of the Good Life* Lewis recommended because it "taught me a lot";[2] by Lewis's longtime breakfast companion John Alexander Smith, the Wayneflete Professor of Moral and Metaphysical Philosophy at Magdalen College from 1909 to 1935; and by W. D. Ross, provost of Oriel College, whose *The Good and the Right* revisited the great Aristotelian moral themes.

These were men who, expecting less than would their juniors by way of strict proof and ineluctable evidence, found in the literature with which an Oxford "greats" man would have been familiar — the Greek and Latin classics — a line of moral reasoning that they developed fruitfully around a set of universally recognizable moral questions. Members of this informal school, who thought in the great philosophic tradition and who doubted that there could be any dramatic new insight into the moral nature of man and his conduct, might disagree about the exact meaning of duty and the good, but they would have agreed that these existed and that the pursuit of them was essential to the human project.

Lewis's Oxford contemporary R. G. Collingwood, whose philosophical mentor had been John Alexander Smith, noted in his *Autobiography* that the Oxford philosophers of the period before 1918 gave their pupils "ideas to live by and ideals to live for," teaching in a way that said, "take this subject seriously, because whether you understand it or not will make a difference to your whole lives."

In contrast, their contemporary at Cambridge University, G. E. Moore, was a moral and metaphysical skeptic, convinced that philosophy could discover no truth not derived immediately from the testimony of the senses or from certain logical relations, and that moral philosophy could do no more than cut away the undergrowth of traditional moral thought and expose the crumbling foundation of ethical theory. To Moore and other realist critics, the differences between the older Kantian moral philosophy of Green and the classical school perhaps seemed unimportant, for Moore believed the issue to be the bankruptcy of the great moral tradition of classical philosophy taught in the universities for seven centuries, and the immediate tasks the necessity that this failure be recognized and the pressing work of revision and reconstruction undertaken.

2. *Letters of C. S. Lewis,* ed. W. H. Lewis (Harcourt, Brace and World, 1966).

In the *Principia Ethica* (1900) he claimed theoretically that good as we know it is simply an object of direct intuition, that nothing could be said or argued by way of defining terms like "good" and "virtue," so that as we face the fact of moral obligation in any given situation no appeal can legitimately be made to general rules. At the same time he insisted on practical grounds that beauty was good in itself, and that the purpose of virtue was the creation of beauty and the pleasurable states of consciousness associated with contemplation of the beautiful. Then in "Does Moral Philosophy Rest on a Mistake?" (1912), H. A. Prichard, an Oxford don sympathetic to Moore's ideas, argued that no reasons at all may be given as to why a certain action is my duty. We are left in our particular situation to originate right action without any reference to the moral traditions, insights, and arguments that most men and women had found persuasive for several millennia.

The practical consequences of the principles of this revolutionary school — a moral subjectivism, to which the name "intuitionism" was soon given — were that pleasurable states of consciousness are the highest good we can know, that moral reasoning is inevitable futile, and that as we stand in any moral situation we simply decide without appeal to any principle. New and radical when Lewis began his Oxford career, they would as the century wore on become popular commonplaces, often the standard assumptions not only of scholars but also of politicians and journalists.

This new morality was good news not only in Bloomsbury, where it fostered an emblematic relativistic society, replete with the "higher sodomy" and serial marriage that set the fashionable moral tone of the twentieth century, but to ordinary folk everywhere, possessed fully of the weaknesses of human nature and fatigued by the quest for virtue, who have suspected that the ancient authorities just might not know as much as they claimed and that a happy consciousness was after all the best one could hope for. Moore's weapon was linguistic, the claim that the older moral philosophy was hopelessly imprecise, necessarily so because its philosophical underpinnings were fallacious, infected as they were with traditional metaphysics — with the moral optimism of Plato and Aristotle, who spoke and wrote as though they expected ordinary readers to be able to discern goodness and duty, and with lingering platitudes redolent of the old Christian moral synthesis.

Of course Moore owed something to the utilitarianism of Mill and Bentham, and he might have found the subjectivism of the Kantian tradition sympathetic, but Kant's stern conclusion that there is an inexorable moral law that though a product of my own thought was nonetheless deducible by all and obligatory for all, would not have suited the purposes of Moore and his Cambridge and Bloomsbury friends. That those purposes were disinterestedly scientific may be doubted. Michael Jones is convincing when he argues in *Degenerate Moderns* that the intellectual biographies of Moore's friends and followers Lytton Strachey and John Maynard Keynes suggest that the popularity, if not the cause, of Moore's moral philosophy was a desire to rationalize sexual misbehavior.

Certainly the followers of Moore and Prichard viewed the classical school with gentle pity, undermining it by controlling the literature of the debate and by assiduously ignoring their idealist predecessors as thinkers nobody could take seriously, a pose that the gentlemanly idealists, with the exception of the ever feisty Collingwood, abetted by failing to imagine that anyone could take the new morality seriously and by refusing to fight it.

Nevertheless, to the intuitionism of Moore and Prichard, Lewis owed the raising of the questions his moral philosophy would try to answer. Are any states of consciousness (or feelings) just, or are all merely pleasurable or painful? Can the words used in moral discourse convey common meanings that rightly bind and instruct our wills, or does conscience stand dumb before every moral question? Are the patterns of virtue one or many, different in different civilizations or the same for all men everywhere?

A Promising Intellectual

His schoolmaster Kirkpatrick said that Lewis read more classics than any boy he had taught, and E. F. Carritt, the University College don who interviewed him when he applied for admission to Oxford, said that Lewis was the best read applicant he had ever examined. At Oxford he was still the boy of books Kirkpatrick remembered, interested in the past and in the things of creative imagination.

But the soldier who returned to studies in January 1919, after being wounded on the front, was also hard at work perfecting what he called in *Surprised by Joy* his new look, a tough-minded stance that exchanged the romantic longing of his prewar days for the somber, stoical belief that this world, as it is, is all that we will know, so that we ought to bear its deep pains and cherish its moderate joys with as much courage as we can muster. He was an incipient modern, a promising intellectual who wrote poetry of a vaguely pessimistic kind founded upon a philosophy in which the fundamental category was "Spirit."

Befriended and promoted by his tutor E. F. Carritt, with Moore's disciple Prichard one of the Oxford realists, Lewis was himself sympathetic to the new no-nonsense philosophy and to the moral philosophy that accompanied it, the first principle of which was the doubt that objective judgments about value were possible. How Lewis appeared in the university as a protégé of Carritt (and, hence, as a realist) and then became successively an idealist, a pantheist, a theist, and finally a Christian is a story told in the last part of *Surprised by Joy* and summarized in the preface to the third edition of *The Pilgrim's Regress*. One step along the way was Lewis's being convinced by his friend Owen Barfield that beauty was not merely subjective but was the experience of something real. If beauty were not in the eye of the beholder, it would follow that things were good that thinking did not make so.

Another step was the move in 1925 to Magdalen College, where the most important philosopher was the great idealist John Alexander Smith, who at least believed the familiar problems of moral philosophy worth thinking about and who displayed a polite skepticism toward anyone who would propose in 1920 to reject the cumulative moral wisdom of over two thousand years on behalf of any conceivable new theory.

From the time he decided that moral value was real, becoming thereby an ally of what I have described above as the classical school, Lewis made unremitting intellectual war on the utilitarians, the idealists, and the moral subjectivists, although, typically, he also took something from each.

His contempt for the utilitarians and their teleological theory was expressed most tellingly in *That Hideous Strength*. This theory proposes always to bring about some desirable future state, the happiness of the greatest number or the perfect society, even at the cost of doing evil, or, as a great twentieth-century practitioner (George Bernard Shaw) wrote, conspired to break the eggs of civilized moral life in order to make the socialist omelet. The leaders of N.I.C.E. (the National Institute of Coordinated Experiments) held the moral theory that existence is its own justification. The theory that in *Out of the Silent Planet* takes Devine and Weston to Malacandra and to murder in order to save the human race, in *That Hideous Strength* drives the Reverend Mr. Straik, an Anglican clergyman, to preach revolution as the fulfillment of Jesus' intentions.

For a religiously convinced utilitarian like Mr. Straik, nothing, not the deaths of millions, is evil if it promotes the great end foreseen. It is tempting to think of utilitarians as harmless folk for whom the greatest happiness of the greatest number means shorter hours and better living conditions, but once the moral question is relocated from "my duty this day" to "my duty to bring about some desirable future state," it becomes clear that Stalin was the greatest utilitarian of our century. Stalin was one who had, in the Reverend Mr. Straik's terms, the courage to sacrifice all "merely human values" for the sake of the coming kingdom of socialist righteousness. Among his late twentieth-century disciples are those who destroy little children so that their lives will not be inconvenienced, and so that we the already born will have enough, the demand upon the society's resources being reduced.

Lewis's argument against the moral subjectivism of Moore and Prichard and the new realists, the ancestor of the modern belief that good-is-what-you-think-it-is, is set forward eloquently in the early chapters of *The Pilgrim's Regress.* There "parrot disease" is the moral disease that, abetted by Freud and his kind, teaches that our ideals are nothing greater than our passions — "argument . . . is the attempted rationalization of the arguer's desires" — and later in the book there are the passages in which Vertue, a fine Kantian himself, insists that the rules must be simply his own.

The Abolition of Man attacks moral subjectivism as it was found in the 1940s, rooted and perpetuated in a philosophy of language. During the years between the wars positivism (the name for the new realism used after about 1930), perhaps justified to some degree by the very loose use of language by idealist philosophers, erected the rule that words, if they mean anything, must have tight, precise, observable referents, a position that does indeed make the definition of good or any other traditional moral term impossible. (Try to define "justice" as precisely and unmistakably as one can define a molecule of water.) In positivist terms the assertion that horses may be noble in some sense in which slugs and sloths are not is meaningless. If it could be granted by a positivist that the word "noble" means anything, this would only broach the truly impossible task of explaining how horses could be called noble.

The realist conviction that moral rules must be the consequence of mere emotion intersects neatly with the idealist proposition that the source of the rules is nothing greater than ourselves. So the new realism or positivism — the doctrine that the only things I can really know are things I can see and touch and describe more or less exhaustively — has a way of turning into subjectivism, the idea that there is nothing outside myself that I can really know at all.

When we ask too much of words, they turn on us, the search for an impossible precision transforming itself into an unmanageable ambiguity. It is hardly surprising that the children of the positivists, who thought they could discover very precisely what words mean in a way that obviated their natural depth and richness, are the deconstructionists, who teach that words mean exactly what you think they mean, nothing more or less. Words, as Lewis knew, are to be listened to because they are doorways to reality, not despised as ineffective instruments because they refuse to yield their substance exhaustively to philosophic propositions. When and as words can no longer be heard, but are treated as operant, merely useful for my purposes now, every attempt to clarify obfuscates, until finally the field is swept clear of common and trustworthy meanings and nothing remains but the irrational power of a sloganeering newspeak.

Reason and Romanticism

Although Lewis, like most dons of his generation, was heavily influenced by the high-sounding themes of Kantian moral philosophy, *The Pilgrim's Regress* devotes a good deal of time to refuting both its intrinsic subjectivism and its dictum that interest or desire is morally disqualifying, that if we obey for any other motive than a high and dry respect for law, for the sake of our own soul's salvation for instance, or for the love of God or neighbor, our motives are compromised by being a kind of bribery.

The Pilgrim's Regress: An Allegorical Apology for Christianity, Reason, and Romanticism is the work Lewis wrote in a few weeks in 1931, just after his conversion to Christianity; it has a freshness and candor that is never again quite so evident. The book describes the pilgrimage leading the protagonist John (obviously Jack Lewis of Ulster) out of Puritania (obviously the moralistic Belfast of Lewis's boyhood imagination), along a road that finally, after many diversions, takes him to Mother Kirk. John of course wanders from the road, so that his pilgrimage takes him through the arid north, populated by high and dry intellectuals, antiromantics like T. S. Eliot and T. E. Hulme; and the swamp-infested south, where in the city of Eschropolis live such representatives of sensuality as the brown girls common to imagination and Glugly the songstress.

At the beginning of his journey John is imprisoned by the Spirit of the Age, who teaches the doctrine that things really are merely that which they can be conceived to be in their most reductive and naturalistic terms. Thus milk is not health-giving but (like dung) a mere secretion of the cow, and attempts at rational argument are merely the rationalizations of the arguers' desires. Along the way John meets the representatives of the living ideologies from Mr. Broad and Mr. Sensible to the political movements that threatened Europe in 1931, the Marxomanni, Mussolimini, and Swastici. The allegory, like all Lewis's works, ranges over the whole terrain of the soul, but the problem that dominates the work is given in its subtitle: the resolution by Christianity of the conflict between the rules delivered by reason and romantic desire rooted universally in imagination.

John is an unhappy child of Puritania, a country half-maddened by oppressive rules nobody can quite keep, but which refuse to desert the heart. The rules have no place for that sweet desire which possesses John and which he tries to satisfy in the arms of the brown girls. His traveling companion Vertue is (we are told) the child of Enlightenment and Euphuia, a Greek name meaning good-heartedness. In another place we are told that Vertue's father is *nomos,* or law.

For John the problem is the taming of desire. This involves sorting through and rejecting the various false desires and setting his heart on the mountains and what lies beyond them, that is, upon God. For

Vertue, the child of law, enlightenment, and goodness of disposition, the problem is the resolution of the Kantian paradox that teaches that duty must be pursued without self-interest. "If there is something to go on to, it is a bribe, and I cannot go to it; if I can go, there is nothing to go to."

Desire — interest in Kantian terms — is morally disqualifying simply because we are doing what we do not simply because it is good, but because we wish to do it. Kantian ethics defeats utilitarianism — there can certainly be no interest in anyone's happiness — but it does so at too high a price, for it leaves the moral world without motive. Once John says to Vertue, "Give in. Yield to desire. Have done with your choosing. Want something." But Vertue cannot.

The resolution of Vertue's paradox lies in the discovery that the existence of the rules does not depend on our knowing the Landlord. The rules are not products of our hearts or consciences, though we may grasp them with conscience. Nor are they products of fear or love. The rules are simply part of the eternal texture of things that we discover, and though they may be rooted in the very existence of the Landlord, we need not know the Landlord to discover them.

This is a first principle that most moral philosophers of the generation before the Great War would have held in some form, the belief that natural law exists and that through conscience everyman might know the first moral platitudes: being is good; do good, avoid evil; honor parents; never steal or lie. Natural law is the theory that unites mankind, law-ridden Jew and libertine Greek, Puritan and humanist, utilitarian and idealist, under a common obligation. It is in fact the basis of every kind of morality and every civil code until the day before yesterday.

Aristotle had assumed it, and Plato. Cicero had spoken of it when he called it the law that is not written down. When St. Paul wrote that even the Gentiles knew that certain kinds of behavior were wrong, he was appealing to natural law. This same idea informed the thought of St. Augustine in the fourth century and St. Thomas in the thirteenth, and influenced Anglicanism at its origin through Richard Hooker's *Laws of Ecclesiastical Polity*.

A Metaphysical Reality

Natural law is not properly, and was not for Lewis, a merely natural idea in the sense intended by our common references to laws of nature. Laws of nature really belong to physics: things fall at a certain velocity; for every force there is an equal and opposite reaction; and the like. Natural law is a metaphysical reality. The fact that the relation between men and women produces children is a fact of nature. That being is naturally fruitful is a principle of natural law. The existence of natural law means that we cannot be good men and women while simply doing as we like. This unwritten law that everyman discovers was the subject of Lewis's lost essay "The Hegemony of Moral Value," written at the beginning of his academic career and before his conversion.

The historical argument, in which the universality of the great moral platitudes is demonstrated by appeal to the moral codes of Hebrews, Sumerians, Greeks, and Norsemen, a method Lewis shared with Gore's *Philosophy of the Good Life,* is given in the appendix to *The Abolition of Man,* and the central argument of the second part of that work is the claim that moral values are a permanent, unalterable moral context that we discover but may not abridge or augment. In the last essay he wrote for publication, Lewis said of natural law, "I hold this conception to be basic to all civilization," noting that without it the laws of the state would become absolute and would lie beyond criticism.[3] Lewis meant even more, for he knew that natural law is rooted in reality in such a way that it describes (by God's will) both the goodness that is God and the good that our intellects discover.

I remind the gentle reader in conclusion that I have said nothing about conversion, grace, holiness, or the theological virtues because these do not belong to moral philosophy or ethics as such. Lewis wrote about these consummate realities in the last chapters of *The Pilgrim's Regress,* and in *Till We Have Faces, The Screwtape Letters,* and *The Great Divorce.*

To a Christian, moral philosophy or ethics based on natural law is at the same time the reflection of God's will for his creation, the moral bond of our common humanity, the accuser of fallen mankind,

3. "We Have No 'Right to Happiness,'" p. 318.

and the indispensable prologue to something greater. In *The Pilgrim's Regress* Vertue plunges into the waters of baptism and is seen no more. This sudden disappearance is hyperbolic — we are creatures who never leave nature behind — but significant. Grace does not destroy but perfects our ever present — if, in human terms and with human means, inevitably frustrated — desire for goodness. But it is true that our pursuit of goodness, with all the condemning discomfort that brings, is transformed into love.

The rules never disappear, but they are, as Our Lord told us in the great fifth chapter of Matthew, made into matters of the heart. The Landlord, Lewis wrote, will help us keep them.

Speaking the Truths Only the Imagination May Grasp: Myth and "Real Life"

STRATFORD CALDECOTT

JOHN HENRY NEWMAN once pointed out that it is very hard for anyone to believe something he cannot first imagine to be true. Today, many people growing up in an industrialized world cut off (physically and intellectually) from the natural environment cannot imagine the milk they drink coming from a cow, let alone how the supernatural claims of Christianity could possibly be true. It seems to bear no relation to the world they inhabit. They have no knowledge of it, nor even any knowledge from which they can draw analogies.

Their imagination (by which I mean that faculty by which they view the world and try to make sense of it) is shaped by technological rather than organic forms. They consequently have difficulty believing that everything in the world grows in order to manifest an inner, invisible unity and to believe that something, some being, created and maintains that unity. For children growing up in a modern city, the world is composed of physical objects jammed together by an external logic or more often by no apparent logic at all: noisy and random, forming no natural order but jostling and fighting for dominance, a unity based on power.

Life was not always so. A life lived close to the earth, to nature in all its forms — plants and animals, rocks and rivers — helps to create in a child the possibility of religious awakening. For those children estranged from nature, the early influence of good literature can have

86

the same salutary effect. Traditional folk and fairy tales, heroic stories, and legends can help prepare someone for what C. S. Lewis referred to as the "baptism" of the imagination; something that for him, albeit not for everyone, was an important preparatory step for receiving the gospel of Christ as Saving Truth.

In my own case, these things helped to wake a longing that could not be satisfied by the kind of knowledge offered by science alone. It was a longing that, once awakened, could not easily be lulled to sleep.

A Longing for Union

This longing has been experienced by men and women of all cultures and times. It is not merely the longing for an explanation of why the world exists at all, although that may come into it. It is a longing for union with something infinitely remote and yet infinitely beautiful; a longing for self-transformation, for the One who entirely transcends our present state. This is the longing that myths evoke, and the fulfillment of which they speak. As Lewis said in his sermon "The Weight of Glory," God has given us such great wonders in nature that we should not want anything else, but

> we want so much more — something the books on aesthetics take little notice of. But the poets and mythologies know all about it. We do not want merely to *see* beauty, though, God knows, even that is bounty enough. We want something else which can hardly be put into words — to be united with the beauty we see, to pass into it, to receive it into ourselves, to bathe in it, to become part of it. That is why we have peopled air and earth and water with gods and goddesses and nymphs and elves.[1]

Yet it would be a mistake to dismiss our myths merely as "wishful thinking" and nothing more. As J. R. R. Tolkien wrote, "legends and myths are largely made of 'truth,' and indeed present aspects of it that can only be received in this mode."[2] In the popular meaning of the

1. "The Weight of Glory," in *The Weight of Glory and Other Addresses* (Eerdmans, 1965), pp. 12-13.
2. *The Letters of J. R. R. Tolkien,* ed. Humphrey Carpenter (Houghton Mifflin

word, of course, a myth is simply a story that is *not* true. I would say rather that a myth is a symbolic story intended to express truth, and a truth perhaps best apprehended and understood through story. Myth, wrote Lewis, "must be grasped with the imagination, not with the intellect." If its characters

> have some touch of mythical life, then no amount of "explanation" will quite catch up with their meaning. It is the sort of thing you cannot learn from definition: you must rather get to know it as you get to know a smell or taste, the "atmosphere" of a family or a country town, of the personality of an individual.[3]

But what is myth designed to express? It concerns not merely the world around us, but the world within us; not so much the surface appearance of the world, but its inner form. For a myth is a way of describing the rules by which the world is made, the rules that govern our lives; whether or not we know them or obey them. In a phrase from *The Lion, the Witch and the Wardrobe,* they reveal "the deep magic from before the dawn of time."

I suppose, even so, that we should properly restrict the name of myth to those stories that encapsulate the religious and cosmological beliefs of an entire community. But the line between myth, folklore, "fairy tales," and fantasy is hard to draw. Stories composed by an individual, such as Hans Christian Andersen's *Snow Queen,* Tolkien's *The Lord of the Rings,* or Lewis's Chronicles of Narnia, seem sometimes to touch the same level of archetypal truth as the myths of a people, and they achieve enormous and lasting popularity as a result. In the case of the leading "Inklings," this amounted to a cult following within their own lifetime.

Fantasy "fandom" may be obsessive, but fundamentally it springs from a healthy response to a sick — a fallen — world. Given the situation in which we find ourselves, even escapism is not necessarily ignoble. To quote Tolkien's essay "On Fairy Stories":

Company, 1981), no. 131. This explains the similarity between the world's myths. "Long ago certain truths and modes of this kind were discovered and must always reappear," Tolkien continued. In particular, "all stories are ultimately about the fall."

3. "Preface to Third Edition," in *The Pilgrim's Regress* (Eerdmans, 1943), p. 13.

In what the misusers [of the term "escape"] are fond of calling Real Life, Escape is evidently as a rule very practical, and may even be heroic. . . . *Why should a man be scorned, if, finding himself in prison, he tries to get out and go home? . . .* Or if, when he cannot do so, he thinks and talks about other topics than jailers and prison-walls? The world outside has not become less real because the prisoner cannot see it.[4]

Lewis put it a similar way: "At present we are on the outside of the world, the wrong side of the door. We discern the freshness and purity of morning, but they do not make us fresh and pure. We cannot mingle with the splendours we see."[5]

What follows is partly an examination of this attempt to "go home," to return to the world outside the prison walls. It is about how we can better understand our own lives in the light of mythic imagination and the relationship of Christianity to mythology. The stories I have chosen to reflect briefly upon are stories of a Quest. The quest is, after all, probably the best-known "plot device" of all folklore and mythology. If the first task of the storyteller is to hold the interest of his listeners, clearly what people find most interesting is a tale that describes a journey in which there is some difficult goal to be achieved, some challenge to be met, some initiation to be undergone, some place or object to be discovered or won.

Why are such tales so endlessly fascinating, so universally told? Perhaps because it is just such a journey that gives meaning to our own existence. We read or listen to the storyteller in order to orient ourselves within — to learn how to behave in order to get where we are going. Each of us knows that our life is not merely a mechanical progress from cradle to grave; it is a search, a quest, even a pilgrimage. There is some elusive goal that motivates us in our work and our play.

Christianity as Myth

The definition of "myth" as a symbolic story designed to express truth is broad enough to apply to the stories we find in the Bible. Of course,

---

4. "On Fairy Stories," in J. R. R. Tolkien, *The Tolkien Reader* (Ballantine Books, 1966), p. 60. Emphasis added.

5. "The Weight of Glory," p. 13.

there is nothing in our definition that rules out the possibility that at least some of these stories may also be true accounts of historical events. The traditional understanding is that they are *both*. Wherever the text of the Bible does not appear to contradict itself, or is not contradicted by human reason or by certain knowledge from some other sources, tradition encourages us to assume that it is *literally* as well as symbolically true — that is, true to the surface as well as to the inner life of the world.

Both the Jewish philosopher Philo of Alexandria and the third-century theologian Origen expressly stated this as a principle of interpretation. We could call it the principle of "Maximum Possible Meaning." Behind it lies the conviction that the divine author of Scripture is also the author of the cosmos, and so the Book of Nature must be reflected in the Book of Scripture, and find there its definitive interpretation.

At one time Lewis regarded the Bible, and the whole Christian story, as no more than a fairy tale dressed up as truth, a "lie breathed through silver." It is easy to see why. Fairy stories as well as many of the classical myths and legends contain many themes, stories, and ideas we also find in the Christian story.

In particular, a hero is generally marked out from birth for a special destiny. He has been born into a time and place in need of some sort of deliverance, usually from an oppressive ruler (who may or may not have supernatural powers). His birth is often marked by some supernatural mark of favor; indeed, he may even be the son of a god. On reaching maturity, he receives his task: a task only he can fulfill. He may have a time of trial before he begins, in which he has to resist temptations that will divert him from his task. The task may involve the recovery of a lost treasure guarded by a dragon, or the undoing of the enchantment that lies over a kingdom, or winning the hand of a princess; often it involves all three.

Jesus Christ fits this pattern for the hero. Just as he fulfills the prophecies of the Old Testament, he also fulfills the universal archetype of the mythic hero (although in both cases he does so partly by turning expectations on their head). He is born to a virgin and is called the "son of God." He enters a world oppressed and enslaved (primarily by sin, but also by the Romans). He receives his mission when he is baptized in the Jordan; the Holy Spirit then drives him into the desert for a time of trial; there he battles spiritually with the "dragon" Satan; he returns from this skirmish to recover the lost treasure of his Father's kingdom, the human race; by giving his life for his friends he succeeds in undoing the enchantment of original sin; finally he is raised to new life and, in the book of Revelation, is rewarded with the hand of the "princess" Israel, the "new Jerusalem . . . prepared as a bride" (21:2). The story of Jesus Christ is, clearly, whatever else it may be, a myth.

Lewis's view that Christianity was merely a fairy tale met with an unexpected response when he discussed it with Tolkien, during a long walk one day around Magdalen College in Oxford.[6] Yes, Tolkien said, the Gospels contain a fairy story — even the sum total of all fairy stories rolled together — the one story we would most wish to be true in all literature. But although we cannot make the story true by wishing, and we must not deceive ourselves into thinking it is true *because we wish it,* we still cannot rule out the possibility that it did all actually happen.

It may be that the very reason we wish it were true is that we were *made* to wish it, by the One who makes it true. God created us incomplete, because the kind of creature that can only be perfected by its own choices (and so through Quest and trial) is more glorious than the kind that has only to be whatever another made it to be.

Lewis was haunted by a comment on the Gospels by a "hard-boiled atheist," a man he very much admired for the toughness and objectivity of his mind: "Rum thing, all that stuff of Frazer's about the Dying God. Rum thing. It almost looks as if it had really happened once."[7] Much later, in a letter to his childhood friend Arthur Greaves, Lewis wrote how he had gradually and with reluctance come to believe that

> the story of Christ is simply a true myth; a myth working on us in the same way as the others, but with this tremendous difference, that it really happened; and one must be content to accept it in the same way, remembering that it is God's myth where the others are men's myths: i.e. the Pagan stories are God expressing himself through the minds of poets, using such images as he found there, while Chris-

6. *They Stand Together: The Letters of C. S. Lewis to Arthur Greaves, 1914-1963,* ed. Walter Hooper (Collier/Macmillan, 1986), pp. 426-28, quoted in *The Quotable C. S. Lewis,* ed. Wayne Martindale and Jerry Root (Tyndale, 1989), no. 243.

7. *Surprised by Joy* (Harcourt, Brace & World, 1955), pp. 223-24 and 225.

tianity is God expressing himself through what we call "real things." Therefore it is true, not in the sense of being a "description" of God (that no finite mind could take in) but in the sense of being the way in which God chooses to (or can) appear to our faculties. The "doctrines" we get out of the true myth are of course less true; they are translations into our concepts and ideas of that which God has already expressed in a language more adequate, namely the actual incarnation, crucifixion and resurrection.[8]

For Christians it is obvious that the life of Christ will fulfill all myths and fairy tales because it is the Way, the Truth, and the Life within all lives. It is the Drama within all drama, the Story that all good stories reflect. The overcoming of death by infinite Love is the Quest at the heart of every quest, and the sacrifice that makes it possible is the essence of all heroism. In the Gospels, literal truth and universal symbolism, history and legend, time and eternity coincide. They are brought together by the "hypostatic union" of divine and human nature.

And this upsets what Lewis called "the whole demythology of our time," the assumption that the biblical stories — the Christian myth — are only symbolic and can be revised or abandoned as needed, if they prove themselves "inadequate to our thoughts."

But supposing these things were the expressions of God's thought? . . . You cannot know that everything in the representation of a thing is symbolical unless you have independent access to the thing and can compare it with the representation. . . . How if we are asking about a transcendent, objective reality to which the story is our sole access? "We know not — oh we know not." But then we must take our ignorance seriously.[9]

8. *They Stand Together,* p. 426.

9. "Modern Theology and Biblical Criticism," in *Christian Reflections,* ed. Walter Hooper (Eerdmans, 1967), pp. 165-66. In the essay Lewis noted that skeptical biblical scholars were "imperceptive about the very quality of the texts they are reading," because they lacked "any standard of comparison such as can only grow from a wide and genial experience of literature in general. . . . If he [a critic] tells me something in a Gospel is legend or romance, I want to know how many legends or romances he has read, how well his palate is trained in detecting them by the flavour; not how many years he has spent on that Gospel."

If the myth comes from God, it is likely to mix symbolic and literal truth in ways that we, fallen creatures, cannot see. "When I know as I am known I shall be able to tell which parts of the story were purely symbolical and which, if any, were not; shall see how the transcendent reality either excludes or repels locality, or how unimaginably it assimilates and loads it with significance. Had we not better wait?"

All this sets the scene for what the Swiss theologian Hans Urs von Balthasar describes as the "theo-drama": a drama *enacted* by God the Son, *written* by God the Father, and *directed* by the Holy Spirit. Each of us is offered a role in this cosmic drama, a mission to perform in mythic space. In relation to Christ, "each individual is given a personal commission; he is entrusted both with something unique to do and with the freedom to do it. Bound up with commission is his own, inalienable, personal name; here and only here role and person coincide."[10]

The English word "person" derives from the Etruscan *phersu* and the Latin *persona,* meaning an actor's role or mask. Thus the word originally referred to the *face* that the actor assumed for the purpose of participating in a drama. For an actor, of course, real life is what happens when he takes the mask *off.* Christianity reverses the relationship. Real life is what happens when he puts it on. The play, the cosmic theo-drama, is more real than what happens out of character and "off-stage." It is only by accepting and carrying out a drama, that is, in the myth, that we can become *persons* who are real for eternity.

Perhaps this sounds strange: that, like the Velveteen Rabbit, we still need to learn to become real. But it is what I have come to see as the distinctive message of Christianity. While agreeing with the oriental religions that we must dissolve the illusion of the "false self," Christianity teaches, not the abolition of the self, but that we may inherit a new self that is not illusory. This new self, the *persona,* is distinct from God by nature, but united with him through grace.

10. Hans Urs von Balthasar, *Theo-Drama: Theological Dramatic Theory,* vol. 3 (Ignatius Press, 1993), p. 51.

Fundamentalism and Myth

In his remark about "doctrines," we see why Lewis, even after he came to believe in the literal, historical truth of the Christian myth, could not be dismissed as a fundamentalist. A fundamentalist is one who reduces religion to the size of his own mind. He mistakes the pointing finger for the moon, relative truth for absolute, the human definition for the reality.

But, as mentioned, believing something to be a historical fact need not prevent us from seeing it as a symbolical truth as well. It is because water is an apt natural symbol of birth and of death that God uses it to *bring about* rebirth in the sacrament of baptism. Lewis was not a fundamentalist; he was a *sacramentalist*. His religion was mystical. A fundamentalist will build a fence around a teaching to "protect" it; but he will never, like Lewis, permit that dogma to sink its roots deep into the earth, nor grow above his fence into the sky. Yet that is what it must do in those people whose faith is a living, growing thing — like the tree of the parable that starts as the smallest of seeds, but grows until the birds of the air can nest in its branches.

Lewis's stories of the land of Narnia (written, of course, twenty years and more after his conversion) revolve around a Quest, reflecting in a hundred ways the understanding he had attained of the human heart and its ways to God — the drama of human and divine freedom. Narnia was the name of Lewis's own "inner kingdom," and the diversity of its talking animal inhabitants subject to a human king expresses the primordial harmony with nature that exists in every rightly ordered soul.

Each story in the series deals with a particular threat to this world within the heart, or test of allegiance to it. The recurrent subtheme of the "royal child" is not merely a device for holding the attention of Lewis's young readers, but has its roots in the Gospel saying: "Unless you become like this child, you will not enter the Kingdom of Heaven." Lewis had perceived that it is only by restoring childlike innocence to the heart that our lives can become capable of fulfillment. "Blessed are the pure in heart, for they shall see God."

In the Chronicles of Narnia the reigns of the usurper Miraz, of the Witches, of the Calormenes, are each in a different way images of what we fallen grown-ups have slipped into calling "real life": the world of adulthood, of cynicism, hypocrisy, "realism," and despair. The "Earthmen" under the spell of the Green Witch work like ants, as though in a great joyless factory. The Telmarines drive the Talking Beasts and magic out of Narnia, building stone bridges to avoid getting their feet wet and regimented schoolrooms for teachers with names like Miss Prizzle. The Calormene rulers speak with great courtesy, but their words cover treachery and deceit and the basest political calculations.

Part of the great power of the books lies in the contrast they paint between "natural" and "artificial" worlds, a contrast that Lewis explained in a more philosophical mode in *The Abolition of Man*. When the White Witch's ice begins to thaw, when the vines tear down the Bridge of Beruna, what we are meant to feel — what we surely do feel — is that here, at last, is real life again; and the "reality" we had previously accepted as inevitable in our own lives is somehow shown up to be nothing but an evil enchantment.

One example will suffice. At a crucial point in *The Silver Chair*, Eustace and Jill, the Prince they have rescued, and their companion the Marshwiggle Puddleglum are trapped by a Witch in her underground kingdom. They almost succumb to her spell, woven of music and smoke. They are almost persuaded that Narnia, Aslan, and even the sunshine of "Overland" are all childish illusions (myths or fairy tales, we would say). "You have seen lamps," the Witch tells them, "and so you imagined a bigger and better lamp and called it the *sun*. You've seen cats, and now you want a bigger and better cat, and it's to be called a *lion*. Well, 'tis a pretty make-believe, though, to say truth, it would suit you all better if you were younger."[11]

With his last strength of will, Puddleglum steps into the fire, and the smell of his burning flesh weakens the spell. Then he replies to the Witch:

> One word, Ma'am. One word. . . . Suppose we *have* only dreamed, or made up, all those things trees and grass and sun and moon and

---

11. *The Silver Chair* (Macmillan/Collier Books, 1970), pp. 151-59. See Peter Kreeft's "C. S. Lewis's Argument from Desire," in *The Riddle of Joy*, ed. Michael Macdonald and Andrew Tadie (Eerdmans, 1989), pp. 249-72. Kreeft wrote that Lewis gave the argument at length in three places: *Surprised by Joy, Mere Christianity* (in his discussion of hope in Book III, chapter 10), and the preface to *The Pilgrim's Regress*. He does not mention Puddleglum.

stars and Aslan himself. Suppose we have. Then all I can say is that, in that case, the made-up things seem a good deal more important than the real ones. Suppose this black pit of a kingdom of yours is the only world. Well, it strikes me as a pretty poor one.

This, he says, is "a funny thing."

. . . We're just babies making up a game, if you're right. But four babies playing a game can make a play-world which licks your real world hollow. That's why I'm going to stand by the play world. I'm on Aslan's side even if there isn't any Aslan to lead it. I'm going to live as like a Narnian as I can even if there isn't any Narnia. So, thanking you kindly for our supper, if these two gentlemen and the young lady are ready, we're leaving your court at once and setting out in the dark to spend our lives looking for Overland. Not that our lives will be very long, I should think; but that's a small loss if the world's as dull a place as you say.

Puddleglum's argument is directed against the "spell" we all fall under the moment we enter (for example) the London Underground, the moment we sit down at a desk to earn money, the moment we forget to pray. It is one of the most powerful arguments for religious faith in the modern world that I have come across. We have faith not because we can immediately prove what we believe, but because it is in some way nobler to believe than to disbelieve.

We are "outside of the world," on "the wrong side of the door." Through myth, we see inside the world, get through the door. And we set about, through a deliberate decision, to act as though the myths were true, as if the greatest and most wonderful possible things were real things that, although they cannot be *dis*proved (for the Witch's clever arguments are no disproof), may take enormous courage to believe. It takes courage to believe, in today's skeptical atmosphere, not that Jesus of Nazareth was a historical figure (for there is respectable evidence of that), but that he died and rose from the dead (for which we have a great deal of impressive testimony but no strictly "scientific" proof, and none that can easily overcome the intrinsic implausibility of the claim), and certainly that there is no other name in Heaven or on earth by which we can be saved (for there is no "proof" of that at all).

We are back with the principle of Maximum Possible Meaning, this time applied to life itself. Religious faith is a categorical refusal to act as though the world were less important, less interesting, less meaningful, than we are capable of conceiving. It may be more; it will not be less. This may be a gamble, but if so it is a gamble that will give our lives meaning *even if we are wrong*. It will create an island of meaning in a sea of unmeaning.

"I'm going to live as like a Narnian as I can even if there isn't any Narnia." I am going to live as though Christ rose from the dead and calls me to follow. In this way, as Lewis found in his own life, Christian myth becomes Christian experience and in due course, in God's good time, the proofs from experience that we lacked in the beginning are ours as well. For we do not walk in the dark forever.

The Romantic Writer: Lewis's Theology of Fantasy

COLIN DURIEZ

A "ROMANTIC THEOLOGIAN," wrote C. S. Lewis in describing his friend Charles Williams (the term was Williams's), "does not mean one who is romantic about theology but one who is theological about romance, one who considers the theological implications of those experiences which are called romantic." Such a theologian believes "that the most serious and ecstatic experiences either of human love or of imaginative literature have such theological implications and that they can be healthy and fruitful only if the implications are diligently thought out and severely lived."[1]

"The imaginative man in me is older, more continuously operative, and in that sense more basic than either the religious writer or the critic," Lewis confessed in a letter written in 1954. His imagination had made him try to be a poet and after his conversion "to embody my religious belief in symbolical or mythopoeic forms." These included *The Screwtape Letters* and the science fiction trilogy, written for adults, and the Chronicles of Narnia, which he wrote for children — not to give them what they wanted, "but because the fairy-tale was the genre best fitted for what I wanted to say."[2]

---

1. Preface to *Essays Presented to Charles Williams* (Oxford University Press, 1947).
2. "Tolkien's *The Lord of the Rings,*" in *On Stories,* ed. Walter Hooper (Harcourt Brace Jovanovich/Harvest Books, 1982), p. 83.

Theologians of Romanticism

What Lewis wrote about Williams applied also to himself, and to his friend J. R. R. Tolkien, author of *The Lord of the Rings*. Their romantic theology led all three to write fantasy, in "a period almost pathological in its anti-romanticism."[3] The Romantic movement beginning in the late eighteenth century had stressed the poetic imagination, instinct, emotion, and subjective experience over against what it saw as cold, reductionistic, materialistic rationalism. However, they were not simply Romantics, valuing these things for their own sakes, because they all belonged to an older world than the Romantic movement, believing as they did in an objective, transcendent reality that the imagination and fantasy explored and revealed but which existed independent of them.

Lewis suggested that comparatively recently we (Western people) lost an ancient sense of the unity of the poetic and the prosaic, the symbolic and the literal.[4] It was this unity that Lewis and his friends tried to regain through their fantasy. The Bible, for example, insists on looking at the natural and human worlds through a multifaceted appeal to our imaginations. It blatantly appeals to our human taste for a story, and to our delight in other unifying symbolic elements such as archetypes. In the Bible, "spirit" is equally "spirit" and "breath" and "wind." Again, the *logos* of John's Gospel is a profound unity integrating many meanings that we today have to separate out. The same is true of the early portions of Genesis.

Christians, not least evangelicals, today tend to read the Bible mainly as if it conveyed (or failed to convey) propositional truth, as if it first and foremost encouraged looking at reality in a theoretical, systematic way. It is undoubtedly (and thankfully) true that the Bible does convey propositional truth and can generate a consistent theoretical model that has far-reaching consequences for all of human knowledge, in the sciences as well as the arts.

Seen as a whole, however, the Bible encourages what might be called a symbolic perception of reality — looking at reality through

3. *The Letters of C. S. Lewis,* ed. W. H. Lewis (Bles, 1966), p. 260.

4. In this, he was deeply influenced by Owen Barfield. See Barfield's *Poetic Diction* (2d ed., Faber, 1952).

narrative, story, image, and other symbolic elements. The Bible begins symbolically with a seven-day creation and the events in the Garden of Eden and ends with the vision of the Holy City, within which is the Tree of Life introduced in Genesis. The hero of heroes of Scripture is the lamb that was slain from the creation of the world.

In a profound sense, such symbols are not merely poetic, but convey reality in a way and at a depth bare propositions cannot. The lamb that was slain, for instance, is linked in myriad ways to actual events in documented history, such as the crucifixion and Resurrection of our Lord. Such symbols are first linked to events and facts, not to concepts, though they provide subject matter for thought (for example, the symbol of the lamb that was slain helps us think about the achievement of the Cross). Their primary function is to bring us into imaginative contact with significant events in history, selected events in our space-time, events of historical importance.[5]

Lewis gave a simple illustration of this in his essay "On Stories," in explaining the logic of the fairy story, which "is as strict as that of a realistic novel, though different." Referring to *The Wind in the Willows,* he asked:

> Does anyone believe that Kenneth Grahame made an arbitrary choice when he gave his principal character the form of a toad, or that a stag, a pigeon, a lion, would have done as well? The choice is based on the fact that the real toad's face has a grotesque resemblance to a certain kind of human face — a rather apoplectic face with a fatuous grin on it. . . . Looking at the creature we thus see, isolated and fixed, an aspect of human vanity in its funniest and most pardonable form.[6]

Biblical symbols, and those in Lewis's own works, are not so easily explainable as this, but the example will give an idea of the unity of

5. This is not to diminish the importance of related events that may be going on in the unseen world, as in the vision of Elisha's servant (2 Kings 6:15-17). Symbols are necessary to capture such visions. John, for instance, drew upon the symbolic language of Daniel and Ezekiel (Daniel 10:1-9; Ezekiel 1:26-28; Revelation 1:12-16) to describe the glorified Christ in the book of Revelation.

6. "On Stories," in *On Stories,* p. 12. See also *Letters to Malcolm* (Harcourt Brace Jovanovich/Harvest Books, 1964), pp. 52-55, where Lewis showed how replacing biblical images with propositions (demythologizing) simply replaced them with poorer and, because less obvious, more dangerous images and mythology.

the symbolic and the literal, and the power of symbol to convey something beyond propositional truths.

The Organ of Meaning

Lewis set forth some of his key ideas on the nature of the imagination in an essay entitled "Bluspels and Flanansferes," in his book *Rehabilitations,* published in 1939.[7] Many he developed and refined in later years, leading to his definitive statement about literature, *An Experiment in Criticism,* published in 1961.[8] We may summarize some of the basic ideas as follows.

First, reason and imagination have distinct roles: reason has to do with theoretical or conceptual truths, imagination with the very conditions of truth. Second, there are standards of correctness, or norms, for the imagination, held tacitly and universally by human beings, just as there are universally recognized rules of logic for the reason. Third, there was originally a unity between image and reality that reflects an objective state of affairs. And fourth, the framing of truths in propositions necessitates the employment of metaphors supplied by the imagination. Language and thought necessarily rely upon metaphor. This is as true in scientific as in religious or in ordinary discourse. Imagination is a maker of meaning, a definer of terms in a proposition, and as such is a condition of truth.

As he put it in "Bluspels and Flanansferes," the imagination is the "organ of meaning" or reality rather than of conceptual truth. He distinguished truth from meaning. Meaning

is the antecedent condition both of truth and falsehood, whose antithesis is not error but nonsense. . . . And thence, I confess, it does follow that if our thinking is ever true, then the metaphors by which we think must have been good metaphors. It does follow that if those original equations, between good and light, or evil and dark, between breath and soul and all the others, were from the beginning arbitrary and fanciful — if there is not, in fact, a kind of psycho-physical

7. *Rehabilitations* (Oxford University Press, 1939).
8. Cambridge University Press, 1961.

parallelism (or more) in the universe — then all our thinking is nonsensical.

The imagination, then, is concerned with apprehending realities (even if they belong to the unseen world), rather than with grasping concepts. Imaginative invention is justifiable in its own right — it does not have the burden of carrying didactic truths.

This is why good works of imagination cannot be reduced to "morals" and lessons, although lessons can be derived from them, and the truer the work the greater the lessons that can be drawn from it. In a review of Tolkien's *The Lord of the Rings,* Lewis noted that "What shows that we are reading myth, not allegory, is that there are no pointers to a specifically theological, or political, or psychological application. A myth points, for each reader, to the realm he lives in most. It is a master key; use it on what door you like."[9] People may ask, Why use fantasy to make a serious point? Because, Lewis answered, the writer wants

> to say that the real life of men is of that mythical and heroic quality. One can see the principle at work in his characterisation. Much that in a realistic work would be done by "character delineation" is here done simply by making the character an elf, a dwarf, or a hobbit. The imagined beings have their insides on the outside; they are visible souls. And Man as a whole, Man pitted against the universe, have we seen him at all till we see that he is like a hero in a fairy tale?

"The value of the myth is that it takes all the things we know and restores to them the rich significance which has been hidden by 'the veil of familiarity,'" he continued.

> The child enjoys his cold meat (otherwise dull to him) by pretending it is buffalo, just killed with his own bow and arrow. And the child is wise. The real meat comes back to him more savory for having been dipped in a story; you might say that only then is it the real meat. . . . By putting bread, gold, horse, apple, or the very roads into a myth, we do not retreat from reality: we rediscover it.[10]

9. "Tolkien's *The Lord of the Rings,*" p. 85.

10. Ibid., pp. 89-90. See also "The Language of Religion," in *Christian Reflections,* ed. Walter Hooper (Eerdmans, 1967), p. 133.

And similarly, he wrote in "Sometimes Fairy Stories May Say Best What Needs to Be Said," although this sort of writing works with some readers but not with others, when it works fantasy can "generalize while remaining concrete" and "at its best it can do more: it can give us experiences we have never had and thus, instead of 'commenting on life', can add to it."[11] This has a special importance for Christians, because fantasy can "steal past" the religious associations and demands that destroy one's ability to feel the truth of the Christian revelation as one should. "[B]y casting all these things into an imaginary world, stripping them of their stained-glass and Sunday school associations, one could make them for the first time appear in their potency." The writer could, then, "steal past those watchful dragons."[12]

An Implied Theology of Fantasy

Out of this belief about the nature and necessity of the imagination, the features of Lewis's theology of fantasy emerge: a sense of otherness, a recognition of the numinous, a longing for joy, the understanding of art as subcreation, and a yearning for recovery and healing.

Otherness. Great stories take us outside of the prison of our own selves and our presuppositions about reality. Insofar as stories reflect the divine Maker in doing this, they help us face the ultimate Other: God himself, distinct as creator from all else, including ourselves. The very well of fantasy and imaginative invention is every person's direct knowledge of the other. As Lewis wrote in "On Stories": "To construct plausible and moving 'other worlds' you must draw on the only real 'other world' we know, that of the spirit."[13]

The Numinous. An all-pervasive sense of the other is focused in a quality of the Numinous, a basic human experience charted by the German thinker Rudolf Otto in his book *The Idea of the Holy* (1923).

---

11. "Sometimes Fairy Stories May Say Best What Needs to Be Said," in *On Stories,* p. 38. See his comments on poetic language in "The Language of Religion," pp. 133ff.

12. Ibid., p. 37.

13. "On Stories," p. 12.

The primary numinous experience involves a sense of dependence upon what stands wholly other to mankind, which is in one way unapproachable and certainly awesome, but also fascinating. The experience of the numinous is captured better by suggestion and allusion than by a theoretical analysis. Lewis realized this, incorporating the idea into his apologetic for the Christian view of suffering, *The Problem of Pain,* and he cited an event from Kenneth Grahame's fantasy for children, *The Wind in the Willows,* to illustrate it.[14] The final part of *The Voyage of the "Dawn Treader"* particularly embodies the numinous, as the travelers approach Aslan's Country across the Last Sea. Where the numinous is captured, its appeal is first to the imagination, which also senses it most accurately. It belongs to an area of meaning that we cannot easily conceptualize.

Joy. A yearning or longing that is a pointer to joy, which Lewis called *Sehnsucht,* was for him a defining characteristic of fantasy. Tolkien, in "On Fairy Stories," makes it a key feature of such stories, related to the happy ending, part of the consolation they endow. Joy in the story marks the presence of grace coming from the world outside the story, and even beyond our world. It denies (in the face of much evidence, if you will) universal final defeat,

> and in so far is *evangelium,* giving a fleeting glimpse of Joy, Joy beyond the walls of the world, poignant as grief. . . . In such stories when the sudden "turn" comes we get a piercing glimpse of joy, and heart's desire, that for a moment passes outside the frame, rends indeed the very web of story, and lets a gleam come through.[15]

In an epilogue to the essay, Tolkien gives more consideration to the quality of joy, linking it to the Gospel narratives, which have all the qualities of an otherworldly fairy story, while at the same time being actual world history. This doubleness intensifies the quality of joy, identifying its objective source.

Lewis saw the unquenchable longing as a sure sign that no part of the created world, and thus no aspect of human experience, is capable of fulfilling fallen humankind. We are dominated by a feeling

14. *The Problem of Pain* (Bles, 1940), p. 6.

15. Tolkien, "On Fairy Stories," in *Tree and Leaf* (2d ed., Unwin Hymen, 1988), pp. 62-63.

of homelessness, and yet by a keen sense of what home means. He speculated that the desire for Heaven is part of our essential (and unfulfilled) humanity.[16] Such longing, thought Lewis, inspired the writer to create fantasy. The creation of Another World is an attempt to reconcile human beings and the world, to embody the fulfillment of our imaginative longing. Imaginative worlds, wonderlands, are "regions of the spirit."[17] For Lewis, joy was a foretaste of ultimate reality, Heaven itself, or, the same thing, our world as it was meant to be, unspoiled by the fall of mankind, and one day to be remade.

Subcreation. This is a key feature of Lewis's preoccupation with fantasy, though one described better by Tolkien. Tolkien believed that the art of true fantasy or fairy-story writing is subcreation: creating another or secondary world with such skill that it has an "inner consistency of reality." A faery-story ("faery" being Tolkien's preferred spelling) is not a story that simply concerns faery beings. They are in some sense otherworldly, having a geography and history surrounding them.

Tolkien's key idea is that Faery, the realm or state where faeries have their being, contains a whole cosmos, a microcosm. Faery is subcreation rather than either mimetic representation or allegorical interpretation of the "beauties and terrors of the world." For in subcreation, Tolkien (and Lewis) believed, we "survey" space and time. Reality is captured in miniature. Subcreative stories give us a renewed view of reality in all its dimensions — the homely, the spiritual, the physical, the moral.

Recovery and Healing. Another feature of fantasy is restoration or recovery, which brings a healing of the wounds caused when we act through the blindness of sin. Through story, the real world becomes a more magical place, full of meaning. We see its pattern and color in a fresh way, we recover a true view of both individual things like hills and stones and of the cosmic things, the depths of space and time itself.

Believing that the writer was a subcreator, Lewis rejected what he saw as the restless quest of the modern world to be original — indeed,

16. See Lewis's speculations in chap. 10, "Heaven," in *The Problem of Pain,* and "The Weight of Glory," in *Screwtape Proposes a Toast and Other Pieces* (Collins Fontana, 1965).

17. "On Stories," p. 35.

it is in being original (as God) in our life and particularly our morals that we sin and become blinded to the true view of things. Meaning was to be discovered in God's created world, not to be created by mankind without him, and in this discovery imagination working through fantasy was an effective aid. Lewis explained: "He does not despise real woods because he has read of enchanted woods: the reading makes all real woods a little enchanted."[18] For Tolkien, fairy stories help us to make such a recovery — they bring healing — and "in that sense only a taste for them may make us, or keep us, childish."[19]

Lewis's Natural Theology

Lewis's theology of fantasy also expressed his belief in natural theology, the idea that truths about God and the world could be known by the unaided human intellect. Only a fuller knowledge of God, the heavenly realm, and the spiritual depended on grace.[20] Lewis's use of natural theology applied to both the reason and the imagination. His apologetic approach encompassed both his popular theology and his fiction. He was vigorous in employing reason in defense of Christianity and of the objectivity of truth and morality.

But it would be a grave mistake to confuse his commitment to objectivity with Enlightenment modernism. For Lewis, imagination can show genuine insight into God and reality independently of the specific revelation of Scripture. However, as Tolkien emphasized in "On Fairy Stories," any such insights are acts of grace from the Father of Lights. They are a kind of pre-revelation, opening the way to receiving the special revelation of the gospel.

Lewis believed that worlds of the imagination are properly based upon the humble and common things of life — what he called "the

18. "On Three Ways of Writing for Children," in *Of This and Other Worlds*, ed. Walter Hooper (Collins, 1982), p. 65.

19. *Tree and Leaf* (Houghton Mifflin, 1965), pp. 3-84.

20. Lewis gracefully portrays the medieval and renaissance world model, a model expressive of belief in natural theology, in his book *The Discarded Image* (Cambridge University Press, 1964). Natural theology was possible because, as Lewis argued in "The Poison of Subjectivism," Scripture itself teaches that our knowledge of the law is not as corrupted as our will. *Christian Reflections*, p. 79.

quiet fullness of ordinary nature." This is why his sort of fantasy was not "escapist." As Lewis said of Kenneth Grahame's *The Wind in the Willows:* "The happiness which it presents to us is in fact full of the simplest and most attainable things — food, sleep, exercise, friendship, the face of nature, even (in a sense) religion."[21]

Such fantasy is the opposite of escapism, because it deepens the reality of the real world for us — the terror as well as the beauty. Tolkien rightly distinguishes between improper and proper escape: the flight of the deserter and the escape of the wrongly imprisoned.[22] In a sense, nature itself induces fantasy. "Nature has that in her which compels us to invent giants: and only giants will do," Lewis wrote.[23]

When the storyteller is building up a convincing "Secondary World," he or she in fact is creating an imaginary world in the image or as a miniaturization of the "Primary World." Such story-making surveys the depth of space and time. Essentially it is the imaginative equivalent of the reason's attempt to capture reality in a single, unified theory. The natural world of God's creating, however, imposes a fundamental limit to the human imagination. We cannot, like God, create *ex nihilo,* out of nothing. We can only rearrange elements that God has already made, and that are already brimful with his meanings.

Paganism and Grace

This understanding of nature helps explain Lewis's interest in paganism and his (surprising to some) use of paganism and pagan or pre-Christian themes in his fantasy. Though to a lesser extent than for Tolkien, for Lewis paganism was a central case study for the intervention and integration of grace in nature. (Most of Tolkien's fiction is set in a pre-Christian world, and Lewis explored a pagan world in his novel *Till We Have Faces.*) Lewis was, like Tolkien, preoccupied with the imaginative fruit of pre-Christian paganism, particularly what might be called "enlightened paganism." It was for him a source of wisdom and a sort of "pre-evangelism."

21. "On Stories," p. 38.
22. "On Fairy Stories," p. 56.
23. "On Stories," p. 31.

In one of his *Latin Letters* Lewis speculated that some modern people may need to be brought to pre-Christian pagan insights in preparation for more adequately receiving the Christian gospel. St. Paul in Athens pointed out a striking insight into the truth on the part of several Greek poets as part of his apologetic strategy (Acts 17:6-31). In Romans 1:18-32 he points to a universal human knowledge of the truth that is inevitably suppressed because of sin. The good may be found in the pagan imagination, a theme also powerfully explored by Lewis in his own great exploration of pre-Christian paganism, *Till We Have Faces*.[24] In holding such a view of what may be called enlightened paganism, Lewis was heavily influenced by Tolkien.

In *Till We Have Faces* Lewis is retelling an old classical myth, that of Cupid and Psyche, in the realistic setting of a historical novel. The story is told through the eyes of Queen Orual of Glome. Having heard a legend similar to the myth of Cupid and Psyche, she recognizes herself and her half-sister Psyche in the newly sprung up legend and seeks to set the record straight, claiming that the gods have distorted the story in certain key respects.

The gods, she said, had called her deep love for Psyche jealousy. They had also said that she saw Psyche's Palace, whereas Orual had only seen shapes in a mist, a fantasy that momentarily resembled a palace. There had been no evidence that Psyche had married a god and dwelt in his Palace. Orual therefore recounts her own version of the story, being as truthful as possible. She had a reader in mind from the Greeklands, and agreed with the Greek demand for truth and rational honesty.

The short second part of the novel — still in Orual's voice — continues a few days later. Orual has undergone a devastating undeception, whereby, in painful self-knowledge, she discovers how her affection for Psyche had become poisoned by possessiveness. In this discovery, which allowed the restoration of a true love for Psyche, was the consolation that she had also been Psyche. She had suffered on Psyche's behalf, in a substitutionary manner, bearing her burdens and thus easing her tasks. By what Charles Williams called "the Way of Exchange," Orual had thus helped Psyche to be reunited with her divine husband. With the curing of her poisoned love, Orual in a

---

24. *Till We Have Faces: A Myth Retold* (Bles, 1956).

vision sees that she herself has become beautiful. She has gained a face in becoming a full person. After this reconciliation, the aged queen Orual dies, her narration ending with her.

A Tale of Two Loves

In this tale, two loves, affection and eros, are especially explored. Another motif is that of substitution and atonement. Psyche is prepared to die for the sake of the people of Glome. Orual is a substitute for much of Psyche's suffering and pain. Psyche herself represents a kind of Christ-likeness, though she is not intended as a figure of Christ. Lewis wrote to Clyde Kilby that

> Psyche is an instance of the *anima naturaliter Christiana* making the best of the pagan religion she is brought up in and thus being guided (but always "under the cloud," always in terms of her own imagination or that of her people) towards the true God. She is in some ways like Christ not because she is a symbol of him but because every good man or woman is like Christ.[25]

This limitation of pagan imagination comes out in the ugly figures of Ungit and the Shadow-brute, deformed images of the brighter Greek deities Aphrodite and Cupid. The truth that these poor images are trying to glimpse is even more beautiful, free of the vindictiveness of the Greek deities. Psyche is able to see a glimpse of the true God himself, in all his beauty, and in his legitimate demand for a perfect sacrifice. Thus Lewis (following St. Paul) endorsed some of the insights of paganism.

This pattern of nature and grace, as exemplified in Lewis's fantasy stories, is a fundamentally premodernist one. This kind of enterprise, with its profound sensitivity to patterns, is rare in contemporary Christian thinking and imagining.[26] Because the source of our author-

---

25. *Letters of C. S. Lewis,* p. 274.

26. The importance of these kinds of patterns or paradigms cannot be overestimated because they concern the fundamental problem solving and social orientation of a culture. The depth of such patterns is only partly captured by the more familiar concept of a worldview as, for example, the excellent study by James Sire, *The Universe Next Door* (3d ed., InterVarsity Press, 1997).

ity is an ancient book, such thought and imagination have primarily a premodernist orientation. Lewis's and Tolkien's successes as contemporary Christian writers conveying the Faith through such a premodernist unity of fact and symbol must be taken seriously by everyone concerned with communicating Christian faith today.

To See Truly through a Glass Darkly: C. S. Lewis, George Orwell, and the Corruption of Language

DAVID MILLS

EVEN WELL-EDUCATED PEOPLE are often startlingly insensitive to language. One reads, even in the better magazines, prose that clanks and clangs, in which words have meanings only in the sense that "Bob lives in Manhattan" is an address, in which all sorts of assumptions the writers may not knowingly hold are conveyed in the words they use without thinking. The words plant themselves in our common vocabulary and grow there quietly till no one realizes what they actually mean, nor how they change minds and actions by making some thoughts more thinkable and others less.

Such a word is "values." Cultural conservatives defend "traditional values" and "family values," thinking they are speaking the language of the past, but in that word "values" lies a revolution in our understanding of goodness, for our ancestors would not have spoken of values but of virtues. The word "values," the historian Gertrude Himmelfarb noted, includes

> the assumptions that all moral ideas are subjective and relative, that they are mere customs and conventions, that they have a purely instrumental, utilitarian purpose, and that they are peculiar to specific individuals and societies. . . . One cannot say of virtues, as one can of values, that anyone's virtues are as good as anyone else's, or that everyone has a right to his own virtues.[1]

1. *The De-moralization of Society: From Victorian Virtues to Modern Values* (Knopf, 1995), pp. 11-12.

A world concerned with values is a very different world from one concerned with virtues. It will be, at the least, a less virtuous world because it will think far less about virtue.

C. S. Lewis saw a similar effect in the change from "ruler" to "leader" as the name for those in authority or power. We ask of rulers "justice, incorruption, diligence, perhaps clemency," but of leaders "dash, initiative, and (I suppose) what people call 'magnetism' or 'personality'."[2] We see this today in the change in the common vocabulary from "piety," which requires submission to God, to "spirituality," which does not; and from "a book," which has a meaning, to "a text," in which the reader may find almost anything he wants; and from "conversion," which assumes the truth is known, to "conversation," which assumes that it is yet to be found.

Our language directs how we understand the world around us and how we react to it and act upon it. Words have consequences, and this is why the corruption of language is such a danger to the common good. "When," Lewis wrote in 1944, ". . . you have killed a word you have also, as far as in you lay, blotted from the human mind the thing that word originally stood for. Men do not long continue to think what they have forgotten how to say."[3]

Orwell and Lewis

George Orwell (1903-1950) and C. S. Lewis (1898-1963) were masters of modern English prose exquisitely sensitive to the misuse of language. Both wrote novels on this subject — Orwell, *Animal Farm* (1945) and especially *1984* (1948), and Lewis, *That Hideous Strength* (1945) — and reflected on the subject repeatedly in their essays.

---

2. *"De Descriptione Temporum,"* in *They Asked for a Paper* (Bles, 1962), p. 18. Lewis traced a similar change from believing love the chief virtue to believing that unselfishness is. "The Weight of Glory," in *The Weight of Glory* (Eerdmans, 1965), p. 1. He also saw that a rejection of objective truth led people to demand of their rulers qualities that could not be defined or measured but were promoted in exciting and compelling words. "The Poison of Subjectivism," in *Christian Reflections,* ed. Walter Hooper (Eerdmans, 1967), p. 81.

3. "The Death of Words," in *On Stories,* ed. Walter Hooper (Harcourt Brace Jovanovich/Harvest Books, 1982), p. 107.

Though they do not seem to have met, and would probably not have liked each other if they had, they had read each other. Writing in 1944, Orwell criticized *Beyond Personality* (the last of Lewis's talks on the BBC, later incorporated into *Mere Christianity*) as an example of "the silly-clever religious book," which he meant as a literary and moral insult.[4] Writing in 1955, Lewis praised Orwell's *Animal Farm* as a masterpiece while judiciously criticizing *1984*.[5] Lewis was the more generous critic, not just because he was a more generous and liberal man, but because he could accept Orwell's observations on society, while Orwell could not accept Lewis's faith, which deeply challenged his materialism and irreligion.[6]

Orwell and Lewis both fought the corruption of language, the attempt to use words to confuse and blind others, to make some actions possible either by making the necessary thoughts thinkable or by making clear thought impossible. Yet Lewis also knew that the problem — the danger — was not only or even mainly one of corrupted language but of corrupted souls.

"Politics and the English Language"

Orwell's most famous short work on language is his essay "Politics and the English Language," published in 1946 and now a standard in anthologies on writing.[7] "The decline of a language must ultimately have political and economic causes," he began, but each makes the other worse. ". . . A man may take to drink because he feels himself to be a failure, and then fail all the more completely because he drinks." This applies to the English language. Our language "becomes

---

4. *The Collected Essays, Journalism, and Letters of George Orwell,* 4 vols., ed. Sonia Orwell and Ian Angus (Harcourt Brace Jovanovich, 1968), 3:263. The passage Orwell ridicules is the third paragraph of chap. 7 of Book IV of *Mere Christianity.* He left out the first two sentences, which put it in context.

5. "George Orwell," in *On Stories,* pp. 101-4.

6. During the last year of his life, Orwell called a seventeenth-century Italian crucifix with a stiletto inside "a perfect symbol of the Christian religion" and wrote that Christianity is "untenable" and "indefensible." *The Collected Essays, Journalism, and Letters,* 4:511, 512.

7. Ibid., 4:127-40.

ugly and inaccurate because our thoughts are foolish, but the sloven-
liness of our language makes it easier for us to have foolish thoughts."

In such English, the images are always stale and the language
always imprecise. "This mixture of vagueness and sheer incompetence
is the most marked characteristic of modern English prose, and especially of any kind of political writing." (He would have included, had
he cared about the subject, religious writing as well.)

> As soon as certain topics are raised, the concrete melts into the
> abstract and no one seems able to think of turns of speech that are
> not hackneyed: prose consists less and less of *words* chosen for the
> sake of their meaning, and more of *phrases* tacked together like the
> sections of a pre-fabricated henhouse.

Rather than taking the trouble to think, "the ready-made phrases
. . . will construct your sentences for you — even think your thoughts
for you, to a certain extent — and at need they will perform the
important service of partially concealing your meaning even from
yourself." What he called "orthodoxy," by which he meant unthink-
ingly following the party line, whatever party you belonged to,
"demands a vague and inflated language and particularly the use of
stale and unrevealing metaphors." Orthodoxy requires such a style
because it does not want people to see clearly, for if they saw clearly,
they might dissent.

They might dissent because "political speech and writing are
largely the defense of the indefensible." Orwell used as examples the
ways Western intellectuals excused the Soviet atrocities. "Millions of
peasants are robbed of their farms and sent trudging along the roads
with no more than they can carry: this is called *transfer of population* or
rectification of frontiers. People are imprisoned for years without trial, or
shot in the back of the neck or sent to die of scurvy in Arctic lumber
camps: this is called *elimination of unreliable elements*."

By ridding oneself of slovenly language, "one can think more
clearly, and to think clearly is a necessary first step towards political
regeneration; so that the fight against bad English is not frivolous and is
not the exclusive concern of professional writers." His answer to the
temptations of "orthodoxy" was simply to write better, in particular to
free one's language of the jargon and images and common phrases that

carry the meaning the orthodox want you to believe. "If you simplify your English, you are freed from the worst follies of orthodoxy. You cannot speak any of the necessary dialects, and when you make a stupid remark its stupidity will be obvious, even to yourself."

He offered several (very good) rules for simplifying your English: "1) Never use a metaphor, simile or other figure of speech which you are used to seeing in print; 2) Never use a long word when a short one will do; 3) If it is possible to cut a word out, always cut it out; 4) Never use a passive where you can use the active; 5) Never use a foreign phrase, a scientific word or a jargon word if you can think of an everyday English equivalent."

"Politics and the English Language" is a great, and given the status of the people he was attacking courageous, essay. Orwell was right as far as he went, but he did not go far enough because he was not a Christian. He recognized good and evil but could not relate them to any transcendent order, and so he could offer only a set of techniques to oppose people who held other views of good and evil. He objected to their calling the murder of political opponents "the elimination of unreliable elements," but he had no *reason* to condemn those who asserted that that was exactly what they were doing — the elements *were* unreliable — and that they were perfectly justified in doing it — you can't make an omelet without breaking eggs, as George Bernard Shaw put it — and thus in using those words to describe what they were doing.

Lewis on Language

Lewis had argued much the same points before Orwell's essay appeared, most famously in *The Abolition of Man* (1943) and *That Hideous Strength* (1945).[8] The crucial difference in their arguments is that

8. Lewis's remarks on the craft of writing can be found in *Letters of C. S. Lewis,* ed. W. H. Lewis (Harcourt Brace Jovanovich/Harvest Book, 1975), pp. 270-71, 291-92; "Christian Apologetics," "Before We Can Communicate," and "Cross-Examination," in *God in the Dock,* ed. Walter Hooper (Eerdmans, 1970), pp. 96-99, 254-57, 263. See also his friend Nevill Coghill's remarks on his style in "The Approach to English," in *Light on C. S. Lewis,* ed. Jocelyn Gibb (Harcourt Brace Jovanovich/Harvest Books, 1976), pp. 59ff.

Orwell was a materialist and Lewis a Christian. As a Christian, Lewis saw the universe in a greater and a clearer light, and therefore saw more clearly the use of language in a fallen world. (This is an offensive claim, perhaps, but as Lewis wrote, "Christianity claims to give an account of *facts* — to tell you what the real universe is like," and if Christianity is true "it is quite impossible that those who know this truth and those who don't should be equally well equipped for leading a good life.")[9]

It was against the degradation of language into an instrument of control that he fought. "Language is an instrument for communication," Lewis wrote in a later work, *Studies in Words*. "The language which can with the greatest ease make the finest and most numerous distinctions of meaning is the best. It is better to have *like* and *love* than to have *aimer* for both."[10] He fought language in which distinctions were not made and false distinctions employed. He wished people would "become aware of what we are doing when we speak, of the ancient, fragile, and (well used) immensely potent instruments that words are." He meant by "well used," skillfully used — because misused words are immensely potent instruments for evil.

In *The Abolition of Man,* he argued that the danger to our language comes not first from political and economic causes but from a philosophical error, the rejection of the *Tao,* rejected as much by artists, intellectuals, and political leaders in England as the Nazis they were fighting. "Traditional values are to be 'de-bunked' and mankind to be cut into some fresh shape. . . . The belief that we can invent 'ideologies' at pleasure, and the consequent treatment of mankind as mere specimens, preparations, begins to affect our very language. Once we killed bad men; now we liquidate unsocial elements. Virtue has become *integration* and diligence *dynamism*."[11]

The process of corruption is hidden "by the use of the abstraction 'man'," he continued. The *Tao* teaches us what it is to be human, but reject the *Tao* and individual men are reduced to examples of "a

9. "Man or Rabbit?" in *God in the Dock,* pp. 108-9.

10. *Studies in Words* (Cambridge University Press/Canto Books, 1990), p. 6. Lewis was also careful to explain what words could not do (pp. 313-26).

11. *The Abolition of Man* (Macmillan, 1955), p. 85. See also Lewis's discussion of the misuse of the word "community" (p. 42).

mere abstract universal" that can be given any meaning you like.[12] One can do to "Man" what one cannot do to the individual man or woman or child. Human nature becomes whatever those in power say it is.

Three years later, Lewis noted that the rationalization of evil as doing good showed itself first in language. "When to 'kill' becomes to 'liquidate' the process has begun. The pseudo-scientific word disinfects the thing of blood and tears, or pity and shame, and mercy itself can be regarded as a sort of untidiness."[13]

That Hideous Strength

It is in *That Hideous Strength,* the third novel in his space trilogy, that Lewis gave the matter his most thorough treatment.[14] (He gives many examples in other books, of course, especially *The Great Divorce, The Screwtape Letters,* and the Narnia Chronicles.)[15] We find, first, the sort of corruption Orwell examined, when stealing people's homes is hidden and defended by calling it the rectification of frontiers. The N.I.C.E. (a conspiracy to take over England disguised as a scientific, humanitarian institute, located in a place called Belbury) wants the legal authority to experiment on criminals but knows the public would

12. Ibid., p. 86. In *That Hideous Strength* (Macmillan/Collier Books, 1965), the good scientist William Hingest explains why this inevitably happens when man is made an object of scientific investigation (p. 71).

13. "A Reply to Professor Haldane," in *Of Other Worlds,* ed. Walter Hooper (Harcourt Brace Jovanovich/Harvest Books, 1966), p. 84.

14. For illuminating treatments of this book and its understanding of language, see Thomas Howard's *C. S. Lewis: Man of Letters* (Ignatius, 1987), pp. 159-206, and Doris Myers's *C. S. Lewis in Context* (Kent State, 1994), pp. 72-111. Michael Aeschliman's *The Restitution of Man* (Eerdmans, 1998), Gilbert Meilaender's *The Taste for the Other: The Social and Ethical Thought of C. S. Lewis* (Eerdmans, 1998), and Peter Kreeft's *C. S. Lewis for the Third Millennium* (Ignatius, 1994) are excellent expositions of Lewis's intellectual assault on scientism, relativism, and the like.

15. In *The Voyage of the "Dawn Treader"* the subject appears in the sufficiency of the Lone Island's defense of the slave trade (using corrupting metaphor) and in the Dufflepuds' sudden clarity when they want something from Lucy; in *The Horse and His Boy* in the Calormene's elaborate but deceitful language; and in *The Magician's Nephew* in Uncle Andrew's rationalization of his sending a little girl to another world.

oppose the plan if they knew. They must change the public's mind by changing its vocabulary. One of their leaders, Feverstone, explains this to Mark Studdock, a young sociologist they want to hire.

> [I]t *does* make a difference how things are put. For instance, if it were even whispered that the N.I.C.E. wanted powers to experiment on criminals, you'd have all the old women of both sexes up in arms and yapping about humanity. Call it re-education of the mal-adjusted, and you have them all slobbering with delight that the brutal era of retributive punishment has at last come to an end. . . . You mustn't experiment on children; but offer the dear little kiddies free education in an experimental school attached to the N.I.C.E. and it's all correct![16]

Feverstone tells Mark that they want him to write such things. Mark's response is only to worry, his professional vanity being touched, whether this would be his main job. Here, in Mark's almost unconscious choices, driven by his desire to get on the inside, Lewis introduced one theme of the novel: that to lie is to reject God and choose the darkness, which leads, more quickly than we realize, to blindness and thus damnation.

In choosing to use words to mean what they do not mean, in order to trick people into approving what they would not approve if they understood rightly, Mark takes a step, a small but decisive step, toward Hell. (Some readers have thought Mark a weakness in the novel because he is such a fool that it is hard to care enough about him to keep reading. We may think that — until we realize that *most* of us are like Mark. We make the same choice to lie or speak truly every day and usually for the same reasons. At that point our interest rises.)

In part, the Belburian method is to force people to think certain thoughts by giving them the words to think them and by destroying the words in which they might think other thoughts, as Orwell described in the appendix on "Newspeak" in *1984*. But the Belburian method is subtler (and Lewis's insight deeper than Orwell's). The

---

16. *That Hideous Strength*, p. 43. In a meeting of the insiders at Belbury, Wither asks the others to call torture "scientific examination" (p. 240), and Frost calls the loss of morals and affections "objectivity" (p. 299).

method Feverstone describes finds within the people he wants to manipulate a prejudice or desire and makes acting upon it respectable by giving it a respectable name. It plays carefully upon the sins of the people, in ways they will not see, by articulating for them what they already believed, or half-believed, or wanted to believe. The good propagandist is a disciple of Screwtape.

Then there is the corrupting language of jargon, which, interestingly enough, is not heard much at Belbury, but is spoken by people like Mark who are, without knowing it, training for Belbury. As a sociologist, Mark was supposed to be concerned with the realities of human life, but he avoided "such words as 'man' or 'woman.' He preferred to write about 'vocational groups,' 'elements,' 'classes' and 'populations': for, in his own way, he believed as firmly as any mystic in the superior reality of the things that are not seen." It is this mental habit of abstraction, I suspect, that made him so easily adopt the language of Belbury.[17]

Jargon is often a technical necessity ("classes" is a useful term for understanding how people act in groups), but one can move very easily from using jargon as a sort of shorthand to using it to avoid those realities. "Compare 'Our Father which are in Heaven' with 'The supreme being transcends space and time,' " Lewis wrote his brother just after his conversion.

> The first goes to pieces if you begin to apply the literal meaning to it. . . . The second falls into no such traps. On the other hand the first really *means* something, really represents a concrete experience in the minds of those who use it; the second is mere dexterous playing with the counters, and once a man has learnt the rule he can go on that way for two volumes without really using the words to refer to any concrete fact at all.[18]

And then there is the corrupting language of metaphor, of rejecting realities you dislike by treating them as metaphors for ideas of which you approve. The Anglican priest Straik, an atheist and self-proclaimed prophet (not, apparently, defrocked), insists on telling

17. Ibid., p. 87. Mark has become a propagandist, and Lewis also shrewdly analyzed their techniques. See pp. 98, 99, 128-30.

18. *Letters of C. S. Lewis,* p. 147.

Mark that the Kingdom of God is to be achieved on this earth, given not by God but by science, that they, the Belburians, are the saints who will inherit the earth, and that Belbury and its programs are the Resurrection.[19] In making realities metaphorical, one steals the attachment and authority of the realities for one's own ends.

An example is the attempt to modernize biblical language in a way that erases the content, either because the modernizer is insensitive to the way images convey truths that cannot be conveyed in propositions, or because he does not like the meaning and wishes to replace it while claiming its authority, or because he simply does not know the realities and thinks his propositions just as good. In *Letters to Malcolm* Lewis noted that the revision of biblical language called demythologizing "can easily be 're-mythologizing' it — and substituting a poorer mythology for a richer." When propositions are substituted for biblical images, the new meanings are "more subtly hidden and of a far more disastrous type."[20]

Making Things Unclear

Then there is the corrupting language of obscurity. It is not quite accurate to say, as some readers have said, that the speech of John Wither, deputy director of the N.I.C.E., makes no sense. When he first meets Mark, he conveys information, but he does not convey the information Mark needs to have — he tells Mark that he may live anywhere, but not whether he has a job.[21] Wither does not speak nonsense but refuses to speak the truth needed.

He intends to manipulate, but his method is different from the one Feverstone explained to Mark. He does not try to adjust the people's vocabulary and therefore their understanding, but tries to cloud their vision and therefore eliminate understanding, leaving his victims to act blindly on instinct and appetite, as Mark does (and Wither knows he will), obeying his almost overwhelming desire to be

19. *That Hideous Strength,* pp. 78-80.
20. *Letters to Malcolm* (Harcourt Brace Jovanovich/Harvest Books, 1964), p. 52. For other examples, see pp. 51-55, 74, 92-93, 96-97.
21. *That Hideous Strength,* pp. 52-53. See also pp. 95, 119-20.

in the inner ring. The director of the N.I.C.E.'s police explains this to Mark: "Making things clear is the one thing the D.D. can't stand. . . . That's not how he runs the place. And mind you, he knows what he's about. It works, Sonny. You've no idea yet how well it works." Wither, after all, can speak plainly to his — not colleagues, for no one at Belbury is a colleague or a comrade — co-conspirators.[22]

At the end of the story, we find that Wither has actually chosen meaninglessness. Belbury has fallen into chaos and death (though to say one is to say the other), but he does not care because "He had willed with his whole heart that there should be no reality and no truth, and now even the imminence of his own ruin could not wake him."[23] He did not want meaning, but he had wanted power; denied power, he had nothing and was satisfied.

A Vision of God

Thus Lewis as much as Orwell exposed the corruption of language, but he saw something more. He knew that to write well we must see rightly, and that to see rightly we must be holy. As St. John says, "Now we are the sons of God, and . . . when he shall appear, we shall be like him; for we shall see him as he is" (1 John 3:2), and, on the other hand, the sinner "is in darkness, and walks in darkness, and does not know where he is going, because the darkness has blinded his eyes" (1 John 2:11).[24]

Orwell saw something of this. "The more I see the more I doubt whether people ever really make aesthetic judgments at all," he wrote four years after writing "Politics and the English Language." "Everything is judged on political grounds which are then given an aesthetic disguise."[25] But for him the causes of corrupted language were economic and political and the solution to simplify your English. He

22. Ibid., p. 97. For Wither's clarity, see p. 240. He is discussing the problems with torture as a way to extract information and the best way to get Mark to tell them where his wife is.

23. Ibid., p. 353. The passage is a frightening description of damnation.

24. See also John 9:35-41; Romans 11:7-10; 2 Corinthians 4:3, 4; Matthew 15:14; Revelation 3:17.

25. *The Collected Essays, Journalism, and Letters,* 4:504.

was a modern man, and his answer was a technique.[26] Lewis saw that the real cause was the corruption of the human soul and therefore that the only lasting answer was redemption and sanctification.

The question is how the vision of the good and of God is gained or lost. Almost everything Lewis wrote addresses this question in some way, and I will take examples only from the Narnia Chronicles and *That Hideous Strength*. In his books, Lewis showed people choosing, but he never explained why they made the choices they did. In the Narnia Chronicles, we see people choose to see or not to see Aslan by choosing to do good or evil. In *That Hideous Strength*, we see Mark choosing to lie.

In *The Lion, the Witch and the Wardrobe*, we see that the state of the heart decides whether we see God and accept him when we do. Peter, Susan, and Lucy respond to the name of Aslan, before they have any idea who Aslan is, with hope; Edmund (who nurtures anger and plots treason) with revulsion and fear. Like Mark Studdock, he is brought to see the good only when his plans fail and he comes close to losing his life. Yet he chooses for Aslan, as Rabadash in *The Horse and His Boy*, given the same choice, refuses him.

Lewis also gave a hint about the nature of images and archetypes. To be saved, the children have to choose to follow a robin, whom they follow because robins are always good in the stories they know. Only Edmund suspects the robin, having through his treachery and greed lost both his discernment and his ability to trust another, because he begins to believe that everyone is as treacherous as he is. His world is turning in upon itself, and he is becoming the only canon or criterion he knows.

In *Prince Caspian*, Lewis showed that we come to see God by accepting the reports of those whom we know are good and have seen him already. Peter, Susan, and Eustace come to see Aslan only by following Lucy, who sees him when they do not. Susan resists most strongly, appealing to her age and the majority against Lucy, and then,

---

26. *The Abolition of Man*, p. 88. As one who would not conform his soul to reality, Orwell was left trying to force reality to fit his wishes, which can only be attempted through technique. Lewis would have seen economic and political forces to be temptations, not causes, and Orwell's treatment itself part of the problem. See "'Bulverism,'" in *God in the Dock*, pp. 271-77.

when the others agree to follow her, threatens to stay behind. She follows, at last, only because she had to or be left by herself in a strange forest. Because she has rejected Lucy's witness but still followed her, she sees Aslan, but sees him last. As George MacDonald tells Lewis in *The Great Divorce,* "If there's one wee spark under all those ashes, we'll blow it till the whole pile is red and clear."[27]

In Caspian we see that the vision comes to those who hope for it, who recognize that this world is not all there is, even if they do not know what else there is. We also see that the vision grows as we grow in the vision. "Every year you grow, you will find me bigger," Aslan tells Lucy.

Aslan Knows Us

Of all the Chronicles, *The Voyage of the "Dawn Treader"* is most clearly a story of the pursuit of the vision of Aslan, but it teaches that the vision is, for most of us most of the time, partial and incomplete, awaiting perfection in the next world and a matter of work, discipline, perseverance, and courage in this one. It also suggests that our vision is not the most important thing, for Aslan knows the children fully, completely, truly. When asked if he knows Aslan, Edmund can only answer, "Well, he knows me."

In *The Silver Chair* Lewis showed the importance of accepting revelation even when it does not seem to work or does not seem clear. In Aslan's Country at the edge of the world Jill receives the four signs she and Eustace are to follow. There the meaning of the signs seems obvious, but they prove not so when she descends into Narnia. Even had Eustace been with her to hear the signs, he would not easily have recognized in the aged king about to board the ship the old and dear friend the first sign told him he was supposed to greet.[28]

The signs are confirmed only when Jill and Eustace follow them,

27. *The Great Divorce* (Macmillan, 1946), p. 74.
28. This explains the need for what Lewis called "obstinacy in belief," in the essay by that title, *They Asked for a Paper,* pp. 183-96. I have taken this insight from Jacques Sys, "Look Out! It's Alive?", in *A Christian for All Christians,* ed. Andrew Walker and James Patrick (Hodder & Stoughton, 1990), p. 184.

through difficulty and in danger of their lives, and find them trust-worthy. They prove to be revelation because they lead them to a world they would not have found or even known about otherwise, and salvific because only by trusting the last sign, to do whatever they are asked in the name of Aslan, do they escape the Witch and return home.

The Horse and His Boy illustrates three lessons about the vision of God. First, Aslan's actions for Shasta and Aravis's good are not per-ceived as such before they know him. He chases them through the country to drive them together because they need each other to complete the mission he has for them. He follows Shasta through the night to save him from falling off the path and dying. Not until Aslan has revealed himself do they understand. Before he reveals himself they simply fear.

Second, those who have not met Aslan tend to explain away his reality. Bree is shocked that anyone would think Aslan a real lion. He tells Aravis that she could not understand such a mystery — she is a "literalist" — but then tries to explain that "Lion" is only an image or metaphor, and all that it means is that Aslan is "as strong as a lion or (to our enemies, of course) as fierce as a lion. . . . it would be quite absurd to suppose he is a *real* lion." Aslan then appears to him, and he quickly repents. (This anticipates Lewis's examination of skeptical biblical critics in "Modern Theology and Biblical Criticism," a paper he would deliver five years later, explaining patiently, on literary grounds, why their reconstruction of the biblical story was so doubt-ful, indeed fanciful.)[29]

Third, some people will refuse to accept Aslan even when they see him. The Calormeme prince Rabadash, whose attempt to kidnap Queen Susan led to the Calormene invasion of Archenland, repeatedly refuses the mercy of the kings who have defeated him even though Aslan tells him to accept. Aslan must, finally, turn him into a donkey, for he is, in reality, an ass. (But even he receives mercy, as Aslan offers him a way to be "un-donkeyed" in the same way that Eustace was "un-dragoned" — the cost for his lack of repentance to be a joke among his people thereafter.)

29. Published in *Christian Reflections,* pp. 152-66.

To Hear Aslan's Voice

In *The Magician's Nephew* we see again that we respond to God as our hearts are disposed. The cabby hears Aslan's voice and says that he would have been a better man had he known about it. Digory and Polly listen with joy. Uncle Andrew convinces himself that since a lion cannot possibly sing, the voice he hears must be only growling and snarling, till all he really does hear is growling and snarling. When, later, he most needs Aslan, he cannot hear him. Andrew "has made himself unable to hear my voice," Aslan tells Polly. "If I spoke to him, he would hear only growlings and roarings. Oh Adam's sons, how cleverly you defend yourselves against all that might do you good!" All he can do for Andrew is to put him to sleep, protected "from all the torments you have devised for yourself."[30]

The Last Battle is set at the end of Narnia when everyone's vision is made clear. It begins in confusion, as the Narnians accept as true what they should have known was false, and even their king is for a time corrupted. A few Narnians remember the truth, most admirably the lamb who asks how Aslan could have anything to do with the murderous god Tash. (How many of us would have had the courage to say so?) It is the obvious question to ask, but only one animal asks it.

Near the end, King Tirian appears and the animals must choose for him and Aslan or for Tash, though Tirian cannot give them evidence that Tashlan is a false god and can only rally his people to himself by reminding them of their history. Some rally to the king's side though it will mean their deaths, others fight for the Calormenes, and the dwarfs fight for themselves, but they have so chosen against the good that they end in Hell even though they are sitting just inside the doorway of Heaven. At the end Aslan makes the reality and the choice clear, and some animals, recognizing him, run away in fear into the shadow.

Vision can be lost not by obvious sins and acts of defiance but by such small acts of the self as pretension and affectation. Susan came to believe that all her years in Narnia had been only a child's game

---

30. See Kendall Harmon's essay in this book (pp. 236-56) for an explanation of God's creation of Hell as a similar act of mercy.

because she wanted to be "grown up," and in doing so she lost true maturity for something far more childish, because imitative. We wonder if this forgetfulness grew from the character she showed in the first two books, where she was the least engaged of the children, and the most proud. It was she who in *The Lion, the Witch and the Wardrobe* asked Aslan to work against the Emperor's magic and later tried to drive away the mice who were chewing apart his bonds. But then we remember her ride on Aslan after his resurrection, and wonder how she could possibly have forgotten.

As in *The Silver Chair,* trust of Aslan is, eventually, confirmed but now only in the next world. Tirian rejects Tashlan and prays to Aslan for deliverance, and Eustace and Polly arrive. Walking through the woods with them "made all the old stories seem far more real than they had ever seemed before . . . anything might happen now." It will, but not in the sense he means. In the other stories, the arrival of children from our world has always been to Narnia's salvation, but now there is nothing they can do but suffer and die and (though they do not know this) be reborn with it.

The Last Battle also teaches that the vision of God will be found through the pursuit of the good, even if the seeker's words are inadequate or wrong. The Calormene soldier Emeth, who has served Tash all his life, recognizes Aslan as "worthy of all honour" and the "Glorious One" as soon as he meets him, and says "it is better to see the Lion and die than to be Tisroc [ruler] of the world and live and not to have seen him." He has the words to say to Aslan because he has, unknowingly, been seeking Aslan all his life, and his reward is to hear Aslan invite him "further up and further in."

A Study of the Corruptible

The Last Battle may also be read as a study of those who would let their language be corrupted.[31] Most of the animals who accept the new Aslan, and then Tashlan, are ignorant and frightened. They know of Aslan only from stories. The false Aslan is shown to them in the

31. *The Last Battle* (Macmillan/Collier Books, 1970). It is also a study in effective lying and propaganda. See pp. 77-78, 101-2.

dark, with such pomp as the ape Shift can manage, accompanied by Calormene soldiers. A few animals protest, but most accept him. He is doing evil — killing the Wood Nymphs and selling them into slavery to Calormen — but convinced that he is Aslan, they assume that he is angry with them and their suffering their own fault. For most, their understanding has been corrupted but not their hearts, but that is enough to set them to serve the ape and the Calormenes and to blaspheme against Aslan.

Others are cowardly or do not love the good enough to resist evil. Puzzle acts out (a form of lying) Shift's lies because he is a moral coward. He later pleads that he is "not clever" and that he was only following orders, but he acted as he did because he did not have the courage to resist Shift's urging to do what he knew was wrong. Only when he sees the Calormen god Tash flying by — witnesses the inescapable reality of evil — does he truly repent. (We sometimes forget that evil may be done passively, as it was done by Puzzle, by not choosing the good when the good must be chosen, or resisting evil when evil must be resisted.)[32]

And some do not see because they have sinned. Even the two heroes, King Tirian and Jewel the unicorn, do not recognize the fake because they have sinned: first by acting in anger and then by murdering two unarmed Calormene soldiers. They had been given enough information to know better: they should have known from the Centaur's report of the stars and the news brought by the Dryad, who died in front of them because someone had cut down her tree, that Aslan has not returned to Narnia.

The sins affect their vision according to their gravity. When acting in anger, Tirian and Jewel forget the evidence they have and cannot decide if the Aslan they hear about is the true Aslan. The mystery that Aslan is not a tame lion, a mystery in the sense of a truth too deep to be grasped, becomes a mystery in the sense of something unknown. It confuses them, seeming to mean that they can know nothing about him, even if he is doing what they know is wrong. (Significantly, perhaps, no one remembers the words that in *The Lion, the Witch and the Wardrobe* followed "He's not a tame lion": "But he's good.") Then

---

32. Another way of understanding Puzzle is to realize that he suffers from the Deadly Sin of sloth or *acedia*.

they fall into deeper sin — murder — and suddenly they are no longer in doubt: they believe the rumored Aslan to be the real Aslan and give themselves up to his justice. Anger dimmed their sight, but murder blinded them.

But they are also repentant and doing penance, and so their blindness lasts only a little while. When the ape declares that Aslan is the same as Tash, Tirian rejects the lie because he knows — he remembers — that Aslan is good and Tash evil. Even so, later that night, when Puzzle/Aslan is exhibited to the animals, Tirian, tied to a tree some distance away, still wonders if he might really be Aslan. After all, "He had never seen the Great Lion. . . . He had not expected Aslan to look like that stiff thing which stood and said nothing. How could one be sure? For a moment horrible thoughts went through his mind: then he remembered the nonsense about Tash and Aslan being the same and knew that the whole thing must be a cheat."

Mark's Rejection of the Vision

The loss of vision in *That Hideous Strength* is shown in Mark Studdock's steady movement to damnation through his choosing to lie: by fantasies of what he will do or would have done (which is a form of lying, though we tend forget this), by pretending to like people he did not like, by saying what he thinks expected and not saying what he thinks will offend, and (in some ways most corrupting) by lying or deciding to lie to his wife.[33] All are small acts, taken one by one, but they build to an act whose significance he had made himself unable to see.

At last he is invited in: to write newspaper stories about a riot that N.I.C.E. will start the next day, to convince the government to grant them emergency powers.

This was the first thing Mark had been asked to do which he himself, before he did it, clearly knew to be criminal. But the moment of his consent almost escaped his notice; certainly, there was no struggle,

---

33. The steps can be found on pp. 17ff., 35-36, 49, 54-55, 69, 88-89, 94, 102-3, 119-21, 124, and 127-35. From that point the story describes Mark's rescue from the damnation he has chosen.

no sense of turning a corner. . . . it all slipped past in a chatter of laughter, of that intimate laughter between fellow professionals, which of all earthly powers is strongest to make men do very bad things before they are yet, individually, very bad men.[34]

Having lost his vision of the good, he is now helping others lose theirs.

The Furnace of Essential Speech

Of language used rightly I will say little here. The best introduction to the language of Heaven, as far as we can speak it on earth, is the stories themselves, because one best learns a language not by reading textbooks and grammars but from the company of those who speak it as natives.

At St. Anne's, the small community opposed to Belbury, language is used to clarify and thereby to heal.[35] There the right word is the word that heals by bringing truth; at Belbury the right word is the word that tricks ("re-education" for "experiment"). The healing word may be a hard word (which breaks the bone to set it again), but a hard word only because the truth is hard to bear. We rarely hear such hard words at Belbury, where conversation is either insider talk or abuse, and usually the sort of insider talk that brings everyone in by defaming those without.

The end and goal is something very hard to describe, and Lewis does so in mystical terms when Mercury descends upon St. Anne's. The lesser mortals (the people like us) become witty and eloquent, and play deeply with metaphor and analogy. Upstairs, Ransom and Merlin, wiser and greater than the others, were living, though even they only for a short time, "in the very heart of language, in the white-hot furnace of essential speech. All fact was broken, splashed into cataracts, caught, turned inside out, kneaded, slain, and reborn as meaning."[36]

34. *That Hideous Strength*, p. 130.
35. A simple example: Mark's wife Jane has had horrifying dreams. The people at St. Anne's recognize them as visions, but she is still frightened. One character tells her to think of them as news, and given only that one small but accurate word, Jane is able to accept them. Ibid., p. 188.
36. Ibid., pp. 321-22.

Less mystically, the people who see truly find their language being deepened. I will give just two examples. First, in the justly famous lines, Aslan is not safe or tame, but he is good. "Wild" and "good" have much deeper meanings than we thought. In explaining this to the children, the Beavers, no intellectuals, articulate a paradoxical truth and mystery theologians have trouble grasping. Second, Aslan, speaking to Lucy in *The Voyage of the "Dawn Treader,"* who wants him to come back soon, tells her that he "calls all times soon." Time, in other words, is not just the movement through history of minute after minute, but part of eternity, encompassed within God.

Training Our Vision

These are all examples of the language of Heaven. Here let me note only that the ability to speak such language is a gift, but it is a gift to be found — or, better yet, received — after and through the cleansing of your language from corruption. From Lewis's writing we may discern ways to train our vision, to learn to choose to see, so that our speech may grow purer. This process of purification is an act for the establishment of man, against his abolition.

The first step in training our vision is obedience: obedience not only to the Christian revelation but to the *Tao*. Lewis commented to his friend Malcolm that one could not explain the mystery of communion, but that we were commanded to "Take, eat: not Take, understand,"[37] and this principle is a central one of the Christian life.

More, we must have an objective standard — the *Tao* and the revelation — to object to propaganda. If there is no right and wrong, those who want to use words as weapons to gain power over others have every right to do so, or, more accurately, since rights themselves reflect a moral order, the rest of us have no right to object. To see, we must believe there is something there to see.

Second, we must accept the revelation and the terms in which that revelation has been given to us, particularly those images we tend to try to put into propositions.[38] The being who is as strong or as

37. *Letters to Malcolm*, p. 104.
38. For an explanation of the necessity of accepting the biblical images, see Mr.

fierce as a lion is not so interesting or glorious — or strong or fierce — as the real lion Aslan, nor as close to us.

Third, we ought to spend as much time as we can in the company of those who see. Not only holy people, but holy books, or rather books in which holiness is conveyed.

Fourth, we ought to enjoy such pleasures as God gives us. Mark is saved at the end of *That Hideous Strength* by the memory of Jane — and, not least, Jane's body — and, less erotically, certainly, by taking enjoyment in a children's book he had enjoyed as a child but stopped reading because he thought it was childish.[39]

All of these together nurture in us "just sentiments," feelings and instincts and responses and emotions all reflecting reality. Until quite recently, Lewis wrote in *The Abolition of Man,* "all men believed the universe to be such that certain emotional reactions on our part could be either congruous or incongruous to it — believed, in fact, that objects did not merely receive, but could *merit,* our approval or disapproval, our reverence, or our contempt."[40] What an object merited was generally established in the *Tao,* and recognized by all. Belbury, not surprisingly, calls these just sentiments "obscurantism" as opposed to the unsentimental "order" and "objectivity" they offer.[41]

We must have just sentiments to see and therefore to speak truly. In losing belief in the *Tao* we have laid ourselves open to accepting without demur any set of reactions, any sentiments, no matter how incongruous with reality. "The right defense against false sentiments is to inculcate just sentiments. . . . a hard heart is no infallible protection against a soft head."[42] As G. K. Chesterton said, when a man ceases to believe in God, he does not believe in nothing, he believes in anything.

Caldecott's (pp. 86-97) and Mr. Duriez's (pp. 98-110) essays in this book, and the references therein, as well as "Modern Theology and Biblical Criticism," pp. 164-66, and *Letters to Malcolm,* pp. 51-56, 92-93, 96-99.

39. *That Hideous Strength,* pp. 359-60.

40. *The Abolition of Man,* p. 25.

41. *That Hideous Strength,* pp. 41, 299. Hingest, the only one who rejects Belbury, does so because it is not to his taste, but his remarks show that his taste has been formed by the *Tao* (pp. 71-72).

42. *The Abolition of Man,* p. 24.

The Call to Holiness

By seeing more clearly, one can think more clearly, and to think clearly is a necessary first step toward regeneration of any kind. And thus the fight against bad English is not frivolous and is not the exclusive concern of professional writers. But the writer's struggle begins in the human heart, Lewis knew, in the choice for or against God. "[W]ith all your innumerable choices," Lewis wrote in *Mere Christianity,*

> all your life long you are slowly turning this central thing either into a heavenly creature or into a hellish creature: either into a creature that is in harmony with God, and with other creatures, and with itself, or else into one that is in a state of war and hatred with God, and with its fellow-creatures, and with itself. To be the one kind of creature is heaven: that is, it is joy and peace and knowledge and power. To be the other means madness, horror, idiocy, rage, im-potence, and eternal loneliness.[43]

Language is best purified not by the writing techniques Orwell offered, as useful as they are, but by holiness. The Orthodox say that a theologian is one who prays and one who prays is a theologian. It may be asserted that a writer is one who says his prayers, and one who says his prayers is (within the limits of his gifts and training) a writer, for poor grammar and clumsy rhythm may yet convey the truth more precisely and deeply than grace and style and wit. "The way for a person to develop a style is (a) to know exactly what he wants to say, and (b) to be sure he is saying exactly that," Lewis wrote.[44] The holy man speaks the truth because he knows exactly what he wants to say, because he sees it in front of him.

---

43. *Mere Christianity* (Macmillan, 1960), pp. 86-87.
44. "Cross-Examination," in *God in the Dock,* p. 263. Lying, Lewis wrote a friend, is saying "what you know to be untrue. But to know this, and to have the very ideas of truth and falsehood in your head, presupposes a clarity of mind." *Letters to an American Lady* (Eerdmans, 1971), p. 51. He would have agreed, I think, that a man can lie so much as to lose that clarity of mind, at which point he becomes a liar, even though he cannot recognize a lie.

The Triumphant Vindication of the Body: The End of Gnosticism in *That Hideous Strength*

THOMAS HOWARD

THAT HIDEOUS STRENGTH is unique in Lewis's fiction, in that there is no "secondary world" into which we are boosted for the landscape of the narrative. Narnia is such a world; it bears no relation to either time or space in our own "primary world." You cannot get there with charts, compasses, or any conceivable hardware.

The Malacandra of *Out of the Silent Planet* is, of course, our Mars: but it is very far from being the dusty, dead planet which shows up in Voyager and Hubble photographs. *Perelandra* whisks us to our Venus, but, again, it turns out to be a world wholly inaccessible to our most advanced technology, ruled as it is by eldila (or, shall we say, more accurately, stewarded by eldila, since it is a world made for human beings). The bus trip in *The Great Divorce* takes us from Purgatory/Hell to Heaven — quite outside of our earthly scheme of distance and chronology. The same is true of *The Pilgrim's Regress* and *Till We Have Faces.*

Primary and Secondary Worlds

A note on this matter of primary and secondary worlds. In his great essay "On Fairy Stories," J. R. R. Tolkien suggested that the power of myth and faerie lies in the fact that they set up a secondary world, with its own laws and qualities, but that these laws, at least, differ not one whit from the laws governing our own planet.[1] (Tolkien, by the way, preferred the spelling "faerie" for the region, since it dismisses summarily and immediately any notion of frivolous creatures flitting about toadstools or the mischievous sprites that even Shakespeare evokes in "A Midsummer Night's Dream" and "The Tempest.")

We are speaking of the moral law, of course, not questions of speed limits and stoplights. In a world uncluttered by diminutive mignons with gauze wings or brownies who curdle the cream, we find ourselves in "the perilous realm." It is perilous since we mortals are there hailed with Reality in such stark shapes and colors that our sensibilities (not to say our souls) are jolted awake.

In the dim murk of our world, Eustace Clarence Scrubb can pass for merely a tiresome and desperately spoiled egoist.[2] In Narnia, he turns into a dragon, not because some great Power has said "What punishment shall we visit upon this wretched child, eeny-meeny-miney-mo," but rather because he *is* a dragon, in any world. It only becomes visible in the sharp clarity of the atmosphere of Narnia. In the hierarchies and orders of our world, Sarah Smith of Golder's Green is a charwoman, but in Heaven she is honored by a great procession of chariots and beasts and music.[3] Her beauty and virtue were hidden under mops and pails and cheap work clothes and a cockney accent before, but now we see who she really was all along. Her simplicity and integrity and faithfulness — this is what those things really look like, but we must be yanked into the secondary world to see them.

The secondary world, for Tolkien, exists in an *analogous* relation to our primary world, and thus throws new light on things here. And, as Lewis made so clear in *The Abolition of Man,* no story in Heaven, earth, or Hell can introduce a new moral scheme. Good and evil are like primary colors: you can deny them by shutting your eyes or turning out the lights, but you cannot replace them.

You cannot make up a fiction that lauds venality, or extols pusil-

---

1. "On Fairy Stories," in *The Tolkien Reader* (Ballantine Books, 1966), pp. 27-84.

2. *The Voyage of the "Dawn Treader"* (Macmillan/Collier Books, 1970), chaps. 6 and 7.

3. *The Great Divorce* (Macmillan/Collier Books, 1975), chap. 12.

lanimity, or celebrates duplicity. Perhaps you can, but your story will fail since it will carry no conceivable reader with it. The coward wants to read about heroes, not cowards. Even the venal and pusillanimous and duplicitous want to see themselves in some semiheroic light. We do not *like* duplicity — neither we, nor fauns, nor eldils — because it is essentially and forever odious.

That is, despite the sundry marvels that our world never encounters — wardrobes that back up onto the land of Faerie, centaurs, Seroni, Pfifltriggi, and mighty beings to grasp whom we mortals have to reach for the category "angel" — despite these marvels, we all find ourselves overwhelmed soon enough with the very strong hunch that what we are reading is a "true" story, true as a tuning fork or plumbline, and that the reality of centaurs and Pfifltriggi are entirely irrelevant when it comes to the very narrow question of the tales' credibility.

On the profoundest level, the tales are, we almost have to say, *more* true than any factual journalism or scholarly history that our own world looks upon as true. This is so because ours is indeed the "Silent Planet," which voluntarily demurred at the choreography and the harmony that mark "real reality" (as Francis Schaeffer put it), and plunged itself into darkness, discord, suffering, and death. In the secondary worlds of these tales, we hear something of the harmony we were meant to hear. The secondary worlds are, in this sense, the real primary world.

Heaven and Hell Break Loose

Now what is *That Hideous Strength?* Judged by the canons that preside over the general discussion of fiction, especially of the novel, *That Hideous Strength ne marche pas,* the French would put it. It is, in some senses, a great ragbag — or, shall we say, treasure chest — of virtually all of Lewis's moral theology. Nearly every topic that Lewis touches on in his essays and discursive books finds itself unfurled in solid colors and solid forms here.

The book is at least prophetic. Written in the 1940s, it finds itself at the very cusp between good and evil as they are manifesting themselves in the 1990s. In many ways, a reader who had only this one of

Lewis's many books would have as excellent a condensing of his thought as could be asked for.

In *That Hideous Strength* we are never outside England. However, the Reality that seems to break through the scrim that divides Thulcandra (Earth) from the blissful choreography apparently visible and audible in the rest of Creation turns out to be the Reality that we have all along been penetrating in *Out of the Silent Planet* and *Perelandra*. In this book the secondary world muscles its way through the scrim that hangs between our ordinariness — a sort of blindness, you might say — and the titanic truth of things. We stay in England; but all Heaven and all Hell have broken loose.

Nothing we see at first is unexpected: Two young intellectuals with a troubled marriage, he trying to advance his career, she left at home feeling unfulfilled; the quiet, cynical plotting of academic politics; a few old-fashioned dons trying to maintain the old ways; some new research institute with vaguely utopian goals — just fundraising, that, we think; an atheistical, left-wing priest of a type not (alas) uncommon. Even the "counter-cultural community" of St. Anne's seems a familiar sight.

The story turns out to be the story of salvation for the two main characters, Jane and Mark Studdock. Their marriage is altogether threadbare. Jane conceives of herself as an intellectual, and resents all the hints that her society cherishes connecting women with hats and tears and domesticity. "Matrimony" is the first word of the book. We meet Jane reflecting, to the disadvantage of her husband, on words from the marriage rite in the *Book of Common Prayer:* "Matrimony was ordained, thirdly, for the mutual society, help, and comfort that one ought to have of the other."

Of the first purpose of marriage, "It was ordained for the procreation of children," we hear, significantly, nothing. For Jane wants to be a "mind." She is busy with her dissertation, which, with exquisite irony, concerns Donne's "triumphant vindication of the body." The irony here is that Jane is a Manichaean or a gnostic, having fallen into the common trap of supposing that the physical realm is in some way inferior to the spiritual realm, and therefore to be eschewed.

Jane's taste for clothes that are "severe" and "really good on serious aesthetic grounds," her dislike of hats and anything else stereotypically feminine, her desire to be seen as "an intelligent adult and not a woman," all this seems harmless enough. It is certainly under-standable. But the drama in this story discloses to us the diabolical horrors that stand at the far end of any division of mind and body. At the end of this gnosticism lies Belbury, and Babel, and chaos, and suicide.

Her husband Mark is busy selling his soul for a mess of pottage. It is quite the worst sort of pottage since it entails one's going to any craven, even groveling, lengths to get "in" — in this case, in to the innermost circle of the faculty at Bracton College. He is an oaf and a cad when it comes to being a spouse, and we all sympathize heartily with Jane's dereliction, even though we cannot but admit that she is a very proud young woman. There is a hint, later, that Mark is also a sort of gnostic, with the irony that his field, sociology, is one that is supposed to deal with realities. "His education has had the curious effect of making things that he read and wrote more real to him than things he saw. Statistics about agricultural labourers were the sub-stance; any real ditcher, ploughman, or farmer's boy was the shadow."

Hovering over the beginning of the story, then, is the possibility of a tearing apart of something that was meant to be whole. Our young couple, who look upon each other with a "laboratory outlook upon love," are moving, almost inevitably, it seems, to divorce, to the gnostic act of tearing "one flesh" into two. (We note, from hints in the book, that these gnostic intellectuals were not so dismissive of the body as not to enjoy its pleasures, even before marriage, and that this misuse — exploitation, really — of the body is a cause of their division.)

The locale of salvation for these two people separates itself out presently into two small communities, Belbury for Mark, and St. Anne's for Jane. Things start innocently enough with some routine business at Bracton College about selling some property. The faculty is discussing the matter. All is carried on in the thin and exalted atmosphere of academia. A faculty meeting: what could be more civilized?

The reader has not gone far, however, before he suspects that something is rotten in the state of Denmark. There is a harshness, and a serpentine wiliness about the attitude of the men who are eager to sell the property. All is tergiversation. Language, that is, is being pressed into the service of deceit. Language, made to be a vehicle of truth, is being unmade. All is thickly coated with euphemism and circuitousness. But euphemism is not the only tool. Brute force will do when needed: when old Canon Jewell, the very archetype of your traditionalist and gentlemanly don, tries to expostulate, he is shouted down.

It is the pro-sale crowd that is clearly the "in" crowd at Bracton, and Mark will do anything — anything — to get in. The reader encounters difficulties here because all the members of this chic group are colossal bores. Why any mortal would want to weasel his way into such a drab coterie defies credibility, we wonder — until we realize, to our own vexation, that what Mark is doing we have done over and over. (The hapless third-grader who sees his fellows in great floppy trousers with the crotch-seam worn at knee level and who manages to get hold of such a garment in the forlorn hope that this will constitute an *entré,* is heading down the track on which Mark has been accelerating for some time now.)

It presently comes to light that Mark's crowd (he seems, early enough on, to be making a success of his efforts) have, as a sort of quasi-headquarters, a great mansion outside of town, whither they resort to pursue plans that dwarf the mere sale of Bracton land. A huge program is afoot. The college, the town of Edgestow, and, it gradually dawns upon us, the whole world, is to be remade according to posttheist, gnostic, virtually Bolshevik "efficiency."

All ancient oaks and elms are to be cut down. Ancient buildings are to be leveled. All winding streams are to be bulldozed into straight canals. "Tradition" is to be annihilated in the interest of the new man, who will be, like all such new men, free of bourgeois prejudices, tradition-born timidity, outdated moral codes, and reverence for anything that hales from antiquity.

This Is Hell

The reader may stifle a yawn here: how many anti-utopian books must I read? They're all the same. H. G. Wells's fantasies, Aldous Huxley's *Brave New World,* George Orwell's *1984* and *Animal Farm* — they have all pictured such a world, the latter two, of course, by way of casting sardonic aspersions on such fatuity. The poor boys in William Golding's *Lord of the Flies* thought you could organize things so that strife and cupidity could be eliminated. Alas. And the reader's yawn is interrupted peremptorily. This is not just another failed utopia. "This is Hell," he finds himself saying about Belbury, the mansion run by the Progressives. Cynicism and perfidiousness are its principal marks, and its denizens embody these qualities.

There is Curry, whom Mark thought might be his *entré*. But presently he meets Lord Feverstone, who, in beguilingly intimate conversation with Mark persuades him that Curry is nothing but window-dressing, and that the *real* people one must get to know are so-and-so, and so-and-so, *ad infinitum*. Naturally, as one moves among the company with Mark, each one is jeeringly dismissed by the newest acquaintance as silly and wholly expendable.

Near the center (but where, we, and Mark, begin to wonder, *is* the center?) we find one Fairy Hardcastle, a burly woman with bobbed hair, police uniform (including jackboots), and a cigar. And there is Straik, an apostate Anglican priest, all-too-recognizable, whose worst fear is that anyone will for a moment suppose that he might possibly mean anything other than the Belburian utopia by such quaint religious language as "the kingdom of heaven."

Filostrato turns up, and we find ourselves meeting a man who has carried gnosticism to hysterical lengths. He will have *all* vegetation shaved right off the planet: metal trees are more efficient; they don't rot and die and so forth. He can't bear the earth being "furred over" this way. And all loam and nests and eggs and all the riotous fruitfulness that makes such a mess of the world — all will be scoured and sterilized. Spiritual man will come into his own. There is also a man with a trim white goatee and eyeglasses that make it exceedingly difficult to see into his eyes. He seems to be, in some sense, the head man; but one is never quite sure. His name is Frost (Freud?).

The most baleful figure by far is one Wither. He is the "Deputy Director," and in many ways seems to control things with very little reference to Frost. We very quickly run aground on his syntax. He is able to utter whole paragraphs of elegant prose that, upon reflection, turn out to have meant nothing. Again, at Belbury language is unmade, is pressed into the service of non-meaning and thus of confusion and alienation.

Wither keeps insisting that "We are a family, Mr. Studdock," and one realizes, with revulsion, that Belbury is the very travesty of family. (And we recall Mark's "unfamilial" marriage to Jane: sterile; drab; joyless. His failures there have, perhaps, suited him for Belbury, or left him specially vulnerable to its seductions.)

At the center of Belbury there is The Head. It is literally a bodiless head. The denizens of Belbury are out to prove that man is, or should be, a pure intellect, untrammeled by all the embarrassing viscera, plumbing, and lymph that ruins our dignity. One recognizes, of course, the shopworn agenda of gnosticism, which is ever the same and ever new and always titillating. Spiritual man!

The Head is kept "alive" with various hoses and spigots and tubes, and it drools imbecilities from its ghastly mouth. It is worshiped by Belbury, and most especially by Wither. Its imbecilities are taken as sibylline wisdom. (Hell again? One recalls the ancient notion that evil is imbecilic, finally.)

One finds one's theology of Hell cruising near: is not Hell the final result of the agenda of evil, which is to unmake the good solidity that marked the original creation, and which is the very mode characteristic of the City of God, with its adamantine foundations? We find "shades" in Hell. Spectres. Damned souls, which are the mere detritus left when evil has leeched and leeched away the good solidity that God made when he made the universe and man.

Thus Belbury, the travesty of travesties. Is this Hell yet once more? Evil can create nothing. It can only ape, with hideous clumsiness, the good solidity that attends the good. We may recall here the ape Shift, in *The Last Battle*. And then we recall, with a start, that some people prefer the shadow, the imitation; some people choose Hell, as indeed we see Mark doing, not without qualms, as he sinks deeper into the society of Belbury.

A Peculiar House

On the other hand, we have St. Anne's. It is a peculiar house, populated by a random assemblage of unimpressive people. There is Ivy Maggs, the Cockney charwoman; and there is McPhee, the Scottish skeptic; and Dr. and Mrs. Dimble, a nice, egregiously ordinary couple — he is a don, and she is a plump, motherly, barren housewife. Arthur and Camilla Dennison are an appealingly civilized youngish couple who love "weather" (instead of grumbling about rain — Belbury's Feverstone, we find out later, "had always hated weather"), and who like nothing better than an outing with sandwiches, coffee, and cigarettes. There is also a bear named Mr. Bultitude (Lewis borrowed the name from the nineteenth-century schoolboy tale, *Vice-Versa*), a jackdaw named Baron Corvo, and a cat named Pinch.

At the center, and the undoubted head of the household, is Ransom, the hero of *Perelandra*. It turns out that he is the Pendragon of Logres, Logres being King Arthur's kingdom conceived of as a place of justice, purity, charity, and even holiness. St. Anne's is the only fragment left, now, fifteen centuries after Arthur, of Logres. It is named after the mother of the Mother of God, and, since it becomes the mother of salvation to Jane, who in turn becomes the mother of salvation for Mark, it seems appropriately named. Jane becomes the *theotokos,* the "God-bearer," to Mark, since it is (as we will see) by the means of her flesh that salvation is mediated to him.

Jane, as a result of some terrifying and apparently clairvoyant dreams that she is having, finds herself at St. Anne's on the recommendation of Mrs. (or, "Mother") Dimble, from whom she has received, in spite of her uneasiness with Mother Dimble's big-breasted motherliness, great comfort and help. She is admitted to St. Anne's through a small door in the wall at the bottom of the garden, and led up a narrow path by one Grace Ironwood.

Lewis teases us here with evanescent suppositions. "Strait is the gate and narrow is the way" — do we hear a fugitive echo of that somewhere? And Ironwood: "sweetest wood and sweetest iron," say the devotions for the Adoration of the Holy Cross on Good Friday. Not to mention Grace. It is sometimes the case that grace seems a bit severe upon our first encounter with it. Remember how daunting the advent of Aslan is in the Narnia Chronicles. Miss Ironwood is a severe spinster dressed all in black. One may pursue such foxfires, or not, according to one's wish.

It eventually becomes clear that Jane is a wanted person because of these dreams of hers. Both Belbury and St. Anne's know about them. Hence we discover Belbury's motive in wooing Mark. He is to bring his wife to Belbury, because she will prove to be the key to their finding Merlin who, returning to England from Logres, still exercises the sort of authority over the creation that we imagine the unfallen Adam to have had.

St. Anne's is equally anxious to get Jane, for the same reason. The sticky bit is that Merlin, being innocent, won't be able to tell the difference between evil and good at first glance, and may therefore be dragooned by Belbury into furthering their schemes with his power. St. Anne's must find him first. This is the thriller part of the story — the race to secure Merlin.

Of course, as is unflaggingly the case with Lewis's fiction, the narrative is suffused with echoes and resonances. Theology spells the matter out according to its particular mode — discursive, proposition-alist, abstract. Narrative spells it out according to its particular mode of indirection and image-making. The matter here is the ancient fight between Hell and Heaven.

The Body Vindicated

Whereas Belbury is busy about unmaking meaning (cf. Wither's syn-tax, or Belbury's travesty of the notion of "family"), St. Anne's is built and sustained by meaning. Nothing but the bald truth is tolerated there. Language, *pace* Wither, is brought to its great herculean glory in its total consonance with meaning. At one point, words come out of Dr. Dimble's mouth "like castles." In another scene, when the gods descend in glory on St. Anne's, we find that Mercury's visit releases the whole company (most of them are down by the kitchen fire; Ransom is upstairs alone with Merlin, whom they have secured, *mirabile dictu*) into glorious and blissful articulateness.

Jane finds salvation from her prim and nettled egoism at St. Anne's. Mark is well en route to Hell at Belbury. But some rag of sanity — actually, it is the mere memory of Jane, most especially Jane's body, the body Jane herself has tried, in effect, to escape — rescues him and sends him fleeing from Belbury. No argument, no exercise of "mind," saves them. They are saved, both of them, from their gnosticism, by their acceptance of the body.

But not, we must be clear, *merely* of the body, if that means (as it tends to, these days) mainly sexuality. That would be to exchange gnosticism for materialism. For Mark and Jane, and indeed for all of us, the body must take its part in the great dance of charity, of which marriage is the great model and image. Mark must come to see himself as he is: a "little vulgarian . . . dull, inconspicuous, frightened, calculating, cold," a "coarse, male boor with horny hands and hobnailed shoes and beefsteak jaw . . . blundering, sauntering, stumping in." He must discover that in taking her body "he had plucked the rose, and not only plucked it but torn it all to pieces and crumpled it with hot, thumb-like, greedy fingers." He must learn to love her, to treat her with reverence: "The word *Lady* had made no part of his vocabulary save as a pure form or else in mockery. He had laughed too soon."

Mark escapes the apocalypse that comes upon Belbury as the natural and inevitable product of their agenda. They have sought unmeaning: they get it, in the bloodiest terms. Babel is visited upon them. They tried to destroy nature; and nature destroys them. Or rather: they have destroyed themselves, as Frost proceeds to do.

As Belbury collapses in babelian chaos around him, Frost knows that all his plans have failed, but the knowledge does not move him, "because he had long ceased to believe in knowledge itself. . . . He had willed with his whole heart that there should be no reality and no truth, and now even the imminence of his own ruin could not wake him." He proceeds to burn himself to death, and after he lights the fire someone (God?) offers his soul an escape. "He became able to know (and simultaneously refused the knowledge) that he had been wrong from the beginning, that souls and personal responsibility existed. He half saw: he wholly hated. . . . With one supreme effort he flung himself back into his illusion." Such, Lewis seems to be saying, is the end of gnosticism.

The fruition of things at St. Anne's, by comparison, is embarrassingly domestic and ordinary. Mark has arrived, and has fallen asleep in a little hut at the bottom of the garden, having scattered his clothes hither and thither. Venus descends. Birds coo and chirp in amorous melody. The greenery thrives in its beds of compost. The director has sent Jane out of the main house to meet her husband, with the instruction to have children. There is the hint here, perhaps, that by fulfilling the first purpose of marriage she shall receive the third as well.

Jane "descends," through the garden, past the piggeries, to the hut. Through the window she sees Mark's clothes strewn about. He needs a wife. "How exactly like Mark! Obviously it was high time she went in." Jane has been saved, and is about to become the bearer of salvation to her poor, proud, craven husband.

Fragmentation and Hope: The Healing of the Modern Schisms in *That Hideous Strength*

LESLIE P. FAIRFIELD

DURING WORLD WAR II the Free World focused intently on defeating the Axis armies, and assumed (not unreasonably) that their own cause represented truth and virtue. With a longer perspective, C. S. Lewis recognized acutely that the Allies were relying on powers that would ultimately turn upon those who wielded them. Once peace came, the forces of technological modernity would threaten England with evils more insidious than Nazism, because less obvious.

So in 1943 Lewis wrote "a 'tall story' about devilry" with a view to warning his culture of the deeper war in progress. That war was a struggle for the soul of Western civilization itself, and in it the powers of modernity were already splitting and fragmenting both society and the souls of individuals.

That Hideous Strength — the third volume in his "space trilogy" — takes place in England after the War, and it depicts both that fragmentation and the healing powers that still sought to mend and unify the West. Fifty years later we are amazed at Lewis's prescience, and the accuracy with which he identified both the problem of modernity and the solution Christianity offers.[1]

---

1. *That Hideous Strength* (Macmillan/Collier Books, 1965), p. 7. As a work of literature, it should be said, *That Hideous Strength* lacks the sureness of touch Lewis would display thirteen years later in *Till We Have Faces*. He compressed too much

The Story of the Two Cities

The novel describes the struggle between two opposing "cities," as St. Augustine terms those two conflicting tendencies in human society, love of self and love of God. One of them is Belbury ("fortress of Ba'al"), a pretentious nineteenth-century mansion, the headquarters of an ominous "National Institute of Co-ordinated Experiments." The other is St. Anne's-on-the-Hill, a village in the eastern Midlands whose heart is a comfortable manor house within (significantly) a walled garden.

N.I.C.E. is ostensibly a humanitarian think-tank, using science to help solve social problems, which in reality masks a conspiracy to dominate England and reduce the population to behavior-modified slaves of the technocratic elite. In the manor at St. Anne's there live a small "Company" of Christians whose calling is to resist N.I.C.E. and its culture, and work for the rescue and the healing of England.

Torn between the two cities are a young couple, Mark and Jane Studdock. Mark is a naive young sociologist at the University of Edgestow, situated (spiritually as well as geographically) between Belbury and St. Anne's. N.I.C.E. is scheming to usurp and dominate both the university and its town, for they believe that certain ancient powers of nature lie buried beneath Edgestow's Bracton College. Hoping to ally the old magic with new technology, N.I.C.E. recruits Mark, exploiting his desire to be on "the inside," and uses him to help undermine the College's resistance to its purchase by the Institute.

But N.I.C.E. have an additional motive in seducing the gullible young man. Mark's wife Jane has powers of "clear sight," dreams that point to the Institute's real intentions, though at first, being an enlightened young woman, she thinks of them only as nightmares. The leaders of the Institute mean to deflect the threat Jane represents, and to bend her clairvoyance to their own purposes. But Jane is terrified by her dreams, and finds her way to St. Anne's through her friendship with two of the Company there, a professor and his wife from Edgestow.

---

into one novel, and the allegorical surnames are too obvious: "Frost" and "Wither" at Belbury, "Ransom" at St. Anne's. And sometimes the heavyweight ideas hold back the pace of the story.

Jane is an independent and superficially liberated young woman, and initially she feels a strong aversion to the manor house at St. Anne's and the ordered, hierarchical life of its Company. But gradually she recognizes the winsome life these Christians represent, and she commits herself (still warily) to their cause.

Ultimately the ancient powers buried beneath Bracton College do break loose, in the person of Merlin, the ancient magician. Raised from his long sleep, he finds his way not to Belbury, as the leaders of N.I.C.E. anticipate, but to the manor at St. Anne's. Sworn to the service of the true King, and strengthened by angelic Powers of Heaven that descend upon St. Anne's, Merlin puts a Babel-curse on Belbury, confusing their language and leaving the Institute helpless when the animals (on whom they have ruthlessly experimented) turn on their tormentors and destroy them.

N.I.C.E. ("that hideous strength") and all its technological devil-try melt down catastrophically, while the healing powers of Heaven rest upon the hilltop manor of St. Anne's. Mark Studdock escapes the inferno, and his reunion with Jane at St. Anne's symbolizes the salvation of England.

The City of Fragmentation (Belbury)

That Hideous Strength is a parable of the centrifugal forces of modernity, the culture that has dominated the Western world since the Enlightenment in the seventeenth century. N.I.C.E. represents the logical conclusion of the modern worldview that has deliberately dismissed the Christian Story, and replaced it with what Lewis elsewhere calls "the Great Myth" of inevitable human progress.[2]

In particular, the Institute embodies four schisms in the modern soul, schisms that divide both individuals and society. These schisms the Christianity embodied in St. Anne's aims to heal.

---

2. "The Funeral of a Great Myth," in *Christian Reflections* (Eerdmans, 1967).

The First Schism: Humans vs. God

In the first place, the ethos of N.I.C.E. represents the schism between humans and God, which also means the alienation of human beings from any stable truth and their exile to the wasteland of pure relativity.

In the worldview of modernity, beginning in 1619 with Descartes's ominous first principle "I think, therefore I am," human reason asserted its omnipotence. Descartes demoted God from the status of Axiom and First Principle, and took God's place in that respect. God became an hypothesis — which Descartes nevertheless thought he could verify, though his successors came to think it was not worth verifying. When Napoleon asked the astronomer Laplace why the latter's great work omitted any reference to God, Laplace replied, "Sire, I had no need for that hypothesis."

Two centuries later at Belbury, the God-hypothesis never appears on the horizon. The sophisticated culture of the Institute takes human primacy and autonomy as given, and assumes that the universe is a closed system. There is no transcendent creator, nothing exists other than the material universe, and human beings dominate their world. Therefore, it is axiomatic that the technocrats have the power to remake the planet after their blueprint, and (God being banished) ethical objections to their work are assumed to be fatuous and non-existent. One of the N.I.C.E. elite, Lord Feverstone, deplores the persistence of "our rivals on this planet. I don't mean only insects and bacteria. There's far too much life of every kind about, animal and vegetable. We haven't really cleared the place yet. First we couldn't; and then we had aesthetic and humanitarian scruples."[3]

These, of course, are now erased by the superior wisdom of modern technology. The schism between human beings and God, our usurpation of autonomy, means that truth and goodness — in fact, all norms of any kind whatever — are merely illusions, residual fantasies left over from humanity's infancy but now outgrown. One of Belbury's leaders tells Mark Studdock that the purpose of the Institute's psychological conditioning "is to eliminate from your mind one by one the things you have hitherto regarded as grounds for action. It is like killing a nerve. That whole system of instinctive preferences,

3. *That Hideous Strength*, p. 42.

whatever ethical, aesthetic or logical disguise they wear, is to be simply destroyed."[4]

Human beings are free from all norms, all constraints — alienated completely from God, from supranature, from any limitation of any sort on the naked human will.

The Second Schism: Mind vs. Matter

The new master of the universe is not humanity per se, however, but specifically the human mind. The N.I.C.E. ethos articulates plainly the second schism in modernity, the chasm between mind and matter.

Descartes's omnipotent "I" was not an embodied human being, but rather a *res cogitans* ("thinking thing") that stood in stark contrast to the Nature on which it operated. From the very beginning of modernity, Enlightenment thinkers like Descartes have made a value-distinction between the probing, analytical, and omnipotent Mind and an inert, vulnerable, and apparently defenseless Nature — to the disadvantage of the latter, which Mind was free to manipulate, even eradicate, as it willed. One of the Institute's scientists gloats over the prospect of "shaving the planet," eradicating the "rivals" of which Lord Feverstone had spoken.

But the logical aim of modernity goes further than that. Technology looks to free human beings from their bodies as well. N.I.C.E.'s Professor Filostrato argues,

> In us organic life has produced Mind. It has done its work. After that we want no more of it. We do not want the world any longer furred over with organic life, like what you call the blue mould — all sprouting and budding and breeding and decaying. We must get rid of it. By little and little, of course. Slowly we learn how. Learn to make our brains live with less and less body: learn to build our bodies directly with chemicals. . . .[5]

The superficial sensualism of modernity — think of the explicit description of sex in modern literature — hides a deeper antipathy to

4. Ibid., p. 296.
5. Ibid., p. 173.

Nature. When we make Eros a god, we quickly discover that he eats his worshipers. Or — to mix the metaphor — we find that playing with sex is like gargling with nitroglycerin while smoking a cigarette. So, like the Heaven's Gate suicides in Los Angeles, we rush to the opposite pole and fear sexuality, and all the unbridled powers of Nature which it represents.

Anything that moves can run out of control. Certainty and security come by progressively eliminating Nature. The irony (as Belbury will discover to its horror) is that in the end, Nature strikes back and wins. But before we look at that great reprisal, we need to notice a third schism in the modern soul.

The Third Schism: Sexuality vs. Androgyny

The profound antimaterialist spirit of modernity entails an attack on sexuality. Superficially we see hedonism and the exploitation of eroticism, a no-holds-barred demolition derby of sexuality, where male predation is the norm and the invariable reality.

There are no women among the predatory Belbury elite, except one: the Institute's head of internal security, a Major "Fairy" Hardcastle who caricatures masculinity and specializes in whips and leather.

> Mark found himself writhing from the stoker's or carter's hand-grip of a big woman in a black, short-skirted uniform. Despite a bust that would have done credit to a Victorian barmaid, she was rather thickly built than fat and her iron-grey hair was cropped short. Her face was square, stern and pale, and her voice deep. A smudge of lipstick laid on with violent inattention to the real shape of her mouth was her only concession to fashion and she rolled or chewed a long black cheroot, unlit, between her teeth.[6]

Jane Studdock discovers that Hardcastle's cheroot (lit) can be an effective tool for interrogation, and that the Major finds sexual gratification through inflicting pain on women, rather than through any sexual encounter with the opposite sex.

6. Ibid., pp. 60-61.

Nor are the male predators of Belbury capable of true sexual meeting, or the reconciliation of opposite sexes. At most, the technocratic elite permit themselves a frigid homosexual embrace. The Deputy Director Wither and his assistant Frost

> were now sitting so close together that their faces almost touched, as if they had been lovers about to kiss. . . . with swift convulsive movement, the two old men lurched forward towards each other and sat swaying to and fro, locked in an embrace from which each seemed to be struggling to escape. And as they swayed and scrabbled with hand and nail, there arose, shrill and faint at first, but then louder and louder, a cackling noise that seemed in the end rather an animal than a senile parody of laughter. . . .[7]

The true conjunction of sexual opposites is far too threatening for the technocratic elite. Eros the god is terrifying to encounter. A sterile androgyny is all the Belbury culture can manage. And even this androgynous sex is threatening. Hence Belbury's ambition to "shave the planet," to eliminate the disgusting physicality of reproduction, to reduce life to Mind. The demon-god of N.I.C.E. is a disembodied head — the head of a decapitated murderer — which the Belbury scientists keep alive artificially, and which they worship. So even the androgynous sexuality of the technocratic elite withers under their profound antipathy to physical Nature, as opposed to immaterial "Mind."

The Fourth Schism: Humans vs. Humanity

The self-contradictions in Belbury's modernity are most obvious in the Institute's attitude toward humanity. At a superficial level, we see modern individualism rampant. Descartes's apotheosis of the individual had become (two centuries later) Darwin's competitive, predatory struggle in which only the fittest individuals survive. Belbury's Lord Feverstone expresses this schism between individual and individual, as he urges young Mark Studdock to join the N.I.C.E.:

---

7. Ibid., p. 243.

Man has got to take charge of Man. That means, remember, that some men have got to take charge of the rest — which is another reason for cashing in on it as soon as one can. You and I want to be the people who do the taking charge, not the ones who are taken charge of.[8]

Even Mark recognizes before long that Belbury "was the world of plot within plot, crossing and double-crossing, of lies and graft and stabbing in the back, or murder and a contemptuous guffaw for the fool who lost the game."[9]

But the schism at Belbury is far deeper even than the merciless struggle of each against all. Man taking charge of man must mean the destruction of what is truly human. *That Hideous Strength,* Lewis would write a few years later, was "an attack . . . on something which might be called 'scientism'," an assertion of what he called "the metabiological heresy," the "belief that the supreme moral end is the perpetuation of our own species, and that this is to be pursued even if, in the process of being fitted for survival, our species has to be stripped of all those things for which we value it — of pity, of happiness, and of freedom."[10]

Modernity not only pits individual against individual, therefore, but abolishes entirely what sets humans apart from nature. As Lewis argued in *The Abolition of Man,* a lecture series given in early 1943, during the time that he was composing *That Hideous Strength,*[11] the modern analytical mind systematically erases all suprapersonal Truth, all virtues and all standards, as illusions of the primitive human imagination, and as unverifiable by the scientific method.

Rigorously "objective" thinking roots out all superstitious notions of this kind. As Frost tells Mark, "it is like killing a nerve."[12] But if

---

8. Ibid., p. 42.

9. Ibid., p. 245.

10. "A Reply to Professor Haldane," in *Of Other Worlds,* ed. Walter Hooper (Harcourt Brace Jovanovich, 1966), pp. 76-77. This unfinished essay contains Lewis's explanation of what he means by saying that Frost worshiped devils.

11. *The Abolition of Man* (Macmillan, 1965). *That Hideous Strength* was finished in late 1943 (the preface is dated Christmas Eve). For a shorter treatment of the same questions, see "The Poison of Subjectivism," in *Christian Reflections,* ed. Walter Hooper (Eerdmans, 1970).

12. *That Hideous Strength,* p. 296.

all "values" are debunked and rejected, individuals have no grounds for action other than raw emotion. The "value" of a value lies only in its emotional intensity. And the more we act solely on the emotional force of our desires, the more we sink back into Nature.

But the irony is even deeper than that. For the modern analytical mind ends by analyzing and dismissing mind itself. By insisting on strict "objectivity," by treating human beings merely as objects to be analyzed scientifically, the Belbury scientist concludes that mind is only a by-product of matter. Following the logic of modernism to its conclusion, Frost mentally abolishes himself.

> For many years he had theoretically believed that all which appears in the mind as motive or intention is merely a by-product of what the body is doing. But for the last year . . . he had begun to taste as fact what he had long held as theory. Increasingly, his actions had been without motive. He did this and that, he said thus and thus, and did not know why. His mind was a mere spectator. He could not understand why that spectator should exist at all. . . . The nearest thing to a human passion which still existed in him was a sort of cold fury against all who believed in the mind. There was no tolerating such an illusion. There were not, and must not be, such things as men.[13]

So the logical end of the Belbury train-of-thought is suicide (which Frost proceeds to commit). The schizoid mentality of modernity ends in self-erasure. And Nature absorbs mind back into herself.

Belbury is a cartoon, but like a good cartoon it highlights features that actually exist, and that are intrinsic and decisive. Lewis saw the essence of modernity fifty years ago. Most Christians in the West today are still struggling toward the critical distance that Lewis achieved. Most of us are still enmeshed in the Belburian culture of schism and fragmentation.

13. Ibid., p. 357.

The City of Hope (St. Anne's)

But of course *That Hideous Strength* presents another "city" over against the Belbury of the modern world. Lewis wants to show us that the Christian Story and the Christian community hold together and preserve all the elements in life that modernity splits and forces apart.

St. Anne's-on-the Hill is the beachhead of healing and sanity in an England threatened by the schisms of modernity.

The First Healing: God and Humans

St. Anne's is first of all a community where humans acknowledge that God is the axiom. Jane Studdock comes to St. Anne's, terrified by her prophetic dreams but clinging to her modern self-image as an independent, autonomous, critical thinker. She assumes the modern closed-system universe. Only naive primitives would believe in what science cannot demonstrate.

But gradually Jane notices that the "Company" at St. Anne's are all more confident, more vivid, altogether richer, more lively human beings than she is. Her friends Arthur and Camilla Denniston enthusiastically sweep her off for a drive in the fog. "We both like Weather," Arthur tells her. "Not this or that kind of weather, but just Weather. It's a useful taste if one lives in England." Soon they left the road

> and went bumping across grass and among trees and finally came to rest in a sort of little grassy bay with a fir thicket on one side and a group of beeches on the other. There were wet cobwebs and a rich autumnal smell all round them. Then all three sat together in the back of the car and there was some unstrapping of baskets, and then sandwiches and a little flask of sherry and finally hot coffee and cigarettes. Jane was beginning to enjoy herself.[14]

But the vividness and cheer of her new friendships are simply prelude to the reality Whom Jane encounters at St. Anne's. The

14. Ibid., p. 113.

"Director" of the Company there, Professor Ransom, persuades Jane to accept the possibility that God exists, and that Jane is not the First Principle of her own universe after all. Could it be, Jane wonders, that "one were a *thing* after all — a thing designed and invented by Someone Else and valued for qualities quite different from what one had decided to regard as one's true self?"[15]

And then Jane meets the Someone Else. She is walking in the walled garden, and suddenly

> . . . at one particular corner of the gooseberry patch, the change came. What awaited her there was serious to the degree of sorrow and beyond. There was no form nor sound. The mould under the bushes, the moss on the path, and the little brick border, were not visibly changed. But they were changed. A boundary had been crossed. She had come into a world, or into a Person, or into the presence of a Person. Something expectant, patient, inexorable met her with no veil or protection between. . . . In this height and depth and breadth the little idea of herself which she had hitherto called *me* dropped down and vanished, unfluttering, into bottomless distance.[16]

But of course the true Jane whom this Person calls out is far deeper and more grownup than the shallow, superficial young woman who had fled to St. Anne's, clinging to her "modern independence." As her life with the community continues, Jane discovers that in confessing herself a creature, she is becoming not less but more human.

The Second Healing: Humans and Nature

As they recognize their creatureliness, the Company at St. Anne's discover that they are once again kinfolk to all of creation. The sterile, manipulative "objectivity" of Belbury has alienated human beings from Nature, who will ultimately turn upon her oppressors and swallow them whole.

But at St. Anne's the primal distinction is not between Mind and

15. Ibid., p. 318.
16. Ibid.

Matter. It is between Creator and creation. And human beings are unequivocally located on creation's side of the distinction. Of course they are separate from unconscious Nature, nor are they wholly part of the preconscious world of the animals. The manor house at St. Anne's does hold a good many animals, including a more-or-less tame bear named Mr. Bultitude. And the bear's life is to the lives of the human Company as a deep pool is to a sunbeam.

> One of our race, if plunged back for a moment in the warm, trembling iridescent pool of that pre-Adamite consciousness, would have emerged believing that he had grasped the absolute: for the states below reason and the states above it have, by their common contrast to the life we know, a certain superficial resemblance. Sometimes there returns to us from infancy the memory of a nameless delight or terror. . . . At such moments we have experience of the shallows of that pool. But fathoms deeper than any memory can take us, right down in the central warmth and dimness, the bear lived all its life.[17]

Human beings are called to a more complicated obedience to their Creator than the bear is. But at St. Anne's, the bear is not simply "clinical material," a specimen to be examined under anesthesia or a "natural resource" to be "managed." He is not part of a Nature that Mind exploits. He is part of the family.

Of course St. Anne's is a prophetic vision of the future — most manor houses would be wise to exclude bears from permanent residence. The "Peaceable Kingdom" is a reality promised in the Word of God, and not an empirical presence. Yet Lewis sees clearly that human beings who acknowledge their accountability as stewards, and treat creation as "brother Sun" and "sister Moon," might meet a friendlier response from Nature than technological rationality had led them to anticipate — or that technological rationality itself receives.

The Third Healing: Masculine and Feminine

As St. Anne's is firmly planted in the creatureliness of the natural world, it is not surprising that the Company there embodies a very

17. Ibid., p. 306.

creaturely sexuality — in a way that surprises Jane Studdock when she first meets the community. For all Jane's "modern" casualness about sex (she and Mark had been lovers as a matter of course before their marriage) she assumes that human beings are fundamentally "souls," and that sexual differences are relatively superficial.

Professor Ransom disagrees with Jane on the equality of the sexes.

> Yes, we must all be guarded by equal rights from one another's greed, because we are fallen. Just as we must all wear clothes for the same reason. But the naked body should be there underneath the clothes, ripening for the day when we shall need them no longer. Equality is not the deepest thing, you know.

Jane responds that equality is the deepest thing and that "it was in their souls that people were equal." But Ransom replies, gravely: "You were mistaken. That is the last place where they are equal. . . ."[18]

Jane is taken aback to discover that the men and the women at St. Anne's take turns cooking and washing up. There is no competitive exploitation of one sex by the other, no predatory jungle of sexual domination as at Belbury, but rather cooperation — in the matter of pots and pans as in every other respect.

But there are distinct differences between men and women, and the weekly routine reflects them. Jane asks Mother Dimble why the men and women at St. Anne's alternate days of working in the kitchen — St. Anne's has no servants — and Mother Dimble replies:

> "it's a very sensible arrangement. The Director's idea is that men and women can't do housework together without quarreling. There's something in it. Of course, it doesn't do to look at the cups too closely on the men's day, but on the whole we get along pretty well."

Jane asks why they will quarrel, and Mother Dimble answers: "Different methods, my dear. Men can't *help* in a job, you know. They can be induced to do it: not to help while you're doing it. At least, it makes them grumpy."[19]

The matter-of-fact (and very unmodern) division of housework

18. Ibid., p. 148.
19. Ibid., p. 167.

at St. Anne's reflects the profound conviction of this community that sexual differences are not only universal throughout creation, but reflect a reality above creation as well. Jane had thought initially at St. Anne's that becoming a Christian would allow her to transcend the sexual bipolarity that had so offended her in her marriage. Now she begins to wonder.

> But she had been conceiving this [Christian] world as "spiritual" in the negative sense — as some neutral, or democratic, vacuum where differences disappeared, where sex and sense were not transcended, but simply taken away. Now the suspicion dawned upon her that there might be differences and contrasts all the way up, richer, sharper, even fiercer, at every rung of the ascent. . . .

The Director confirms Jane's suspicion that reality is fundamentally gendered, that the sterile androgyny of Belbury is a mutant and a sport, the ironic and unforeseen product of a culture that professed to be materialistic and therefore misunderstood matter. No, says Professor Ransom, gender is the rule everywhere in reality, and inescapable. "The male you could have escaped," he tells her, "for it exists only on the biological level. But the masculine none of us can escape. What is above and beyond all things is so masculine that we are all feminine in relation to it. You had better agree with your adversary quickly."[20]

And the secret to this reconciliation is submission and obedience. Jane needs to renounce her prim independence (so casual about sex, so uneasy with sexuality) and receive her husband's masculinity. Mark in his turn needs to confess his male oafishness, his blundering inability ever to attend to Jane (perhaps his fear of Jane's femininity?), and submit the urgency of his physical desires to her timidity — and so truly meet her.

The novel ends with an *epithalamion,* in which Jane turns to embrace her sleeping husband. The healing of the sexual wars takes place not through sterile androgyny, but through the reconciliation of opposites.

---

20. Ibid., p. 316.

The Fourth Healing: Human Beings and Humanity

And the reconciliation of ultimate opposites (Heaven and Earth, God and human beings) brings the restoration of true humanity, not its abolition. The schizoid world of modernity, Belbury and its Institute, forever seek to pick reality apart and to separate it into isolated particles. When this analytical mentality reaches its logical and psychotic conclusion, analysis turns its beam on mind itself and abolishes thought. Analytical science teaches us that analytical science is an illusory by-product of matter, and does not exist.

The crown of evolution, the scientific mind, proclaims its own abolition. (Can modern science long survive the denial of the Christian Story, on which modern science is built? Can the scientific method operate outside the Story of a wise and all-powerful Creator God, who fashioned an orderly world and gave human beings rational minds that can know that world?) At Belbury the modern mind turns upon itself and commits suicide.

By contrast the world of St. Anne's strengthens and establishes true humanity. Living within the Christian Story, in proper obedience to the Creator, the Company at St. Anne's have depth and color and vividness. At the end of the story Mark begins to wonder why the Company are so alive, and he feels so weak and squalid. How, he asks himself, did they

> find it so easy to saunter through the world with all their muscles relaxed and a careless eye roving the horizon, bubbling over with fancy and humour, sensitive to beauty, not continually on their guard and not needing to be? What was the secret of that fine, easy laughter which he could not by any efforts imitate? Everything about them was different. They could not even fling themselves into chairs without suggesting by the very posture of their limbs a certain lordliness, a leonine indolence. There was elbow-room in their lives, as there had never been in his. They were Hearts: he was only a Spade.[21]

The secret (as Mark discovers) lies in recovering our true place in the universe, and renouncing our proud claims to be Axioms and First Principles, obsessively murmuring our modern mantra, "In the

21. Ibid., p. 360.

beginning, Me. . . ." As we turn from our futile rebellion and resume our place as creatures, says Professor Ransom, "We are now as we ought to be — between the angels who are our elder brothers and the beasts who are our jesters, servants and playfellows. . . ."[22]

Recovering our true humanity requires that we recognize ourselves as creatures — neither First Principles nor disembodied minds, but part of Nature. Yet in the Christian Story we are also "a little lower than the angels," true persons made for fellowship with God and with each other. True humanity involves true meeting, and Mark's reconciliation with Jane symbolizes the restoration of our own true nature after the Fall.

Lewis and Modernity

Although the schizoid fragmentation of Belbury's modernity is powerful, there are moments of purest hope and beauty in Lewis's England. Once when Jane approached the walled garden of St. Anne's she rose above the smoke and the fog that were choking the land, and

> a luminous blue was showing overhead, and trees cast shadows (she had not seen a shadow for days), and then all of a sudden the enormous spaces of the sky had become visible and the pale golden sun, and looking back, as she took the turn to the Manor, Jane saw that she was standing on the shore of a little green sun-lit island looking down on a sea of white fog, furrowed and ridged yet level on the whole, which spread as far as she could see.[23]

There are islands of sanity and vision in the incoherence and fragmentation of post-Christian modernity, islands from which healing may one day spread out to the nations. St. Anne's-on-the-Hill helps us recognize those islands when we see them.

22. Ibid., p. 378.
23. Ibid., p. 138.

The Abolition of God: Relativism and the Center of the Faith

SHERIDAN GILLEY

WHILE C. S. LEWIS never came to share his friend J. R. R. Tolkien's devotion to the saints, he complained in his final work, *Letters to Malcolm,* that "the 'low' church *milieu* that I grew up in did tend to be too cozily at ease in Zion." In looking forward to "some very interesting conversations" with St. Paul in Heaven, his grandfather never foresaw "that an encounter with St. Paul might be rather an overwhelming experience even for an Evangelical clergyman of good family. But when Dante saw the great apostles in heaven they affected him like *mountains.*"

He did not agree with Catholic devotion to the saints, but saw that the saints "keep on reminding us that we are very small people compared with them." He thought that such prayers *to* the holy dead *could* be lawful, and he had no compunction about praying *with* them, "with angels and archangels and all the company of Heaven."

Toward the Center

In this, as in the other issues dividing the churches, as in his own habit from 1950 on of making his private confession to an Anglo-Catholic priest, Lewis moved from his original Protestantism in a Catholic direction toward the center of the Christian tradition. In this,

161

he tried to make sense of the whole of the orthodox inheritance, and to find the mean between what the Church of England's *Book of Common Prayer* calls too much refusing and too much admitting.

What he perceived with uncanny accuracy and foresight (most of his peers did not see it at all) was that the modern world contains a phenomenon infinitely more sinister than the issues that divide Protestant from Catholic. That is the common enemy of all good Christians, the evil that I can only call in the vaguest terms liberalism, which leads to what Lewis called "the abolition of man" in the name of an ultimate ethical and religious relativity.

Yet Lewis's starting point was rather the modern abolition of *God*. He discovered that the inconsolable longing that had come to him in myth and fantasy, the Joy for which he watched and waited, was ultimately futile without an Object. He saw that his essential mistake had been to desire the subjective sensation of Joy instead of him who gave it. Religious experience is like all other experience: not an end, but a key or clue or an opening to something other, indeed, as Lewis came to see it, as an avenue of divine self-disclosure, in which God reveals and offers himself.

Thus Lewis identified his original error in the modern elevation of subjective experience over objective truth, an error that eliminated God from consideration. In *The Abolition of Man*, he unveiled the modernist snare of Satan in the apparently innocuous statement, made by two schoolmaster authors of an elementary textbook on English, that when we call a waterfall sublime, we are speaking simply of our own emotions and not of a quality belonging to the waterfall itself. We may feel that a waterfall is sublime, but sublimity is not an objective property of the waterfall. Thus beauty is only a matter of perceptions and feelings developed from cultural conditioning and individual taste — and not only beauty, but all ultimate moral and spiritual values are subjective and relative.

Lewis opposed to such subjectivity the notion of the *Tao* or the way, a universal body of moral and spiritual truths, antecedent to Christianity, that constitutes a kind of logic or grammar in terms of which the human reason has always interpreted the world. In all cultures there is a witness against lying and stealing and treachery and murder. As he wrote in a later essay, "The Poison of Subjectivism," a short study of the history of ethics will reveal the massive unanimity of the practical reason in man. From the Babylonian *Hymn to Samos,* from the *Laws of Manu,* the *Book of the Dead,* the Analects, the Stoics, the Platonists, from Australian aborigines and Redskins, he will collect the same triumphantly monotonous denunciations of oppression, murder, treachery and falsehood, the same injunctions of kindness to the aged, the young, and the weak, of almsgiving and impartiality and honesty.

The reader may, he concluded, "be a little surprised (I certainly was) to find that precepts of mercy are more frequent than precepts of justice: but he will no longer doubt that there is such a thing as the Law of Nature."

The Law of Nature

Of course, Lewis knew that while the law of nature was universally acknowledged, it was also universally disobeyed. Yet the enormous underlying realm of sheer agreement outweighs any differences, and though a particular culture may be lamentably defective in one or other of the truths of the *Tao,* there is a sufficient common factor among all human cultures to tell us what all mankind believes.

"Those who know the *Tao,*" he wrote, "can hold that to call children delightful or old men venerable is not simply to record a psychological fact about our own parental or filial emotions, but to recognize a quality which *demands* a certain response from us whether we make it or not." When he wrote this, Lewis did not relish the society of young children, but he recognized this as a kind of color-blindness in himself to a truth of the *Tao.* In short, the proper emotional reaction to the *Tao* may be present in an individual by grace, nature, or education; but the value is not simply a result of instinct, nor is it reducible to our subjective response to it, for it existed before us and exists beyond us, and like God it abides forever.

Subjectivism about values is eternally incompatible with democracy and freedom. We and our rulers are of one kind only so long as we are subject to one law. But if there is no law of nature, the *ethos* of any society is the creation of its rulers, educators, and conditioners; and every creator stands above and outside his own creation. Without some eternal values that bind ruler and ruled alike, "what barrier remains between us and the final division of the race into a few conditioners who stand themselves outside morality and the many conditioned in whom such morality as the experts choose is produced at the experts' pleasure?"

Like G. K. Chesterton, Lewis embodied his teachings on the ultimate evil of subjectivity in fiction, in his science fiction novels *Out of the Silent Planet* and *Perelandra* and above all in *That Hideous Strength*. The principal villain of the last, Frost, wishes to reduce everyone else to his own blind subjectivity, though he is in the hands of diabolical powers beyond his own complete imagining. He hopes to enslave the nation to the Devil by harnessing to N.I.C.E. (the National Institute for Co-ordinated Experiments), a semiscientific instrument, the mysterious force of the Celtic magician Merlin, who lies buried but still sleeping somewhere nearby. Yet Merlin, when awakened, becomes the focus for the awakening of the virtue of that other ideal buried under Britain, Logres.

Logres, a theme suggested by Lewis's Anglo-Catholic friend, the poet and novelist Charles Williams, is the sleeping embodiment of all that is best and highest in the national spirit, and Merlin's resurrection heralds the defeat of evil. For human resources by themselves are unavailing. When Merlin asks what good is left in the world, he is told that the Saxon king at Windsor is powerless, that the "Faith itself is torn in pieces . . . and speaks with a divided voice," that only one in ten of the population is Christian, and that there are no other Christian Princes and no Emperor. "If all this west part of the world is apostate," protests the magician,

> might it be lawful, in our great need, to look farther . . . beyond Christendom? Should we not find some even among the heathen who are not wholly corrupt? There were tales in my day of some such: men who knew not the articles of our most holy Faith but who worshipped God as they could and acknowledged the Law of Nature.

His hearer has to disillusion him: "The poison was brewed in these West lands, but it has spat itself everywhere by now." Above all, it is ascendant in the university, though the teachers there never thought that anyone would *act* on their theories: all the philosopher's lectures were "devoted to proving the impossibility of ethics, though in private life he'd have walked ten miles rather than leave a penny debt unpaid."

Lewis insisted that he had written about the corruption of a college not because teachers were more likely to be more corrupt than anyone else, but because he knew his own profession best. On the other hand, he did feel intensely the *trahison des clercs,* even in his own university, and he pointed to the modern tendency of the priests of the shrine, the guardians of the tradition, to betray it from within.

The Liberal Theologians

The worst of these were the liberal theologians, so active among his fellow Anglicans. Such a Christianity, popular in Lewis's day as in ours, was Arianism, which denied the divinity of Christ and treated him as a man who had experienced God in some special way. It had been, in the fourth century, the highly special prerogative of highly cultivated clergymen and *clercs manqués,* and for the most part remained such in Lewis's day, while the orthodox Athanasius stood then where his disciples still stand today. The modern Arians had, in effect, abolished God by rejecting the Incarnation.

The effect of this Arianism, as Lewis saw, was to make the average Englishman or American think that scholars have shown that the New Testament story of the Resurrection was only a way people long ago expressed their feelings for their teacher after he died; a man who has never heard of *The Myth of God Incarnate* is still sure that Jesus is merely a man about whom miraculous stories came to be told. He will never, unless corrected, come to face the claim of Jesus Christ to his obedience. Arguing against this vulgarized Arianism was one of the purposes of *Mere Christianity*.

Indeed, since Lewis wrote, the treason of the clerics has gone as far as he had foreseen in many of the Western churches, in which the generation of skeptical clerics who have ruled since Lewis's death have sapped the very foundations of mere Christianity. "Liberal Christianity can supply an ineffectual echo to the massive chorus of agreed and admitted unbelief," he noted in *Letters to Malcolm*. ". . . did you ever meet, or hear of, anyone who was converted from scepticism to a 'liberal' or 'de-mythologized' Christianity?"

There are, of course, some honorable exceptions. But many of the powers that be within the churches have acquiesced and even assisted in the relativization and paganization of popular culture and the wholesale destruction of the disciplines of home and family life. The people of England and America have been robbed of their religion and morals at least in part by their religious and moral leaders. Bishops have defended abortion and homosexuality, on the grounds either that we have been given no clear teaching on these matters or that the teaching we have been given is now irrelevant. And with this has gone a ruthless subversion of the doctrinal content of the Faith, in the name of pluralism, openness, and inclusivity — new names for that very subjectivity and relativism in which Lewis saw the flames of Hell.

Lewis was, of course, familiar with modernist bishops; as with the notorious Barnes of Birmingham, himself the persecutor of men more orthodox than he, whose biography a few years ago appeared under a title — *Ahead of His Age* — encapsulating the very worst of the liberal chronological snobbery that Lewis loathed. In *The Great Divorce,* Lewis drew an immortal picture of a modernist bishop, who refuses the glories of Heaven because Heaven denies him the liberty to speculate. This prelate is told that there is no need for an "atmosphere of inquiry," for Heaven is "the land not of questions but of answers" because there men see God. But the bishop objects that "The free wind of inquiry must *always* continue to blow through the mind, must it not?" and declares that "to travel hopefully is better than to arrive." If there is no final truth to find, is the reply, "How could anyone travel hopefully? There would be nothing to hope for."

In short, the bishop's radicalism is rooted not in "honest opinion," but in a wholly intellectual pride that Lewis thought the very worst of all sins, and which the bishop will not even sacrifice for the Beatific Vision, preferring to read papers to his Theological Society in Hell. "When the doctrine of the Resurrection ceased to commend itself to the critical faculties which God had given me, I openly rejected it. I preached my famous sermon. I defied the whole chapter. I took every risk!" "What risk?" comes the response. "What was at all likely to come of it except what actually came — popularity, sales for your books, invitations, and finally a bishopric?"

I think Lewis was right to locate the heart of this treason in the heresies of New Testament scholarship, of which he said that it was

bound to make an uneducated man either an atheist or a Roman Catholic. At the moment in the Church of England, it is making large numbers of *educated* men Roman Catholics. I discovered for myself that, in Lewis's words, being "Missionary to the priests of one's own church" is an embarrassing role, though, he concluded, "I have a horrid feeling that if such mission work is not soon undertaken the future of the Church of England is likely to be short."

Heaven and Hell

Lewis regarded much liberalism as demonic, because in abolishing God it was doing, quite literally, the Devil's work. It is thus well to remind ourselves that he came to Christianity through the intensity of his vision of Heaven, that "The Weight of Glory" is surely one of the greatest sermons in our language, and that outside the Revelation of St. John the Divine and Dante's *Paradiso,* there can be few anticipations of Paradise more moving than the last chapter of *The Last Battle,* or the last lines of *A Grief Observed.* Yet the clarity of this picture is the other side to the intensity of his vision of Hell, the description of self-devouring selfhood in the *Screwtape Letters,* and the endless waste of bleak mean rainy streets that opens *The Great Divorce.*

There is a saying of Kierkegaard that communication may either give us information or change us from what we are. Lewis's works are pervaded by the sense of the agony of the naturally egotistic and selfish soul in its struggles to escape from its own selfhood, its petty self-preoccupations, lusts, pride, and self-obsessions, and the desperate reality of its choices for or against Almighty God.

Lewis constantly reminds us that every human being is created for either bliss or torment. In this, reading Lewis can, God willing, help to change us from what we are. To read Spenser, he said of his best-loved poet, is to grow in mental health. Like Spenser, he is a gracious writer in the older sense of that lovely word, as one whose writings convey the grace of God.

And he has, I believe, the answer alike to infidelity and bigotry in "mere Christianity." What the world needs, in different manner and measure, is the orthodox irenic that he preached; and my prayer is that his vision may find a home.

Awakening from the Enchantment of Worldliness: The Chronicles of Narnia as Pre-Apologetics

STEPHEN M. SMITH

LET ME BEGIN with two stories. As a child, the wife of one of my students had read *The Lion, the Witch and the Wardrobe.* She loved Aslan deeply and became a devoted fan of Narnia. In college, she was converted. She discovered that Lewis was a Christian, and had written six *more* of the Narnia books. She thought life could not get any better. Later, reflecting on her conversion, she saw that *The Lion, the Witch and the Wardrobe* had not only made her a friend of Narnia but had made her fundamentally open to the vision of reality in the Christian message. Narnia *predisposed* her to the gospel. When the explicit gospel message came to her, her mind and imagination were ready to hear and understand it.

I had a similar experience — while teaching in seminary! Like many male adults, I thought I should be more interested in Lewis's apologetic writings. *Miracles* I considered particularly acute. Then my wife and I started reading the Narnia Chronicles to our children. After a few volumes, I was hooked. I felt the spell of my own naturalistic prejudices being dissolved. Reading Narnia became a spiritual adventure.

When we read the stories together, I read the parts related to Aslan, not because I am a better reader than my wife, but simply because I can get through them. The depiction of Aslan is so powerful for her that she simply cannot read it aloud. I know of no other imaginative depiction of the Divine more authentic and moving.

Predisposed to the Gospel

The forties was the decade of Lewis's great apologetic writings. With the publication of *The Lion, the Witch and the Wardrobe* in 1950, he shifted his focus from apologetics to fictional pre-apologetics. The other six books in the series were published one each year until *The Last Battle* appeared in 1956.[1]

What is Lewis doing in these stories? Let me suggest a word: pre-apologetics. As we speak of creating a disposition to *hear* the gospel as "pre-evangelism," we can speak of creating a predisposition to *believe* the truth of the Christian vision and to doubt the alternatives as "pre-apologetics." Because it attempts to change the readers' vision or imagination, to give them new assumptions about what is, or can be, true, pre-apologetics is done primarily through story, through stories that undermine the secular story and make believable the Christian story.

"The story does what no theorem can do," Lewis wrote in "On Stories." A story "may not be 'like real life' in the superficial sense: but it sets before us an image of what reality may well be like at some more central region."[2] As he wrote in "Christian Apologetics," a talk given a few years before he began writing the Narnia Chronicles, we do not need more books on Christianity, but more "books by Christians on other subjects — with their Christianity *latent*. You can see this most easily if you look at it the other way round. . . . It is not the books written in direct defense of materialism that make the modern man a materialist; it is the materialistic assumptions in all the other books."[3]

---

1. One difficulty should be noted. Some biographers contend that, after a debate at the Socratic Club at Oxford in 1948, Lewis felt himself soundly defeated by the Roman Catholic philosopher Elizabeth Anscombe. Some have argued that Lewis's response was never to write an apologetic work again. I am not prepared to adjudicate this issue. There is a full and satisfying discussion in the essay "Did C. S. Lewis Lose His Faith?" by Richard Purtill in *A Christian for All Christians,* ed. Andrew Walker and James Patrick (Regnery Gateway, 1992), pp. 27-62. See pp. 8-11 for the philosopher Basil Mitchell's judgment (he was a founding member of the Socratic Club).

2. "On Stories," in *Of Other Worlds,* ed. Walter Hooper (Harcourt, Brace and Jovanovich, 1966), p. 15.

3. "Christian Apologetics," in *God in the Dock,* ed. Walter Hooper (Eerdmans, 1970), p. 93.

We know that Lewis wanted to commend the Faith through the Chronicles of Narnia. As Aslan says to the children at the conclusion of *The Voyage of the "Dawn Treader"*: "The very reason you were brought to Narnia is that by knowing me for a little [in Narnia] you may know me better there [on earth]." Through these stories Lewis intended to awaken in us a hunger for "Something More" and make us dissatisfied with what we have. He wanted to open our hearts to the reality of God as the one in whom power and goodness, majesty and compassion meet, and to recognize as counterfeits all the worldly things we naturally put in God's place. Hear his words in his famous sermon preached at Oxford in 1941:

> Do you think I am trying to weave a spell? Perhaps I am, but re-member your fairy tales. Spells are for breaking enchantments as well as for inducing them. And you and I have need of the strongest spell that can be found to wake us from the evil enchantment of worldli-ness. . . . Almost our whole education has been directed to silencing this shy, persistent, inner voice, almost all our philosophies have been devised to convince us that the good of man is to be found on this earth.[4]

One goal of the Chronicles of Narnia is to break the enchantment of worldliness, including the deep naturalistic prejudice against the supernatural. Narnia is Lewis's pre-apologetics; it is his attempt to predispose the reader to hear the truth without being biased against it by secular prejudices when he is called through the explicit gospel message.

Let me give three illustrations of Lewis's pre-apologetics in the Narnia Chronicles. In them Lewis gave an answer to what we might call the problem of belief, the problem of projection, and the problem of syncretism.

The Problem of Belief

The first comes from *The Lion, the Witch and the Wardrobe*. We might call it the problem of belief: how does one believe that which seems

---

4. "The Weight of Glory," in *The Weight of Glory* (Eerdmans, 1965), p. 5.

unbelievable? This is the epistemological dilemma, as philosophers would call it, that faces anyone who wants to believe in the supernatural and miraculous.

Take the Resurrection. Everything we know from our senses tells us that when a person dies, he is gone forever. Bodies do not rise from the dead. So do we follow the English philosopher David Hume's famous contention that the idea of the Resurrection is so implausible that *any* alternative explanation is more likely to be true, or do we try to give the evidence such weight as will create the possibility of affirming the Resurrection, as for example the German theologian Wolfhart Pannenberg has done?

That is the issue in *The Lion, the Witch and the Wardrobe.* The story begins early in World War II as the four Pevensie children are shipped off to a house in the country to protect them during the German bombing of London. They explore the house on a rainy afternoon and find it full of "unexpected places." Lucy hides in an old wardrobe, and before we know it, she is crunching on Narnian snow and pushing tree branches aside.

We can never forget this wonderful scene: the unexpected chill, Lucy's surprise at finding herself in a new world, and then her meeting with the kind faun, Mr. Tumnus. In his home she learns of the tyranny of the White Witch, who has all Narnia under an icy spell, so that in Narnia it is "always winter and never Christmas." Lucy learns that the Witch will do anything to keep the four thrones at the castle of Cair Paravel from being filled with humans (Lucy and her sister and brothers) because it will mean her destruction.

Lucy has entered a strange new world, but it is not totally strange. Had not Mr. Tumnus been Christmas shopping? (By the way, one never sees shops in Narnia.) Lucy is caught up in this world as Mr. Tumnus reveals that he is to report to the Witch any human he sees. Lucy must leave. At the risk of his life, Mr. Tumnus escorts her back to the lamp, and she returns through the wardrobe to the professor's house. "I'm here," she shouts.

The other three — Peter, Susan, and Edmund — cannot see what she is shouting about. She tells them that she has been away for hours, but they stare at one another, wondering what happened to her, because she has been away only for a few seconds in this world's time. She explains, but her story, of course, is impossible to believe. (Would *you* have believed Lucy?) She gets the others to enter the wardrobe, but all they do is bump into the back. That settles the question for Peter, Susan, and Edmund. Narnia does not exist.

A Story Likely to Be True

Worried about Lucy, Peter and Susan try to resolve matters by talking to the owner of the home, Professor Kirk. The evening with him turns out to be very illuminating. They tell Lucy's story, and then the professor asks them "the last thing either of them expected, 'How do you know . . . that your sister's story is not true?'" The children are in a quandary, but the Professor exclaims,

> Logic! Why don't they teach logic at these schools? There are only three possibilities. Either your sister is telling lies, or she is mad, or she is telling the truth. You know she doesn't tell lies and it is obvious that she is not mad. For the moment then and unless any further evidence turns up, we must assume that she is telling the truth.

But this overloads the children's sense of plausibility. It is not at all likely that Lucy is lying, but it is just not possible that she is telling the truth. The Professor is telling them to believe something they just cannot believe, and they ask, "But how could it be true, Sir?"

That is the question. The Professor tries to expand their plausibility structure and the prejudices that keep them from believing Lucy's testimony. He explains that another world might exist with its own time structure, and if so, there might be doorways from it to our world, but that these doorways might not be open all the time. When Peter objects, "If things are real, they're there all the time," the Professor answers "Are they?" and leaves Peter speechless. Indeed, it is the very strangeness of Lucy's witness that moves the Professor to believe that her story is probably true.

Meanwhile, Edmund has himself got through the wardrobe and been corrupted by the White Witch, who promises to give him treats and make him a king if he brings his brother and sisters back to Narnia. He meets Lucy there and returns with her through the wardrobe. Coming back to our world, he not only denies the existence of Narnia but sneers at Lucy for believing in it. He tells Peter and Susan that they had been pretending. As we know, Peter and Susan are never convinced of Lucy's story, until they go through the wardrobe themselves and the adventure begins.

Lewis is dealing with two issues here. The first is the question of how we are to judge witnesses. We see in Edmund a boy who is willing to deny the truth (to himself as much as to others) to get what he wants, and in Lucy a girl who sticks to the truth at any cost. Lewis seems to be telling us that our ability to judge the witnesses depends on our ability to recognize goodness, and to question our assumptions when someone good tells us something we think we cannot believe.

He also seems to be warning us that some skeptics may be lying, for reasons not apparent to us. As the Professor implies, should not Peter and Susan believe Lucy rather than Edmund? So the question is not just, How can we believe the unbelievable? but, Should we believe someone who is telling us the unbelievable? In response to the witness given by Lucy, the other children must clarify and weigh the options. Is she lying, insane, or telling the truth?

This exercise in weighing evidence is a crucial component of Lewis's apologetic strategy. In a famous passage in *Mere Christianity,* he uses the same strategy to assess the gospel witness.[5] The question to be asked about Jesus Christ is: Is He mad, a myth, or the Master? Lewis knows the facts will not allow any other alternative, especially not the common "compromise" of saying that Jesus was not the Son of God but was a wise human teacher. One can see in this the possible outline for a response to the Jesus Seminar, in which Jesus is reduced to a shadowy sage who never claimed to be the God the church later made him into.

The second issue is how can we believe the report of an event that lies outside what we know (or think we know) to be believable or plausible. Lewis seems to be responding to the skeptic David Hume's famous *Essay on Miracles* (published in 1748), whose influence continues to this day. Hume's strategy was to show how implausible is the testimony concerning a miracle given what we know about nature. Therefore, any witness to an event radically outside our world of meaning (like a resurrection) is *essentially* unbelievable. Lewis ex-

5. Book II, chap. 3.

plicitly responded to Hume's argument in his book *Miracles,* published just three years before *The Lion, the Witch and the Wardrobe.* He described "the ordinary procedure of the modern historian" as admitting no miracle

> until every possibility of natural explanation has been tried and failed. That is, he will accept the most improbable "natural" explanations rather than say a miracle occurred. Collective hallucination, hypnotism of unconsenting spectators, widespread instantaneous conspiracy in lying by persons not otherwise known to be liars and not likely to gain by the lie — all these are known to be very improbable events. . . . But they are preferred to the admission of a miracle.[6]

Look at Lewis's pre-apologetic strategy here. He sets up the story so that we as readers know the truth — Narnia is really there — because we had a privileged place in its discovery by Lucy. We watch the skepticism of the Humes of the world (Peter and Susan in the story) proven wrong. We see that the witnesses to another world might be right even though they cannot prove their case, and we see that skepticism itself requires an unprovable assertion of faith in human knowledge: that we know all there is to know.

In *The Lion, the Witch and the Wardrobe,* Lewis is preparing his readers for the time when they will consider Christianity and decide for or against its apparently implausible claims. They will have to go through the same process with the gospel witness to Jesus Christ as incarnate Savior and risen Lord as Peter and Susan (and the Professor) went through with Lucy's witness to the reality of Narnia. Will they be open to this new reality, or will they keep the wardrobe door closed forever?

The Problem of Projection

The second illustration of pre-apologetics comes from *The Silver Chair.* We might call it the problem of projection. The insight I will present is not original with me. Others have seen the scene to be described as an

6. *Miracles* (Macmillan, 1947), pp. 103-4.

illustration of a crucial aspect of nineteenth-century atheism's challenge to belief in God. The theory of projection, given by the German philosopher Ludwig Feuerbach and later used by Marx, Freud, and others, asserts that "Religion is simply the projection of human nature onto the illusory transcendent plain. Human beings mistakenly objectify their own feeling. They interpret their experience as an awareness of God, whereas it is in fact nothing other than an experience of themselves. God is the longing of the human soul personified."[7] As Freud put it, the eternal things we believe in are "fulfillments of the oldest, strongest and most urgent wishes of mankind."[8]

The encounter of Puddleglum, Jill, and Eustace with this theory, in the mouth of a Witch intent on keeping them imprisoned in her world by convincing them there is no other world, is the climax of the story. Their decision to accept or reject it determines whether good or evil triumphs. The story of *The Silver Chair* is a dramatic and wonderful quest. While hiding from bullies at Experiment House (their "progressive" school), a cousin of the Pevensies named Eustace Scrubb and his schoolmate Jill Pole end up in Aslan's country. They are given a special task, to find the kidnapped Prince of Narnia (though only Jill hears it, because through showing off she caused Eustace to fall off the cliff). She is given four signs to memorize and obey and sent to Narnia. (Eustace had already been there, and had been transformed from a selfish, spoiled little boy, in *The Voyage of the "Dawn Treader."*)

The signs are not easy to follow, and they miss the first one, but even so they begin their journey. As they start they are joined by the unforgettable Puddleglum, a Marshwiggle, a glass-half-empty sort if ever there was one. Along the way, passing through giant country, they see some rocks that look like giants. Jill, who does not really believe Puddleglum and Eustace's testimony to the existence of giants, thinks that "all the stories about giants might have come from those funny rocks," noting how one could be fooled by them in the twilight, how the stuff that likes hair must be heather or birds' nests, and so on,

---

7. Alister McGrath, *Intellectuals Don't Need God: And Other Modern Myths* (Zondervan, 1993), pp. 94-95.

8. Quoted in Angus Menuge, "The Temper of an Apostle," in *Lightbearer in the Shadowlands,* ed. Angus Menuge (Crossway, 1997), p. 136. The essay is an excellent discussion of Lewis's ability to "debunk the debunkers."

until "her blood froze. The thing moved. It was real giant." This is an important foreshadowing of the questions they will face later.

After many adventures they arrive in Underworld in a dark cavern deep under Narnia. They are brought to a castle — they pass Father Time on the way! — and find a Prince, but he claims to know nothing of the Prince they are seeking. But there is one strange thing about him. He is bound by a spell that, he tells them, horribly changes him for an hour every day. To keep him from hurting himself and others during that hour he is bound to a silver chair till he returns to normality.

The Prince is bound and the fit begins. In the midst of his moaning, he begins crying out the truth. He is the Prince they sought. He was trapped by a wicked Witch Queen who wants to use him to take over Narnia. He cries for mercy and release. But they are not completely sure that he is the Prince they seek. He could truly be bewitched. He could be a madman. They could be killed if they let him go. Aslan told Jill that she would know the Prince if he asked for something in his name. The Prince cries out for freedom "by Aslan himself." The three cry out, "It's the sign."

But what to do? Can they believe the Prince tied to the chair? Is he not out of his mind? Perhaps his using Aslan's name was an accident — anyone in Narnia might call upon Aslan. Puddleglum marvelously answers that they must obey Aslan's word even if they do not know what will happen. (Here is another answer to the problem of belief, and an important one throughout the Chronicles.) They cut the cords binding the Prince, who comes to his senses, smashes the silver chair, and then identifies himself as the true Prince. The Queen had kidnapped him to use in her plan to conquer the "overworld" of Narnia.

Just then the Queen of the Underworld, the Emerald Witch, enters. She graciously seeks to engage the four in dialogue. The Prince renounces her and her plans of conquest. He declares that he is leaving. She throws some green powder on the fire and begins to play soothing music. "The very sweet and drowsy smell" and the "steady, monotonous strumming" make it hard to think.

The travelers explain that they come from the world up there, but they find that they cannot prove that such a place exists. The Witch suggests that this idea of an overworld might be a dream. Jill then insists that they come from the world above ground, but her thoughts become foggier as the enchantment deepens. ("At this time it didn't come into her head that she was being enchanted, for now the magic was in its full strength; and of course, the more enchanted you get, the more certain you feel that you are not enchanted at all.") She even finds "herself saying (and at the moment it was a relief to say): 'No. I suppose that other world must be all a dream'."

Puddleglum Remembers the Sun

Then Puddleglum, who was "fighting hard" against the enchantment, declares, "I have seen the sun coming up out of the sea of a morning and sinking behind the mountains at night. And I've seen him up in the midday sky when I couldn't look at him for brightness." At this they all "looked at one another like people newly awaked."

Their testimony having failed to convince the Queen, the Prince then tries to explain his memory of the overworld by way of analogy with a lamp. Her response is a classic statement of the theory of projection. They cannot tell her what the sun is: "You can only tell me it is like the lamp. Your *sun* is a dream; and there is nothing in that dream that was not copied from the lamp." This seems convincing. About to be seduced again, Jill declares, "There's Aslan." And again the Witch replies:

> I see that we should do no better with your *lion,* as you call it, than we did with your *sun.* You have seen lamps, and so you imagined a bigger and better lamp and called it the *sun.* You've seen cats, and now you want a bigger and better cat, and it's to be called a *lion.* Well, 'tis a pretty make-believe . . . look how you can put nothing into your make-believe without copying it from the real world, this world of mine, which is the only world.

At that moment, the frustrated Puddleglum stomps out the fire. The pain clears his brain and he is able to resist all her attempts to deny the reality he knows. As he starts to walk away, the enraged Witch turns into a horrible snake and the four are able to fight and kill it.

This debate and confrontation are the turning point of the story. The travelers and the Prince then escape from the underworld, and the Prince sees his dying father, King Caspian. The two children return to Aslan's Country and from there to the horrible Experiment House, where, with the help of a risen King Caspian and Aslan, they exact a delicious revenge on the bullies who had been tormenting them. (This story has the most interesting journey of all the Narnia Chronicles: from a London school to Aslan's Country — which is Heaven — to Narnia to the Underworld and back again through each, completing the circle.)

Lewis's pre-apologetic strategy here is to help readers question the projection theory and realize there may be something in the "projections" after all. In *The Silver Chair* it is a patently false and evil enchantment designed to trap Jill, Eustace, Puddleglum, and the Prince in a dark world and prevent them from trying to find their way home. This theory is profoundly evil because it denies reality and thereby traps its devotees in a dark, grim, depressing world — and, worse, encourages them in the service of evil by preventing them from recognizing it as evil. Rejection of this theory is liberation from a great and destructive lie.

Why did Lewis make an example of the projection theory the turning point of the story? He clearly saw that it is central to modern atheism, and he knew its destructive power.[9] By exposing the theory's falsity in the fictional world at Narnia, he wanted to inoculate his readers against the claim that the gospel story is mere projection. He is trying to break the enchantment of the naturalistic worldview and its claim that all concepts of the Divine are merely fabrications of the imagination or dreams with no real cognitive status.

Much of the intellectual world in which Lewis was formed dismissed the Christian claims as some form of projection. Even within the church the claims of transcendence are often denied as mere projection. Bishop J. A. T. Robinson's *Honest to God* — millions of copies sold! — was seminal at the popular level for doing just this in the 1960s. Bishop John Spong's works do this today. In the terms of the world of *The Silver Chair,* a bishop may be a witch. Be forewarned!

---

9. He had himself felt its power under the cover of "the new Psychology," in which he rejected the hints of another world given in his experiences of "Joy," convinced he had seen through them. *Surprised by Joy* (Harcourt, Brace & World, 1955), pp. 203-4.

This is pre-apologetics. Lewis is trying very dramatically to create a counterprejudice opposed to the naturalist spirit of the age by showing how frighteningly tempting the projection theory is even when it is completely wrong. He is preparing his reader for the time when, fearing the claims of transcendence, someone brushes them aside as nothing more than projections.

The Problem of Syncretism

The third illustration comes from *The Last Battle*. We might call it the problem of syncretism. Syncretistic philosophies claim that all religions participate in the same reality and that all their particular doctrines and claims are merely inadequate expressions of a universal being or spirit or force that transcends them all. Bishop John Spong has put this very well in describing his praying at a Buddhist shrine about ten years ago:

> I do not believe, however, that the God I worship has been captured solely in my words, my forms or my concepts. . . . My conviction is that the true God, the divine mystery, the essence of holiness, is within and beyond all these ancient worship traditions.

God "is pointed to by all [religions], captured by none," argued the bishop. God "lives, I believe, beyond the images that bind and blind us all."

In *The Last Battle,* set in the last days of Narnia, the crucial issue is: Who is Aslan and what is his relation to Tash, the foul god of the Calormenes, the traditional enemies of Narnia? Is Tash a false god, or is Aslan only the Narnians' name for Tash, and Tash the Calormenes' name for Aslan? The story begins when the deceptive ape Shift disguises a donkey as Aslan to dupe the other animals. Then, to cement an alliance with Calormen, he has the idea of uniting Aslan with Tash into "Tashlan." When a lamb asks how Aslan could be friends with a brutal god like Tash — which is the right question to ask — Shift hisses:

> Baby! Silly little bleater! Go home to your mother and drink milk. What do you understand of such things? But you others, listen. Tash

is only another name for Aslan. All that old idea of us being right
and the Calormenes wrong is silly. We know better now. The Calormenes use different words but we all mean the same thing. Tash
and Aslan are only two different names for you know Who. That's
why there can never be any quarrel between them.

The chant from the dwarfs and the animals he has fooled goes
up, "Tash is Aslan; Aslan is Tash." However, the last King of Narnia,
Tirian, is not deceived. He knows that Tash "fed on the blood of his
people," while Aslan loved Narnia and Narnians. But before he can
protest he is struck down and dragged away.

Despite King Tirian's resistance and the help of Eustace and Jill,
who have come back to Narnia in response to King Tirian's prayer to
Aslan for help, the deception and confusion get worse and worse until
the few still loyal to King Tirian and Aslan are defeated by the Calormenes and their new Narnian allies. Then, as "night falls on
Narnia," Aslan judges Narnia and opens the way to his own country
(Heaven) for those who have remained loyal to him — brings them
"further in and higher up!" But the others, who had followed Tashlan,
now looked in Aslan's face with "fear and hatred." They lost their
ability to talk and become ordinary animals. They did not enter into
Aslan's country but swerved away from him into darkness.

In this story Lewis is illustrating the profound conflict of two
worldviews, Christian particularism and universalism. Particularism
claims that the Father sent his only Son into our fallen history to
accomplish our salvation through his sacrifice. This truth judges all
other claims. The gospel is universal in its call, certainly, but the call
comes only through the particular person of Jesus Christ. What similarities there are between Christianity and other religions "may well
be a *preparatio evangelica,* a divine hinting in poetic and ritual form at
the same central truth which was later focussed and (so to speak)
historicized in the Incarnation."[10]

Universalism claims that a universal spirit or force permeates all
reality and finds each religion mainly a different form of expressing this
universal spirit in thought, morality, and worship. All religions lead up
the same mountain (although some may go up faster than others).

10. "Religion without Dogma?" in *God in the Dock,* p. 132.

Fundamentally, the gods of all religions are particular, culturally and historically determined, expressions of "the power of Being" or "the Great Life Force" or "the Divine." No matter how different their historical manifestations, they are in essence the same. Aslan is Tash, Tash is Aslan.

In *The Last Battle,* the reader is taught that Aslan is not Tash and that to equate them or mix them is absolutely wrong, a confusion that comes from the bosom of darkness itself, that brings a darkness in which the true God cannot be distinguished from his enemies. The reader sees that it is precisely a spirit of deception that would claim that Aslan is Tash. To be faithful to Aslan one must renounce Tash. Good and evil are real. Narnia is a place where a real spiritual and moral battle is being engaged. Even for the earth there may come a time that will be known as our Last Battle.

Lewis saw this. In *The Last Battle* he prepared us to reject the power of "religion" since it would deny any ultimate value to the profound differences between the various faiths. *The Last Battle* is a particularly effective antidote to New Age metaphysics and religious monism.[11]

Knowing the Gospel Better

These three stories from the Chronicles of Narnia are some of the most conspicuous and compelling illustrations of Lewis's pre-apologetics. They show one side of his strategy as a defender of and evangelist for the Faith, the side he stressed in the 1950s, after finishing his major traditional apologetic works.

In the Chronicles of Narnia, Lewis created a disposition to hear the gospel by showing us the plausibility of the Christian worldview, while undermining our faith in the claims of the alternatives. By bringing us to Narnia and helping us see the Truth and its enemy there, he helped us to recognize it, and to know it better, on earth.

11. For an explanation of monism, see my "Inside the Whirlwind: Christian Theism and the Monism of John Spong," in *Can a Bishop Be Wrong?* ed. Peter Moore (Morehouse, 1998), pp. 151-68, and "God's Body or God's Creation?" *Mission & Ministry* 8, no. 2, pp. 12-15.

APPENDIX:

THE STRUCTURE
OF THE NARNIA STORIES

IN EXAMINING the Chronicles of Narnia I discovered that each story seems to be made up of four books, each containing three to five chapters. We do not know if Lewis intentionally used this pattern, but it seems too consistent and regular to have been accidental.

An introduction to the history and characters and the revelation of the heroes' appointed task is the purpose of book one. Book two describes the adventures and dangers the heroes experience while pursuing their task. Book three continues the description of their adventures, but now the adventure is focused, so to speak, on the central conflict, the battle that will decide whether or not the task is completed. Book four describes the completion of the task (whether the end of a quest as in *The Voyage of the "Dawn Treader,"* or a victory over evil as in *The Lion, the Witch and the Wardrobe* and *Prince Caspian*) and the reconciliation and redemption that completion brings.

The turning point or climax of each story comes at the end of book three or at the beginning of book four. It is then that the conflict comes to the decisive point, and we see how and why the task will be completed. The work of completion usually takes up most of book four, with the children returning to our world at the end (with the exception, of course, of *The Last Battle*).

Let me illustrate this pattern from several of the Chronicles. The pattern appears in the first book in the series, *The Lion, the Witch and the Wardrobe*. In book one (chapters one to five), we meet the four Pevensie children and learn something of their characters. In book two (chapters six to nine), they all enter Narnia, escape the White Witch's servants, and learn that they have been called to Narnia as part of its restoration from the rule of the White Witch — although one of them, Edmund, rejects the adventure and task to serve the Witch. In book three (chapters ten to thirteen) we see the central conflict between Aslan and the Witch played out. In book four (chapters fourteen to seventeen) the Witch's spell is broken, Aslan leads the Narnians to victory over the Witch's servants, and the children begin their reign as kings and queens of Narnia.

The crisis or turning point in the story comes at the end of book three, when Aslan offers himself to the Witch in exchange for the traitor Edmund and she, in a great and foolish act of hubris, releases Edmund and accepts Aslan as a substitute. At the moment she kills Aslan on the Stone Table her doom is sure. She and her servants still have to be defeated in battle (the subject of much of book four), but when Aslan rises from the dead we know that they will be, and the task given to the four Pevensie children will be completed.

In book one (chapters one to three) of the *Magician's Nephew,* we meet the heroes, the ordinary school children Digory and Polly, and in Digory's Uncle Andrew the type of evil they will have to fight. Book two (chapters four to seven) tells the story of their encounter with the Witch and the doom of Charn. In book three (chapters eight to eleven), we see the creation of Narnia, and in book four (chapters twelve to fifteen) we watch the temptation of Digory, the healing of his mother, and the completion of creation. The turning point in this book is Digory's confession that he brought the Witch into Narnia and Aslan's enlistment of him to undo the damage he had done. This happens in chapter eleven, the last chapter in book three.

In *The Horse and His Boy* we again find this structure used. (In this story each book has its distinctive geography as well.) Book one (chapters one to three) introduces Shasta and Calormene culture and takes Shasta to the gates of Tashbaan. In book two (chapters four to eight) he and Aravis escape Tashbaan and flee to the tombs, having discovered a secret they must deliver across the desert to King Lune of Archenland. Book three (chapters nine to eleven) takes the travelers across the desert to warn King Lune and save Archenland from the Calormene invaders. At the end of book three Shasta has the meeting with Aslan that changes and reorients his life, and that forms the climax of the story. Book four (chapters twelve to fifteen) describes the victory of the Narnians, the defeat of Rabadash, and the establishment of Shasta's identity and the beginning of his true calling.

In *The Silver Chair* the four books are distinguished by their relation to the mission given the children, Jill and Eustace. Book one (chapters one to four) describes the mission given to them and their

rocky start. Book two (chapters five to nine) covers their travel overland with Puddleglum, till they discover the way to the Underworld.
In book three (chapters ten to twelve) we read of their travels through
the Underworld, their discovery of the Prince and their risk in freeing
him, and the crucial victory over the Witch. The turning point comes
in the last chapter of book three, when the children, Puddleglum, and
the prince confront the witch and defeat her. Book four (chapters
thirteen to sixteen) gives us their escape from the Underworld, the
return of Jill and Eustace to their world, and their revenge on the
bullies at their school, Experiment House.

In the other three chronicles, *Prince Caspian, The Voyage of the
"Dawn Treader,"* and *The Last Battle,* we see the same pattern used to
structure the story, particularly clearly in *The Last Battle* though a bit
more strained in *The Voyage of the "Dawn Treader."*

Growing in Grace:
The Anglican Spiritual Style
in the Chronicles of Narnia

DORIS T. MYERS

THAT C. S. LEWIS'S Chronicles of Narnia continue to appeal to people of other times and places is a measure of their greatness. One reason, perhaps, is that the seven books, read in order of original publication, describe the emotional climate of Christian commitment at various ages, from very young childhood to old age and death. This insight is most accessible to a reader who is familiar with an Anglican style of spirituality, and specifically the Anglican style of Lewis's time and place.

The 1994 American edition of the Chronicles is arranged in internal chronological order, beginning with the creation of Narnia in *The Magician's Nephew* (the sixth book published) and followed by the two stories of the Golden Age, *The Lion, the Witch and the Wardrobe* and *The Horse and His Boy* (the first and fifth published). The claim that this order complies with Lewis's wishes is an interpretation, perhaps an overreading, of his remarks to a young correspondent in *Letters to Children,* but in his magisterial *Companion to Narnia* (beginning with the third edition), Paul F. Ford has cautiously preferred the original order to the chronological order.[1]

---

1. Readers using this edition should rearrange them in the following order: volumes 2, 4, 5, 6, 3, 1, 7. Lewis's remarks appear in *Letters to Children,* ed. Lyle W. Dorsett and Marjorie Lamp Mead (Simon & Schuster, 1985), pp. 68-69. Two decades

The Anglican Style

Distinctive spiritual styles, made up of devotional practices, customs, turns of phrase, and doctrinal and moral emphases, develop spontaneously within Christian communities. Although the *substance* of belief — what Lewis called "mere Christianity" — is always and everywhere essentially the same, spiritual *styles* change, sometimes very rapidly. Modern Roman Catholics, for example, have gone from Gregorian chant, Friday fish, and Latin to folk music, steak, and the vernacular in one generation.

Lewis was not an American evangelical of today, but a British Anglican of the early twentieth century. Through all of his journeying from nonbelief to belief recounted in *Surprised by Joy,* he remained a member of St. Mark's Church, Dundela, where his father's family had attended since 1870, where his parents were married, and where his grandfather was rector.[2]

The aspect of the Anglican style of Lewis's time most relevant to the Chronicles is the Anglican emphasis on the individual's gradual growth in faith, in contrast with those traditions that emphasize a personal peak experience of conversion.[3] In these traditions, even people nurtured in Christianity from infancy are expected to have this experience, and it is regarded as the beginning of their Christian commitment. In Anglican, as in Roman Catholic, Lutheran, and some other churches, the individual is baptized as an infant and gradually, through contact with the yearly round of liturgical practices and prayers, builds up what Stephen Neill calls "a settled resolute will to

ago Peter J. Schakel pointed out that reading them in the chronological order lessens the emotional impact of the individual stories. *Reading with the Heart: The Way into Narnia* (Eerdmans, 1979), pp. 143-45. For Ford's remarks, see the "Preface to the Fourth Edition."

2. Roger Lancelyn Green and Walter Hooper, *C. S. Lewis: A Biography* (Harcourt Brace Jovanovich, 1974; first Harvest ed., 1976), pp. 13-18.

3. Stephen Neill, in *Anglicanism* (Penguin Books, 1958), pp. 417-18, speaks of a typical "Anglican attitude" and "atmosphere" that "defies analysis," adding that "it must be felt and experienced in order to be understood." Lacking direct experience, the investigator discovers that the best way to develop a feel for it is to study the *Book of Common Prayer* used in Lewis's time, and to read the novels and essays of such writers as Vera Brittain, Dorothy L. Sayers, and Rose Macaulay.

holiness."[4] Individual Anglicans may have a peak experience of conversion, but gradual growth in faith is the norm.

Readers familiar with the spiritual style that emphasizes a dramatic conversion experience are likely not to notice the extent to which the Chronicles deemphasize it. In *The Lion, the Witch and the Wardrobe,* for example, the conversion of Edmund is dismissed with the words, "There is no need to tell you . . . what Aslan was saying, but it was a conversation which Edmund never forgot." In *The Voyage of the "Dawn Treader,"* Eustace's rebirth as a human boy happens offstage, and the drama of it is deemphasized by having Eustace relate it in his understated, schoolboy style. In *The Horse and His Boy,* Shasta's experience is not a rebirth, but a recognition: he realizes that Aslan has been with him all along.

It is important to examine spiritual style rather than doctrinal proposition because Lewis wrote in a spirit of play, casting "all these things into an imaginary world, stripping them of their stained-glass and Sunday School associations," in order to show what it feels like to be a believer — to smuggle religious emotions "in their real potency" past the "watchful dragons" of boredom and embarrassment.[5] He was not writing allegory, which by correspondence shows us what is true, but fairy story, which through narrative shows us what is desirable and ideal.[6] When critics reduce Lewis's fairy stories to allegory, especially an allegory of certain doctrinal propositions, they diminish the specific literary pleasure the stories were designed to give and obscure his masterly portrayal of religious experience, and the mode or form of sanctification and redemption at different stages in life. These stages become clear as we examine the books in order.

4. Neill, *Anglicanism,* p. 418. See also Gilbert Meilaender, *The Taste for the Other* (Eerdmans, 1978), p. 38, concerning Lewis's theology as "a process of sanctification." What he attributes to Lewis individually is normative to Anglicanism.

5. "Sometimes Fairy Stories May Say Best What's to Be Said," in *Of Other Worlds,* ed. Walter Hooper (Harcourt, Brace & World, 1966), p. 37.

6. Lewis cited J. R. R. Tolkien's famous essay "On Fairy Stories" in support of his purpose and method of writing. The essay is most easily found in *The Tolkien Reader* (Ballantine Books, 1966).

The Lion and the Prince

For children born into an Anglican-style religious home, the first awareness of Christianity comes through its two great festivals, Christmas and Easter. The young child does not know why these holidays are so important; he simply accepts the joyous celebration, feeling it more as a physical than a mental or spiritual event. This is exactly what we find in *The Lion, the Witch and the Wardrobe,* the first book in the series. The arrival of Father Christmas in Narnia is a lovely surprise for the children, a physical experience of receiving presents and having a good dinner. Mr. Beaver understands the *evangelium* of Aslan on the move, of an end to the always-winter-but-never-Christmas stagnation, but the children are less aware of it.

The Narnian analog of Easter also focuses on physical sensations: the delicious languor of the spring thaw; the cold, horror, and weeping of the girls' all-night vigil; the joyous resurrection-morning romp and lion-back ride. These sensations, rather than a cognitive grasp of the theology of incarnation and sacrificial redemption, are the message of *Wardrobe.* It is Christianity on the very simplest level.

This perhaps explains the rightness of the Father Christmas episode, which some critics have regarded as a flaw.[7] It fits the sensitive reader's perception, felt rather than consciously realized, that a story about the young child's first awareness of Christianity needs Christmas as well as Easter. Lewis's decision to include the episode must have been just as intuitive. The episode bothers people, not because it is unnecessary but because the sudden shift in narrative pace makes it sound a little out of key. The Beavers and the children are embarked on a tense, hurried journey; the arrival of Father Christmas signals the loss of their reason for hurrying, a narrative weakness made worse by Lewis's long, rather gratuitous discussion about the meaning of the word "solemn." An unsolved artistic problem thus mars the episode; but its presence is thematically necessary.

The first book of the series thus represents the beginning of Christian commitment according to the Anglican style of spirituality, a style that begins with the celebration of holidays (holy days) rather than personal conversion. Lewis regarded the conversion experience as

7. See Green and Hooper, *C. S. Lewis,* p. 241.

moving and real: he described it in *The Pilgrim's Regress* (his first book, written soon after his own conversion) and *The Screwtape Letters*. But in the Chronicles he shows the Christian child growing up in an established church and gradually becoming aware of his religious heritage.

Prince Caspian represents the second stage of spiritual development according to the Anglican pattern. As the child becomes a little older, the simple joys of Christmas and Easter may begin to dim. He becomes aware that the events recounted in the Old and New Testaments happened a very long time ago, and that many people even doubt whether they happened at all. This mood of doubt and disillusionment is well dramatized in the way the four children return to a Narnia whose Golden Age is long past. It is a mood associated with early adolescence, the usual age of confirmation, in which children are (ideally) to make a personal commitment to the faith they know already.

Ironically, Anglican children are confirmed in their faith just at the time that they often begin seriously to doubt it. Lewis himself was confirmed "in total disbelief."[8] Many Anglicans remain in disbelief while admiring the beauty of Christian tradition for the rest of their lives. They listen to the stories, but the woods are dead to them, and they are not convinced that the talking beasts really do exist.

But for some there is a turning point when the growing religious consciousness separates the "What we do (according to tradition)" of early childhood from the "What *I* must do" of maturity. In *Prince Caspian* this turning point comes when Lucy is the only one who sees Aslan and finds that she must follow him whether the others do or not. Her decision is not like the conversion experience described as "asking Jesus into your heart." She and the other children already knew Aslan and the living reality of Old Narnia, although their indifference and self-will kept them from perceiving Aslan when he first appeared to them.

As soon as that was overcome, through a mixture of repentance and trust in their sister Lucy's insight, they were ready to embrace and follow him. Instead of a peak experience that is the beginning of Christian development, the Anglican style of spirituality involves a series of commitments, each deeper and more mature than the last.

It must be emphasized that *Prince Caspian* is not an allegorical

8. *Surprised by Joy* (Harcourt, Brace & World, 1955), p. 161.

representation of confirmation; instead, it simply expresses this spiritual stage in mood and tone. There is a definite impression that the age described is different from that of the first Chronicle, largely given by the emphasis on independent action. When the children enter Narnia in the first book, someone — Mr. Tumnus, the White Witch, the Beavers — takes charge of them. Edmund's treachery involves going off on his own and rejecting the "What I must do (according to tradition)."

But in *Prince Caspian,* when the children come into Narnia, no one takes care of them. Their first task is to survive, and when the dwarf Trumpkin appears, he is a companion rather than a caretaker; when they join the Old Narnian forces, they remind even the King that they do not submit to him. Lucy's virtue — and through her, the completion of the children's task — requires following Aslan on her own.

A Member of the Church

An individual appreciation of what Christianity is all about leads naturally to an inquiry into what it means to be a member of the church, and this is the theme of the third book, *The Voyage of the "Dawn Treader."* It explores two aspects of membership: ethical behavior and participation in the sacraments of baptism and communion.

The givens of the story are admirably suited to exploring the experiences and duties of being a member. The story takes place on a ship, a traditional image of the church. Like the church, the *Dawn Treader* has a hierarchical government, a mission to seek the lost, and a rather specialized vocabulary and code of behavior. Although the *Dawn Treader* does not stand for the church, since this is a fantasy rather than an allegory (in which parts of the ship and/or the actions of the characters would be described so as to draw parallels with the church), the traditional symbolism produces overtones of meaning for the adult reader.

Since the story is fantasy, Lewis explored the meaning of membership through contrast with an annoying marginal member, Eustace the jerk. The comic culture shock he experiences is presented as a contrast between "modern" values and those of Narnia, but the contrast can be seen equally well as the gap between the church's values and those of the world. The outward manners of Anglicanism, especially in Lewis's day, were admittedly archaic: kneeling for prayer, wearing vestments, and using words like "vouchsafe" and "Septuagesima" and "vicar."

Its ethical values may also seem archaic, but Lewis would say they seemed old simply because they are timeless.[9] Timeless, even universal, as they may be, the ethical principles set forth in the adventures of *The Voyage of the "Dawn Treader"* are, to some extent, reflections of a specifically Anglican style of spirituality. First, they center on practical temptations rather than consideration of more abstract principles of right and wrong,[10] and second, they address the temptations important to members of a ruling class. In spiritual style, Anglicans expect everyone to behave as a spiritual aristocrat, as commoners like the Pevensie children become kings and queens. (Similarly, in *The Last Battle,* as he dies Roonwit the centaur reminds the king that "noble death is a treasure no one is too poor to buy.")

In England, although the ministrations of the Established Church are theoretically open to everyone, in practice less advantaged people tend to be Roman Catholics or members of other Protestant churches. As the church of the ruling classes, the Church of England needs members who are inwardly noble rather than venal, secure against the temptation to misuse their wealth and position.

Thus the quest deals again and again with the temptations of money and power: the overturning of the slave trade and of the corrupt bureaucrat, His Sufficiency of the Lone Islands; the escape from Goldwater Island; the rejection of dragon gold; and, finally, Lucy's refusal of excessive beauty, one of the chief means of power for a woman on the Island of the Dufflepuds. Indeed, the Dufflepuds' revolutionary (or perhaps simply revolting) tendencies, and their being put by Aslan under the care of the magician, provide a subtle argument in favor of aristocracy.

Between adventures, the aristocratic members of the ship's company model the ancient elitist virtues of elaborate courtesy, truthful-

9. For example, in *That Hideous Strength* Jane says to Ransom, "Your masters must be very old fashioned," and he replies, "They are very, very old" (chap. 7)

10. We see this characteristic in the way Lewis dismissed an inquiry about freewill and predestination with the words, "*in any concrete case* the question never arises as a practical one." *Letters of C. S. Lewis,* ed. W. H. Lewis (Harcourt Brace Jovanovich, 1966/Harvest Books, 1975), p. 245.

ness, courage, and generosity.[11] Eustace is a misfit at first because he practices the bourgeois virtues of financial prudence, efficiency, scientific nutrition, insisting on his rights, and blowing his own horn. With a touch of Anglican self-mockery, Lewis presents as the best example of aristocratic, ethical behavior Reepicheep the mouse. Through him, Lewis introduces into the story the Renaissance model of a gentleman as set forth in Spenser's *Faerie Queen,* a work written during the age of Elizabeth, when the tone of a specifically Anglican spirituality was first being set.

Reepicheep defends his honor, remains courteous even when punishing Eustace with his rapier, and demonstrates his courage at every opportunity. It is his courage that leads to the rescue of the Lord Rhoop and the adventure of Aslan's Table on Ramandu's Island. He has been well trained in such gentlemen's books as *Mirror for Magistrates,* so that he pities Eustace (who has so mistreated him) in his dragon plight and comforts him with philosophical observations about the Wheel of Fortune.

Lewis's treatment of the adventures as a training for rulership augments the Renaissance feeling we get from the characterization of Reepicheep.[12] The *Dawn Treader*'s voyage, like Guyon's in the *Faerie Queen,* is a mishmash of the adventures of Aeneas and Ulysses. According to the interpretation of medieval and Renaissance poets and critics, the theme of these two heroes' adventures was training for rulership.

Sacramental Analogs

But the emphasis on aristocracy and the virtues of rules applies only to the adventure segments of the Narnia story; there is no aristocracy

11. For a discussion of Lewis's use of language to convey courtesy, nobility, and goodness, and their opposites, see my *C. S. Lewis in Context* (Kent State University Press, 1994), pp. 64-65.

12. In the Renaissance, like the medieval period, it was believed that rulers ought to realize the uncertainty of human fortune so that they would be humble in their prosperity and merciful to the less fortunate. One of the most popular books was Boethius's *The Consolation of Philosophy.* See E. M. W. Tillyard, *The Elizabethan World Picture* (Random House, Modern Library Paperbacks, n.d.), pp. 52-60, for a discussion of fortune with especial reference to Sir Walter Raleigh's *History of the World.*

in the Narnian analogs of baptism and communion. The rescue from the sea, an analog of baptism, happens to the three English children. And the Breakfast of the Lamb, the analog of communion, does not occur until they are reverting to their ordinary, nonroyal personalities. The story is framed by the two sacraments as experienced by the English children: the dunking in the sea at the beginning and the Breakfast of the Lamb at the end.

The inadvertent bath is a good image of baptism as practiced in Anglican churches. The children are, like infants being baptized, drawn into the picture through no choice of their own, without doing anything to become "worthy," without even understanding what is happening to them. They join the *Dawn Treader* in the course of its voyage and are immediately treated as members, as shipmates. Even Eustace, who rudely rejects everything the ship has to offer, is treated courteously.

Many readers see the undragoning of Eustace as an image of baptism, but Lewis's use of these images in this book is more complex than that. In the first place, Eustace gets into trouble because he chooses to leave the company of which he is a member instead of helping with the needed repairs to the ship. When he gets lost, he fears the others will leave him, for he does not understand their motives nor their idea of fellowship. Even after he turns into a dragon (and what church does not have at least one resident dragon?), there is no thought of leaving him, but of somehow fastening him to the ship.

Caspian and the crew's kindness shows him that he has been an "unmitigated nuisance" from the beginning. His undragoning is an image not of baptism but of repentance, the Christian's repeated return to the grace of baptism, which, despite all his efforts to rid himself of the dragon skin, can be accomplished only by Aslan.

Likewise, it is Aslan who provides the Breakfast of the Lamb, the Narnian analog of communion. The framing of the story between the two great sacraments has often been misunderstood because readers too quickly assume that the feast on Ramandu's Island is the Narnian analog of communion.[13] Despite the many details that suggest com-

---

13. Among those who do are Martha C. Sammons, *A Guide through Narnia* (Harold Shaw, 1979), p. 132; and Schakel, *Reading with the Heart*, p. 62. Other critics are less definite. Paul F. Ford, *Companion to Narnia* (Harper & Row, 1980), p. 81, calls it "a less focused although very lovely representation." Evan K. Gibson, in *C. S. Lewis:*

munion — the knife as a reminder of Aslan's sacrifice, the Table's purpose as a refreshment, its magic renewal — the mood is simply wrong. The feelings aroused by the episode are quite different from the one Anglicans associate with communion. The distaste and fear with which the Narnians respond to the bounty, the discomfort of having to eat fancy, "evening" food at breakfast, and the absence of Aslan himself from the meal — all these are quite opposed to the homely, almost routine attitude Anglicans have toward communion.

A hint that Lewis's own experience of communion was not, like the episode of Aslan's Table, an adventure, is found in his 1949 letter to his godchild: "For years after I became a regular communicant I can't tell you how dull my feelings were."[14] Griffiths noted that Lewis had "little interest in liturgy," "never showed any interest in ritual as the dramatization of the myth," and "found any kind of ceremony awkward."[15] It is obvious, then, that the Aslan's Table episode has an entirely different tone from Lewis's fairly typical experience of being "a regular communicant."

Finally, Aslan's Table is set at "the beginning of the end" for the use of "those who come so far," which makes it highly inappropriate as an analog of a sacrament "generally necessary to salvation." It makes much better sense to treat it as one more adventure. Like the rescue of the Lord Rhoop, it deals with courage — the courage required to sit at the table, to taste the food, and to decide on continuing the voyage eastward. It demonstrates how much Caspian has matured as a ruler since his first trial on the Lone Islands, and provides the last

---

Spinner of Tales (Eerdmans, 1980), pp. 180-81, says: "In some ways it seems to represent the central feast of the Christian faith . . . [but calling it an enactment of] a Narnian Holy Communion goes too far."

14. *Letters of C. S. Lewis,* p. 216.

15. Alan Bede Griffiths, "The Adventure of Faith," in *C. S. Lewis at the Breakfast Table,* ed James Como (Collier Books, 1979), p. 20. Although Lewis denied, in *Surprised by Joy,* p. 172, that the externals of Christian practice made any "appeal to my sense of beauty," he defended the Anglican tradition of "decency" (*Letters,* pp. 177-78). In "Priestesses in the Church?" in *God in the Dock,* ed. Walter Hooper (Eerdmans, 1970), p. 236, he defended the customary postures of the priest as having symbolic significance. I suspect that his attitudes were more affected by "externals" than he admitted, or even suspected, especially in the later years when the Chronicles were being written.

great achievement of the quest, the finding of the three Narnian lords and Caspian's future bride.

The Breakfast of the Lamb, on the other hand, has many features of the Anglican style. First, the meal is a simple breakfast. In Lewis's time, "early service" was a synonym for "communion." It was observed in the simplest possible way, since the main Sunday service was normally Morning Prayer. Second, it is a meeting with Aslan, neither a remembrance of him, the aspect of communion emphasized by many Protestant churches, nor a reenactment of Christ's death, which the Roman Catholic spirituality of Lewis's day emphasized. It is a meeting with the resurrected Christ and as such lacks the element of sadness associated with a focus on sacrificial death.

The Narnian breakfast of fish, recalling the twenty-first chapter of John's Gospel, is consonant with the aspect of communion most often emphasized in Anglican spirituality. For Christians who regard it as a mental experience, the episode of Aslan's Table may resemble communion, but Lewis was a thoroughgoing sacramentalist.[16] Another bit of evidence is the homely, familiar tone of the breakfast episode. When the lamb reveals himself as Aslan, the children do not fall on their faces in awe, but address him with natural friendliness. This down-to-earth quality is part of Anglican spiritual style, a style that Lewis criticized for sometimes becoming too cozy.[17]

Again, the literary mode of the Chronicles is fantasy, not allegory. Eustace's falling into the sea does not "stand for" baptism — it is a baptismal experience; the Breakfast of the Lamb does not "stand for" communion — it *is* communion as the children experienced it in Narnia.

In addition to presenting the two sacraments, *The Voyage of the "Dawn Treader"* describes two phases of the Christian life, the active and the contemplative, and the individual's movement back and forth between them.[18] The stay at Ramandu's island provides the transition, finishing the search for the lost lords and, in the feast and their conversation with Ramandu, preparing the children, Caspian, and

16. *Letters to Malcolm* (Harcourt Brace Jovanovich/Harvest Books, 1964), pp. 104-5.

17. Ibid., p. 13.

18. *C. S. Lewis in Context*, pp. 147-48.

Reepicheep for contemplation as they continue sailing east. He turns their thoughts to the great dance of the stars and suggests to them that the universe is larger and stranger than they can know. He corrects Eustace's modern belief that the scientific account is the whole story; when Eustace says that a star is "a huge ball of flaming gas," Ramandu replies, "Even in your world, my son, that is not what a star is but only what it is made of."

The last stage of the voyage is an image of the contemplative experience, with the shipmates' eyes becoming "as strong as eagles'," the eagle being a medieval image of contemplation. For Reepicheep, the chosen one and the most spiritually mature, the experience of sailing the Silver Sea is a prelude to his entry into Aslan's Country. He has fulfilled his calling to the active life by serving as lord to the talking mice of Narnia; now it is time for him to fulfill the Dryad's prophecy. Caspian, in contrast, is called back to the active life — to marriage and rulership. For him and for the English children, the contemplative experience at the end of the world provides guidance and encouragement in doing the tasks that await them at home.

The Young Adult's Task

The Voyage of the "Dawn Treader" depicts a high level of spiritual experience, culminating as it does with the glimpse into Aslan's country. But as the modern proverb has it, "Every good idea sooner or later degenerates into hard work," and the same is true of mystical experience. Thus the next two Chronicles return to the mundane problems of living according to Christian values in a hostile environment. *The Horse and His Boy,* though written fourth, was published after *The Silver Chair* so as to keep the three books dealing with Caspian's reign together.[19] Both deal with the spiritual tasks of young adults. In both, the protagonists learn about God's providence and the need for self-discipline.

The Silver Chair depicts the young adult's task of discerning truth in the midst of confusing appearances and embracing it despite the blandishments of secular ideas that seem to explain the appearances more accurately. The peak of the action, the children's decision to

19. Green and Hooper, *C. S. Lewis,* p. 244.

loosen Rilian's bonds at the risk of their lives, is such a task. So is the next adventure, in which they must resist the Witch's persuasive arguments that what they know is only an illusion. Young adults who go to the university are especially likely to have this experience as they attempt to develop their own settled system of beliefs.[20]

Several minor details also contribute to the prevailing tone of young adulthood in *The Silver Chair.* Eustace's horror at seeing Caspian as an old man suggests the disturbance young people feel when they realize that their parents are aging, that the passage of time is inexorable. The responsibility that Jill and Eustace take for catching and cleaning their own food also suggests the daily life of someone older than a child, whose food is provided.

Furthermore, in *The Silver Chair* the protagonists are without a leader for the first time in the series. In *The Lion, the Witch and the Wardrobe* and *Prince Caspian,* there was the leadership of Peter, older brother and High King of Narnia. In *The Voyage of the "Dawn Treader"* there was shipboard discipline and the rulership of King Caspian. But now Jill and Eustace are equals, and Puddleglum, although older, is a helper rather than a master. With no leader to receive their complaints and solve their problems, they must either change their situation themselves or put up with it. Their independence points up the need for cheerfulness. This aspect of young adulthood is focused in Puddleglum, who talks dolefully but is dependably hopeful.

While *The Silver Chair* depicts the maturation of intellect and will in the young adult, *The Horse and His Boy* focuses more on social maturity. The four protagonists all have to find out who they really are and how they fit into the structure of their world. At the beginning, all four are outsiders in Narnia, strangers to its code of behavior. During their journey to Narnia they learn to avoid the false pride and servility of Calormen and gradually begin to behave well.

The story of Aravis allows Lewis to develop an additional concern of the young adult, making the right marriage. Aravis has to reject the false goal of a socially advantageous, superficial marriage with a Cal-

---

20. John D. Cox, "Epistemological Release in *The Silver Chair,*" in *The Longing for a Form,* ed. Peter J. Schakel (Kent State University Press, 1977), pp. 159-68, interprets their fight against the Witch in terms of the danger of atheistic, positivist philosophy.

ormene noble for marriage with Shasta based on friendship. In *The Voyage of the "Dawn Treader,"* King Caspian's increased maturity is marked by his engagement to Ramandu's daughter, but this relationship is not depicted. In *The Horse and His Boy,* Lewis presents as much of the emotional climate surrounding true marriage as his child readers can receive, strengthening the point by contrasting it with Rabadash's courtship of Queen Susan and Lasaraleen's grotesque marriage to the grand vizier.

Other details suggest the mood of young adulthood. The self-consciousness of this age is focused in Bree's skittish, touchy self-concern, his fear that he will not be acceptable to other talking horses in Narnia. In this story also, no one is in charge of the others. Hwin is the dependably cheerful member of the party. The relationship of the young adults to their parents is explored more fully in this book than in *The Silver Chair.* Bluff, hearty King Lune, the epitome of the English squire, is the warm but nonsmothering parent every young adult wants. The significance of this element is defined partly by contrast, in Shasta's poor relationship with his abusive foster father and Rabadash's hypocritical one with the Tisroc.

The Middle-aged Christian

From young adulthood the Chronicles seem to move toward mature middle age in *The Magician's Nephew.* In middle age, the Christian is usually preoccupied with nurturing, with sustaining both the new generation and aging parents. Digory's quest is concerned with both. The golden apple will protect Narnia's youthful innocence and also heal the sickness of his mother. Likewise, the installation of the cabbie and his wife as the first king and queen of Narnia, sometimes criticized because it is inconsistent with the role of human beings explained in the first two books, is remarkably congruent with the tone of the sixth book. They are the first parents, the parents all middle-aged people would like to be and have. The joyful emphasis on the freshness of Narnia is equally appropriate, since it is middle-aged people who admire the freshness of youth: young people are either ashamed of it or take it for granted.

The Magician's Nephew depicts the sins of middle age as well as its

tasks and longings: the sins of lust, self-indulgence, and an overween-
ing desire for power or financial security. It is the only one of the
Chronicles to depict lust rather than marriage. In this book, the sins
appear in their most ordinary, unromantic aspect. Uncle Andrew's
infatuation with Jadis is foolish rather than frightening. So are his
self-indulgent weakness for brandy (a common middle-aged strategy
for dealing with frustration) and his plans for the economic "development" of Narnia. Middle age takes some of the mystery out of evil:
although Jadis, with her lust for power, is terrifying in Charn, she is
ridiculous in London; even in Narnia, she does not command the fear
we feel for the White Witch (supposedly the same person) in *The Lion,
the Witch and the Wardrobe*.

The middle-aged Christian, burdened by duties and disappointed
in his ability to adhere consistently to the precepts of his faith, is apt
to see life with sober realism, as an exercise of the will. This is the
prevailing tone of *The Magician's Nephew*. In the first three Chronicles,
the protagonists begin their quests with a desire for adventure; in the
fourth and fifth, out of need to escape an unpleasant, confining life
situation; but in this sixth book, Digory goes to the enchanted garden
simply because he is sent. His original desire to explore has been
soundly crushed by the disaster at Charn.

The three middle books, those dealing with young and middle
adulthood, manifest the Anglican style of spirituality in a more subtle
way than the first three Chronicles. Their emphasis on manners
perhaps reflects the Anglican love of ritual, of doing things "decently
and in order" (1 Corinthians 14:40). One recognizes villains such as
Rabadash, Uncle Andrew, and the "good" giants, not by their black
hats, but by their lack of courtesy. When Prince Rilian is bound by
the evil enchantment, his conversation is boorish; after the enchantment is broken, "there was something in his face and air which no
one could mistake."

These books also continue to emphasize gradual growth — by
following the Signs, by persistently riding and running, by carrying
out an assigned errand — and de-emphasize peak conversion experiences. For example, Jill has a peak experience in her conversation with
Aslan on the holy mountain, but it is immediately placed in the context
of the daily discipline of repeating the Signs, something that would
suggest to an Anglican the repeated round of liturgical prayer. To

interpret Jill's experience as a sudden conversion is to mistake the mood of the book and distort its structure.

The Last Days

The emotional impact of the last two Chronicles may also be missed because of their resemblance to Genesis and Revelation. Indeed, one scholar makes this biblical resemblance the principle of unity of binding the Chronicles together, calling their literary form a "scripture."[21] This is to emphasize a cognitive principle of unity rather than the more important emotional principle. Although the end of the world occurs in *The Last Battle,* the feelings explored in the book are those experienced by the elderly Christian in his own last days.

Although the protagonists are said to be young, their behavior and many of their attitudes are those of the old. King Tirian, described as under twenty-five, sounds like an old man who sees the beautiful world of his youth being destroyed. He says, "If we had died before today we should have been happy," and his friend Jewel the Unicorn replies, "Yes, we have lived too long." The friendship of Tirian and Jewel *feels* elderly: "each had saved the other's life in the wars," and because they knew each other so well "they did not try to comfort one another with words." Eustace and Jill are first seen participating in one of the chief pleasures of the elderly, remembering old times with the other Friends of Narnia. Later Jewel tells Jill about the history of Narnia, and "all those happy years . . . piled up in [her] mind" become a great comfort to her.[22]

The elderly person experiences the world as changing for the worse. Although it is almost axiomatic that the policies of any nation, university, or business enterprise will be planned by guileful, selfish Shifts and executed by good-hearted but stupid Puzzles, the elderly person increasingly realizes what is happening, so that the world seems worse than it did in his innocent youth. Changing customs and en-

21. Charles A. Huttar, "C. S. Lewis' Narnia and the 'Grand Design,'" in *The Longing for a Form,* pp. 119-35.

22. It is perhaps not an accident that the elderly don in *That Hideous Strength,* published in 1945, is also named Jewel.

vironmental damage also cause pain, the kind of pain Tirian experiences when he sees the sacred forests cut down, the talking horses in harness.[23]

Although every generation has both believers and nonbelievers, the elderly person perceives a loss of faith, the service of the beautiful lion replaced by false ecumenism and superstition. Furthermore, events seem to move too fast for the elderly. Thus the news of the trees comes before Roonwit can give Tirian the advice he needs, and every plan Tirian devises is rendered useless by a rapid change in the situation.

The pain evoked by the loss of former customs and pieties is common among all old people; however, the love of tradition is a particularly strong aspect of the Anglican style of spirituality. Lewis's commitment to tradition is seen in the first chapter of *Letters to Malcolm,* his Cambridge Inaugural Address, and his numerous private letters protesting changes in liturgy and customary observances.[24]

The sense that the individual is another link in a continuous tradition is an important element in Anglican style, especially in England, where the church seems to the casual observer to have occupied the same buildings, functioned with the same hierarchical structure, and read the same prayers since time out of mind. In *Prince Caspian* we saw the young person coming to terms with tradition and deciding to accept it; in *The Last Battle* we see the old person, deeply committed to tradition, fighting to keep it.

The Scope of the Christian Life

The Last Battle is justly praised for its tactful, nonthreatening presentation of death to children. If the argument of this chapter is correct, through the whole series Lewis did the same thing for other crises of life: the experience of doubt and the commitment to faith, indepen-

---

23. Lewis expressed such a perception in "Delinquents in the Snow," first published in 1957, one year after the publication of *The Last Battle.* This essay is reprinted in *God in the Dock,* pp. 306-10.

24. See, for example, "A Village Experience" and the letters on the church's liturgy, pp. 329-30 and 331-35, in *God in the Dock.*

dence, marriage, the mid-life blahs, the contemplative vision — crises equally beyond the experience of child readers. He was able to do this partly because of the deeply held conviction set forth in the second half of *The Last Battle:* that in Aslan's country, where they are completely themselves, people are not of any particular age.

The Chronicles of Narnia present, in a form attractive to young and old alike, the whole scope of a Christian life according to the Anglican style of gradual growth rather than sudden conversion, of love of tradition, and of emphasis on codes of courtesy and ethical behavior. Lewis was doing in his new fairy stories what Bruno Bettelheim told us the old fairy stories do: raising and resolving adult problems for children.[25] He was also following his conviction, set forth in *The Abolition of Man,* that the didactic purpose of literature is not to teach doctrines and concepts, but values and feelings.[26]

Of course, a person can enjoy the Chronicles without being aware of the Anglican spiritual style, or even the most obvious Christian implications. But an accurate critical appreciation of the stories must take into account the differences between one style of Christianity and another. In "On Stories" Lewis discussed at length the difference between types of danger — from giants, from Indians, from pirates, and from extraterrestrials.[27] The emotional tone, the flavor of each one is different. In the same way, the flavor of the mourner's bench is different from that of the confessional. Insofar as the Christian life is depicted as an adventure or fantasy, the choice of episodes and their details will mirror the types of spiritual excitement to which the author himself responds.

Indeed, in "On Three Ways of Writing for Children," Lewis said, "The matter of our story should be a part of the habitual furniture of our minds."[28] When Lewis wrote theological essays, he wrote as a "mere Christian"; but when he wrote fairy stories, the content was colored by the Anglican style of spirituality in which he was nurtured. To this extent style — Anglican style — was the man himself.

25. Bruno Bettelheim, *The Uses of Enchantment* (Knopf, 1976), passim.
26. *The Abolition of Man* (Macmillan, 1947; rpt. 1977), pp. 25-27.
27. *Of Other Worlds,* pp. 4-11.
28. Ibid., p. 34.

The War of the Worldviews: H. G. Wells and Scientism versus C. S. Lewis and Christianity

THOMAS C. PETERS

THE RECENT POPULARITY of such movies as *Contact* and the *Star Trek* series, the enormous appeal of Carl Sagan's *Cosmos,* and the best-selling works of Darwinists like Stephen J. Gould and Richard Dawkins have all exemplified the perennial conflict between the worldviews of scientism and Christianity. It is a controversy that of course predates both H. G. Wells and C. S. Lewis, but it was Wells who first raised scientism to the stature of a worldwide cult by imbedding its principles and visions into his best-selling science fiction stories and Lewis who answered in kind by writing a science fiction trilogy directly controverting the doctrines of scientism.

Wells and His Critics

H. G. Wells is widely known as one of the founders of the science fiction genre and as the author of such best-sellers as *The Time Machine* (1894), *The Invisible Man* (1897), and *The War of the Worlds* (1898). Many are not aware, however, of the remarkable breadth of Wells's work and the full impact of his ideas on the post-Victorian Western world. By the year 1900, when he was just thirty-four, the name Wells had become a household word by virtue of the great popularity of his imaginative stories. Over the next decades he began to diversify his works, writing romance novels, treatises on world politics, and serious speculations on the future of humanity.

In his romance novels, beginning particularly with *Ann Veronica* (1909), Wells promoted what he called "sexual liberation" from the "hypocritical" norms of monogamous marriage. In a series of didactic works, including notably *A Modern Utopia* (1905) and *Socialism and the Family* (1906), he waged a conscious campaign to abolish the nuclear family and the traditional restrictions on sexual love. It was in *A Modern Utopia* that he described the traditional household as a place where "men and women are lashed together to make hell for each other; children are born abominably, and reared in cruelty and folly."[1]

As the twentieth century progressed, Wells became increasingly involved in politics. For a brief period he was a fellow member with George Bernard Shaw of the Fabian Society, a group of English socialists who sought gradual change in society through reasonable persuasion, but he did not have the patience for their endless debates and lack of action. His own political thoughts were not always easy to pin down: he was a radical socialist and yet a thorough individualist; he could be the German-hating patriot and yet the cosmopolitan pacifist; he advocated free love in his private life and yet strict control of the passions in his utopian writings.

Wells's most persistent cause, however, was his utopian vision for humanity's future. To this he turned repeatedly not only in his science fiction, but in a series of prophetic books including *Anticipations* (1902), *The World Set Free* (1914), *The Outline of History* (1920), *The Fate of Homo Sapiens* (1939), and others. Many of his specific predictions about technologies and wars proved to be remarkably accurate; others, of course, did not.

Wells's writings and ideas attracted a worldwide legion of admirers, who came to hold a cultlike faith in his notions of human history and progress through science. To millions in the reading public, Wells was the imaginative tour-guide to the coming age of scientific wonders. To many young people he became the welcomed guru of liberation from Victorian sexual norms. To others he was something like a prophet, calling for a new kind of life under a new kind of government. In all, his enormous popularity thrust him into

1. H. G. Wells, *A Modern Utopia* (University of Nebraska Press, 1967), p. 131.

the limelight as one of the world's most prominent advocates of the doctrines of scientism.

With all of his fame and popular adoration, however, Wells was certainly not without his detractors. There were many, particularly among Christian thinkers, who found his writings troubling and objectionable, and who attacked his approach and (in some cases) his abilities. In a letter C. S. Lewis once described Wells's writings as "first-class pure fantasy . . . and third-class didacticism" and to the Socratic Club dismissed him as one of "those faddists . . . whose indefensible naïvete forbade them to understand the actual condition of man."[2] It was of Wells that his friend G. K. Chesterton once said: "I think he thought that the object of opening the mind is simply opening the mind. Whereas I am incurably convinced that the object of opening the mind, as of opening the mouth, is to shut it again on something solid."[3] Chesterton's friend Hilaire Belloc replied to Wells's worldwide best-seller *The Outline of History* in a point-by-point attack that was said to have handed Wells an intellectual defeat from which he never fully recovered.[4] In a review of this controversy, T. S. Eliot wrote in 1927 that

> Mr. Wells has not an historical mind; he has a prodigious gift of historical imagination . . . but this is quite a different gift from the understanding of history. That demands a degree of culture, civilization and maturity which Mr. Wells does not possess. . . . Mr. Wells merely panders to the unthinking desire to have one's cake and eat it too, to have a religion without believing in anything except the latest theories of comparative anatomy, anthropology and psychology.[5]

2. *Letters of C. S. Lewis,* ed. Warren H. Lewis (Harcourt, Brace and World, 1966), p. 222; a precis of "If We Have Christ's Ethics Does the Rest of the Christian Faith Matter?" from *The Socratic Digest,* no. 1, quoted in Walter Hooper, *C. S. Lewis: A Companion and Guide* (HarperCollins, 1996), p. 330.

3. G. K. Chesterton, *Autobiography* (Sheed and Ward, 1936), pp. 228-29. See also "H. G. Wells and the Giants," in *Heretics* in *G. K. Chesterton: Collected Works,* vol. 1 (Ignatius Press, 1986), pp. 71-83.

4. Michael Coren, *The Invisible Man: The Life and Liberties of H. G. Wells* (Atheneum, 1993), pp. 158-70.

5. T. S. Eliot, in *The Monthly Criterion: A Literary Review* 5.2 (May 1927): 253-55.

Thus, in the early decades of this century, as the controversy between scientism and Christianity raged, the name H. G. Wells seemed always to be somewhere near the center of the storm.

Scientism and Science

Though the distinction is not widely understood, it is important to notice that scientism is not the same thing as the practice or the philosophy of science. Wells's creed involved a great deal that is not only beyond the ability of science to assert, but is patently unscientific. None of his Christian critics opposed legitimate science, but they all strongly objected to scientism, which Lewis saw in that specific cult which developed in the work of H. G. Wells and has persisted ever since.

Scientism refers not to the careful and painstaking empirical methods by which scientists seek to establish facts and their causes, nor to the marvelous discoveries and technological fruits of science. Scientism is that unique combination of atheism, materialist philosophy, evolutionism, hostility to religion, and doctrinaire adherence to the universal validity of the scientific method which has become the gospel according to Wells, Thomas Huxley (the famous nineteenth-century Darwinist), Carl Sagan and Stephen J. Gould (both university professors and best-selling authors), and a great many others to this day. In a reply to a criticism of his books by J. B. S. Haldane, one of the great advocates of scientism of his day, Lewis noted that scientism was a view of things "casually connected with the popularization of the sciences," although held less often by real scientists than by the scientific laity. It is not "formally asserted by any writer: such things creep in as assumed, and unstated, major premises."[6]

In Michael Aeschliman's excellent book *The Restitution of Man* can be found a fine discussion of the historical and philosophical foundations of scientism and its opponents, particularly C. S. Lewis. Aeschliman refers to scientism most generically as the "misapplication of scientific method" and traces the progressive displacement of moral

6. "A Reply to Professor Haldane," in *Of Other Worlds: Essays and Stories* (Harcourt Brace Jovanovich, 1966), pp. 76-77.

and spiritual values by an exclusive concern for quantity and material fact.[7] Giving as an example of this displacement the statement of Jacob Bronowski that "Man is a part of nature, in the same sense that a stone is, or a cactus, or a camel," Aeschliman noted that naturalism confused "*nature* as the essential character of a person, reality, or thing," from which morality and purpose can be derived, and "*nature* as the vast mechanism of the universe," from which they cannot. Thus

> the essential character of man amounts to nothing more than his physical existence within the larger soulless ticking mechanism of the "natural" world, constituted by accident and impelled toward eventual entropic dissolution. Within the bounds of such a philosophy, free will, purpose, and rational thought itself are drained of any significant meaning and rendered absurd, for of what possible value are reason and action if they are merely the necessary consequents of implacable natural laws?[8]

In *The Abolition of Man* (1943), Lewis pointed out that the primary intention of scientism is "to extend Man's power to the performance of all things possible."[9] In particular, Lewis noted in his reply to Haldane, scientism asserts

> that the supreme moral end is the perpetuation of our own species, and that this is to be pursued even if, in the process of being fitted for survival, our species has to be stripped of all those things for which we value it — of pity, of happiness, and of freedom.[10]

It is toward the amoral aspects of this "performance of all things" and to the godlike pretensions in the effort that Lewis addressed most of his fire in his science fiction stories.

As distinct from science, then, scientism is an ideology in which the model of the natural sciences is seen as the only acceptable test of the validity of all things and all ideas. Tested by this standard, such immaterial realities as God and soul and spirit become mere imagi-

7. Michael Aeschliman, *The Restitution of Man: C. S. Lewis and the Case against Scientism* (Eerdmans, 1983), p. 20.

8. Ibid., pp. 11-12.

9. *The Abolition of Man* (Macmillan, 1955), p. 88.

10. "A Reply to Professor Haldane," pp. 76-77.

native constructs of the active brain — a psychological need, an economic construct, a projection of human life onto the cosmos. Values and morality become relative only to culture and situation. Humanity can claim no divine origin or direction, but through the power of science and rational government it can reach toward its own perfection and divinity. Indeed, the title of Wells's *Men like Gods* (1923) was not intended as hyperbole, but as an accurate description of the final outcome of scientism.

As Evelyn Waugh put it in a review of one of Wells's late novels, if you do not believe in the Fall and "have a sanguine temperament, you must believe that only the most flimsy and artificial obstructions keep man from boundless physical well-being."[11] For the advocate of scientism, religion thus becomes the enemy. "We must learn not to take traditional morals too seriously," Haldane declared in 1923 in *Daedalus: or, Science and the Future*. "And it is just because even the least dogmatic of religions tends to associate itself with some kind of unalterable moral tradition, that there can be no truce between science and religion."[12]

War of Worldviews

The striking contrast between Wells's and Lewis's science fiction stories reflects the greater war of worldviews that spans at least the past two centuries. However, wars are won or lost by local battles, and both Wells and Lewis knew that the stakes of this battle were very high: our very minds and souls, and therefore the very future of England and Western societies.

In Wells's early science fiction stories, such as *The Time Machine* and *The War of the Worlds,* we find a somewhat tentative exploration of scientific possibilities and questions. Wells's imaginative adventures struck a welcome chord for a generation who had grown weary of

11. "Machiavelli and Utopia — Revised Version," a review of Wells's *The Holy Terror,* in Evelyn Waugh, *The Essays, Articles and Reviews of Evelyn Waugh* (Little, Brown and Company, 1983), p. 246.

12. Quoted in Doris T. Myers, *C. S. Lewis in Context* (Kent State University Press, 1994), p. 41.

Victorian predictability and smugness, and an eager readership thrilled to his depictions of hideous underground cannibals and seemingly invincible invaders from Mars. Indeed, by the turn of the century science was fully enthroned in the popular mind, and Wells caught the wave of its popularity by toying with the questions and fears lurking behind scientific enthusiasm in the popular mind.

In *The Time Machine* — which sold 6,000 copies in a few weeks — Wells explored the compelling question: What will become of the human race? Through his clever use of time travel, Wells laid before his readers two possibilities. The first is embodied in the gentle Eloi, whose ease and security have rendered them physically weak and incapable of defending themselves. The second possibility is illustrated in the terrible Morlocks, a subterranean race who maintain and feed upon the helpless Eloi. In both cases human intelligence has atrophied from disuse.

Wells deliberately upset his readers in order to spur them into action. He meant his science fiction stories as a wakeup call to a society asleep in its own smugness. His Time-Traveler laments: "I grieved to think how brief the dream of human intellect had been. It had committed suicide. It had set itself steadfastly toward comfort and ease, a balanced society with security and permanency as its watchword, it had attained its hopes."[13] This theme was prominent in his science fiction from beginning to end. He felt that the twentieth century was humanity's moment of crisis, and that it was imperative for humanity to wake up and seize control of its own destiny through science.

To follow his thoughts through the corpus of his science fiction stories is to witness an increasing clarity and urgency of purpose. In *The Island of Dr. Moreau* (1896) the author's antireligious theme takes center stage, and in *The Food of the Gods* (1904) it enjoys its full, malicious play. There the Vicar is portrayed as a man who is prejudiced, reactionary, fearful, hypocritical, and highly ignorant; and one of the young giants complains that the point of religion is to "shelter the weak and little."[14] From that point onward it seems as if Wells never tires of portraying Christian believers as ignorant, foolish, cowardly hypocrites who stand in the way of scientific progress.

13. H. G. Wells, *Seven Famous Novels* (Alfred A. Knopf, 1934), pp. 56-57.
14. Ibid., p. 650.

It is also in *The Food of the Gods* that Wells's doctrine of humanity taking control of its destiny through science comes to full expression. He wrote of a new generation of giants, who are the progeny of scientific discovery and the hope of the future. These young giants embody the spirit of progress, of the inexorable growth of science and technology. In the end they take their heroic stand against the combined forces of ignorance, conservatism, religion, and tradition. In a dramatic final scene, the young giant leader speaks to the assembled warriors: "We are here, Brothers, to what end? To serve the spirit of the purpose that has been breathed into our lives. . . . We fight not for ourselves, but for growth, growth that goes on forever."[15]

In both his fiction and nonfiction Wells drew his lines of battle clearly between those with the courage to embrace the future and those whose fears drive them to conservatism, tradition, and especially religion, whose resistance to the "irreversible process . . . will only prolong the tale of our racial disaster."[16]

Hope in the World State

Possibly Wells's most eloquent statement of hope in the coming world-state appeared in his wildly popular *The Outline of History*. In this 1,200-page tome Wells views the broad sweep of human history as "a long struggle between rational innovation and tradition."[17] In A. N. Wilson's summary, the book "was written at great speed in little over a year," by someone who was not a historian and took much of the material from the *Encyclopaedia Britannica*. The book

> is not informative, it is discursive. It is peppered with generalizations, and it makes no secret of its Evolutionary Utopianism. It presents a Human Race . . . marching away from the repressive darkness of the past, onwards and upwards towards a classless world, rid of its superstitious religious systems and its sexual taboos, state-educated, enlightened, and free. . . . He gazes optimistically towards the future,

15. Ibid., p. 688.
16. H. G. Wells, *Experiment in Autobiography* (Macmillan, 1934), p. 197.
17. H. G. Wells, *The Outline of History* (Garden City Publishing Company, 1931), p. 1154.

convinced that "clumsily or smoothly, the world, it seems, progresses and will progress."[18]

In the final pages of this remarkable history, the author made his pitch for the necessity and inevitability of a scientifically controlled world government.

> Our true state, this state that is already beginning, this state to which every man owes his utmost political effort, must now be this nascent Federal World State to which human necessities point. Our true God is now the God of all men. . . . Sooner or later that unity must come, or else plainly men must perish by their own inventions.[19]

In Wells's expected future, humanity becomes its own god, and the scientific world-state solves all human problems. "Nothing is needed but collective effort," he argued. "Our poverty, our restraints, our infections and indigestions, our quarrels and misunderstandings, are all things controllable and removable by concerted human action."[20]

In his final years (he died in 1946) Wells wrote *Things to Come* (1935), a screenplay that would become the first major science fiction movie with sound. This production is important in that here in abbreviated form the author brings together all of his favorite themes and adds a touch of his utopian vision as well. It is a story of the triumph of scientific progress over ignorance and conservatism, but here he adds the dream of a new world government as discussed in his *Outline of History* and *A Modern Utopia*. The only hope for the human race, he insisted, lies in a world government under the firm control of scientific planners. The protagonist Cabal puts it this way:

> And we, who are all that is left of the old engineers and mechanics, are turning our hands to salvage the world. . . . We have ideas in common; the freemasonry of efficiency — the brotherhood of science. We are the natural trustees of civilization when everything else has failed.[21]

18. A. N. Wilson, *Hilaire Belloc* (Atheneum, 1984), p. 298.
19. Wells, *The Outline of History,* p. 1157.
20. Ibid., p. 1168.
21. H. G. Wells, *Things to Come* (G. K. Hall, 1935), p. 60.

This political theme in Wells's science fiction is far from a frivolous fancy in the interest of a good story. He waged a lifelong campaign for his desired scientific-socialist world state. In fact, his polemics on this subject eventually drew critical attacks not only from his usual adversaries like Chesterton, Belloc, and Lewis, but also from his former allies such as George Bernard Shaw and other members of the Fabian Society. Despite such widespread opposition, Wells never wavered in his belief (his scientistic belief) that the way to human salvation lay in a scientifically planned and controlled world government.

The Prophet of Science

As his fame became worldwide, Wells had truly come to see himself as the prophet of science, but as his fame faded he came to feel himself a prophet without honor. In his final years his arguments became increasingly urgent, and his attacks upon his opponents even more virulent. Wells typically referred to the Christian faithful as people who "betake themselves to the comfort and control of such refuges of faith and reassurance as the subservient fear-haunted mind has contrived for itself and others throughout the ages."[22] In his autobiography, published in 1934 when he was sixty-eight, he declared that

> by a bold handling of stupidity, obstruction and perversity, we may yet cut out and file and polish and insert and turn the key to the creative world community before it is too late. That kingdom of heaven is materially within our reach.[23]

Cowardice, fear, subservience, stupidity, obstructionism, perversity, ignorance, indolence, and complacency were among the many derisive labels that he freely ascribed to his religious opponents.

At the same time, his decreasing output of science fiction stories and increasing production of sociopolitical polemics cost him millions of his former fans, as his readers were less inclined to admire his world socialism than they were his amazing science fiction stories and his racy romantic novels. In his mature years Wells met with Lenin and

---

22. H. G. Wells, *Mind at the End of Its Tether* (William Heinemann, 1945), p. 17.
23. Wells, *Experiment in Autobiography,* p. 12.

later Stalin and Franklin Roosevelt in an effort to realize his dream and forge a worldwide socialist government. It is hardly surprising that they rejected his proposals. In the end he became a bitter man, as his popularity continued to decline and the world refused to follow his lead into socialistic scientism. In his autobiography Wells complained:

> That universal freedom and abundance dangles within reach of us and is not achieved, and we who are Citizens of the Future wander about this present scene like passengers on a ship overdue, in plain sight of a port which only some disorder in the chart room, prevents us from entering. Though most of the people in the world in key positions are more or less accessible to me, I lack the solvent power to bring them into unison. I can talk to them and even unsettle them but I cannot compel their brains to see.[24]

And in his last book, published in 1945, the year before he died, Wells declared that the universe "is going clean out of existence, leaving not a wrack behind. The attempt to trace a pattern of any sort is absolutely futile."[25]

Here is the picture of a man who has seen himself as the prophet of the future, but who has in the end been compelled to give up the fight. Faced with the failure of all his dreams, "Wells turned his face to the wall, letting off in *Mind at the End of Its Tether* one last, despairing, whimpering cry which unsaid everything he had ever thought or hoped," wrote Malcolm Muggeridge, who as a young man had shared Wells's utopian hopes. "Belatedly, he understood that what he had followed as a life-force was, in point of fact, a death wish."[26]

Lewis's Space Trilogy

C. S. Lewis's science fiction stories begin where those of Wells leave off. For in 1938 appeared *Out of the Silent Planet,* the first story in his

---

24. Ibid., p. 702.

25. Quoted in Coren, *The Invisible Man,* p. 222.

26. Malcolm Muggeridge, *Conversion* (Collins, 1988), quoted in Coren, *The Invisible Man,* p. 226.

space trilogy, which directly and deliberately replies to the themes and doctrines Wells had promoted so energetically in his science fiction.[27] As Wells employed his imaginative genius in proclaiming scientism in his stories, so Lewis applied his genius to the imbedding of Christian doctrine in his. To read the stories of Wells and Lewis as point and counterpoint in an argument is a singular delight, because each author intentionally sought to controvert the essential doctrines held by the other.

Out of the Silent Planet delineates the issues to be explored in the space trilogy. The reader meets Professor Weston, who embodies the Wellsian ideal of evolutionary progress and the survival of the human species through the triumph of science. Most of the action takes place on the planet Mars. Speaking to the great overseer of Mars, Weston explains:

> I bear on my shoulders the destiny of the human race. Your tribal life . . . has nothing to compare with our civilization — with our science, medicine and law, our armies, our architecture, our commerce, and our transport system which is rapidly annihilating space and time. Our right to supersede you is the right of the higher over the lower.[28]

Here is Lewis's rendition of Wells's scientism, complete with its evolutionary trappings, its enthusiasm for material progress, its concern for the destiny of the human race, and its "end justifies the means" morality. Throughout the space trilogy, the doctrine of scientism is called Westonism.

Though *Out of the Silent Planet* is arguably the most engaging story in the trilogy in terms of plot, not until *Perelandra* (1943) do we begin to see where Lewis was taking his fundamental argument against scientism. Weston is now on the planet Venus, again seeking a future home for the human race. In the first story Lewis questioned the right

27. In *C. S. Lewis in Context,* Myers compares the characters and plots of Lewis's *Out of the Silent Planet* with Wells's *The First Men in the Moon* and *Perelandra* with *The Time Machine.* In both stories, she argues, "Lewis starts with Wells's premises and builds on them to produce a more philosophical and artistical work of fiction." *C. S. Lewis in Context,* pp. 39-65.

28. *Out of the Silent Planet* (Macmillan, 1965), p. 135.

of humanity to conquer the universe; in this second story he explored the interplay of knowledge, power, and ethics.

For Wells knowledge demands the power and creates the ethics. In *Perelandra* Lewis argued that ethics directs (or ought to) our knowledge and limits our power. *Perelandra* reads like poetry and has the feel of mythology. Imagining a situation parallel to the biblical story of Eden, Lewis set Professor Weston as the tempter and his scientism as the pernicious doctrine because it is, indeed, a promise that "you shall be as gods." Lewis brought his readers to explore the questions of human knowledge, human pride, and God.

Here he employed the Faustian theme, as in his pursuit of knowledge Professor Weston makes a bargain with the powers of darkness. A chilling episode portrays the formerly rational Professor Weston in his metamorphosis, coming to claim his godlike powers. In a slavering fit he howls, "Do you see, you timid scruple-mongering fool? I am Universe. I, Weston, am your God and your Devil."[29] What began in the professor as a simple belief in scientism becomes, in fact and inevitably, a losing bargain with Satan. In the end, the unfortunate Weston is overwhelmed by his mentors and is transformed into a devilish monstrosity called the Un-Man.

In this episode Lewis reflected, of course, the Christian aversion to the great vanity that often hides within human knowledge. The terrible image of the Un-Man illustrates Lewis's warning — as developed that same year in *The Abolition of Man* — that scientism amounts to an annihilation of what is truly human in human beings. Lewis's use of the term Un-Man for this final stage in evolution is significant because Wells, Shaw, and many others believed in the possibility of man developing into Super-Men. (One of Shaw's most famous plays is called *Man and Superman*.)

Wells had looked for a new, superior kind of man — which he called the "Samurai" in *A Modern Utopia* — who would rise to absolute power on the wings of science. Lewis argued that to achieve such a "hideous strength" would require the relinquishment of what it means to be truly human — thus effecting the emergence not of the Super-man, but of the Un-Man. For Lewis man is indeed perfectible, but not by his own efforts. The only hope for human

29. *Perelandra* (Macmillan, 1965), p. 96.

perfection is through repentance and the Creator's gracious act of renewal.

No one can accuse either Wells or Lewis of subtlety in their science fiction stories. Certainly Lewis's third story, *That Hideous Strength,* published in 1945, the same year as Wells's *Mind at the End of Its Tether,* has the touch of a sledgehammer; for here the author takes the Faustian theme from Perelandra and proceeds to pound his message home. Weston is gone, of course, but his allies are up to their old tricks under the guise of the National Institute of Co-ordinated Experiments (N.I.C.E.). In the N.I.C.E. Lewis portrays the Wellsian dream of giving complete political power to an elite group of scientific planners. In the story Lewis calls this organization "the first-fruits of that constructive fusion between the state and the laboratory on which so many thoughtful people base their hopes of a better world,"[30] and shows what its last fruits will be like. Thus having personified this doctrine of scientism, Lewis then treats his readers to a spine-tingling spectacle of the consistent consequences of such a fusion of applied science and political power.

From Scientism to Evil

In the end, Lewis's argument against Wells's scientism is grounded in a realistic recognition of human nature as fallen and flawed. The real problem with the Wellsian, scientistic dream of humanity "taking control of its destiny" lies in the human propensities toward greed, lust, and pride — propensities that neither science nor politics is capable of changing. As Lewis argued:

> Let us not be deceived by phrases about "Man taking charge of his own destiny." All that can really happen is some men will take charge of the destiny of others. They will be simply men; none perfect; some greedy, cruel, and dishonest. . . . Have we discovered some new reason why, this time, power should not corrupt as it has done before?[31]

30. *That Hideous Strength* (Macmillan, 1965), p. 23.
31. *God in the Dock* (Eerdmans, 1970), p. 311.

In other words, left to their own ethics and their own devices, the strong will always bully the weak. History has more than proven this. Perhaps the most unsettling of Lewis's arguments against Wells is that scientism leads in the end to evil. This theme is found throughout the trilogy, but it is especially strong in the final two stories. In *Perelandra* Lewis explores the slow, corrosive force that uses Professor Weston's pride and will to power to destroy his humanity and create a demon:

> The forces which had begun, perhaps years ago, to eat away his humanity had now completed their work. The intoxicated will which had been slowly poisoning the intelligence and the affections had now at last poisoned itself and the whole psychic organism had fallen to pieces.[32]

Man's will for godlike power comes to dominate and destroy the very things that define his humanity; thus the man becomes the un-man.

In *That Hideous Strength* the hapless professors at Bracton College stumble into a nightmare of evil, as the proponents of scientism gain the political power to do whatever they please. Lewis explains the process:

> The physical sciences, good and innocent in themselves, had already . . . begun to be warped, had been subtly manoeuvred in a certain direction. Despair of objective truth had been increasingly insinuated into the scientists; indifference to it, and a concentration upon mere power, had been the result. . . . And now, all this had reached the stage at which its dark contrivers thought they could safely begin to bend it back so that it would meet the other and earlier kind of power.[33]

The Wellsian doctrine of scientism includes precisely that rendering of truth to be merely relative and mutable, and that misuse of science in the effort to gain godlike power for human beings. In all three stories Lewis's argument is essentially the same: When mere humans reject God and the absolute moral values of the Tao, they

32. *Perelandra*, p. 130.
33. *That Hideous Strength*, p. 203.

eventually seek absolute power over others in order to achieve what they think is a higher good, and then they inevitably do great evil.

Though Wells would object to this terminology, the controversy between Lewis and Wells really does come down to the question: God or gods? Christian doctrine states that God exists — outside humanity, other than humanity, and absolutely superior to humanity. The doctrine of scientism holds that there is no such God, and that in his place emergent evolution will, through science, come to produce the Super-Man who will rule the future. In other words, humans will become their own gods. In *That Hideous Strength* Lewis put it this way:

> Dreams of the far future destiny of man were dragging up from its shallow and unquiet grave the old dream of Man as God. . . . What should they find incredible, since they believed no longer in a rational universe? What should they regard as too obscene, since they held that all morality was a mere subjective by-product of the physical and economic situations of men?[34]

Thus Lewis identifies the essence of scientism as the deification of humanity — Wells's "Men like Gods."

Certainly Lewis was not alone in warning against the cultic aspects of popular scientism, but few have been so bold as to equate scientism with the Satanic temptation to reject God and set oneself up as a god instead. While Wells is widely recognized as a founder of science fiction — though his role in propagating scientism is largely forgotten — Lewis had the audacity to use Wells's own genre to controvert the tenets of scientism.

Reading Wells's and Lewis's science fiction stories is a fascinating adventure in imaginative argumentation. Having read Wells's stories, who cannot sympathize with the dream of humanity finally putting an end to wars, to disease, to hunger, and to social chaos? Who can resist the heady dream of humankind reaching out toward the challenges and mysteries of the vast cosmos?

Yet, having also read Lewis's stories, who can help but stop and wonder who will control the controllers, and from whence will come these elite leaders who will rule scientifically but with wisdom, justice, and mercy? Who does not feel the cold breath of evil lurking in that

34. Ibid.

absolute power, that hideous strength, that is the dream of H. G. Wells and his scientism?

The Great Contrast

Finally, are we really surprised to find that Wells, having invested all of his faith in human achievement, concluded his life in disillusionment and bitterness despite all his success and honors; while Lewis — having put his faith in the grace of the loving God — found cause for peace and hope in his waning years despite the excruciating loss of his beloved wife?

In his final years Wells wrote *Mind at the End of Its Tether* (1945), wherein — in contrast to the optimism of his whole career — he despaired of any chance for human survival against the destructive onslaught of nature. Referring to himself as "he," Wells wrote:

> in the past he has liked to think that Man could pull out of his entanglements and start a new creative phase of human living. In the face of our universal inadequacy, that optimism has given place to stoical cynicism. . . . Man must go steeply up or down and the odds seem to be all in favour of his going down and out. . . . Ordinary man is at the end of his tether.[35]

In contrast to Wells's final years of hopelessness and despair, Lewis's last days were brightened by the grace of hope in the Resurrection and faith in the Creator's love. Even in his pain and mourning over the tragic loss to cancer of his beloved wife, Lewis's journal contained entries such as this:

> Praise is the mode of love which always has some joy in it. Praise in due order; of Him as the giver, of her as the gift. Don't we in praise somehow enjoy what we praise, however far we are from it? . . . But by praising we can still, in some degree, enjoy her, and already, in some degree, enjoy Him.[36]

---

35. Wells, *Mind at the End of Its Tether,* p. 30.
36. *A Grief Observed* (Bantam Books, 1961), p. 72.

In the writings and lives of H. G. Wells and C. S. Lewis we see the two major conflicting worldviews of scientism and Christianity. Scientism portrays human life as a material struggle for survival and power, the only ultimate hope lying in the perpetual survival of humanity as a species. But Christianity looks beyond the grave in a different way, giving hope to every individual soul for a resurrection into the wonders that lie just beyond the door. This hope is captured in Lewis's famous sermon "The Weight of Glory," where he said:

> At present we are on the outside of the world, the wrong side of the door. We discern the freshness and purity of morning, but they do not make us fresh and pure. We cannot mingle with the splendours we see. But all the leaves of the New Testament are rustling with the rumour that it will not always be so. Some day, God willing, we shall get in.[37]

---

37. *The Weight of Glory* (Eerdmans, 1965), p. 13.

Tools Inadequate and Incomplete: C. S. Lewis and the Great Religions

JERRY ROOT

IN HIS POPULAR BOOK *Mere Christianity* C. S. Lewis observed, to the surprise of many, "If you are a Christian you do not have to believe that all the other religions are simply wrong all through."[1] Of course questions immediately follow. If, as Christians maintain, the atonement of Christ alone can provide access to God, what could Lewis have had in mind when he asserted that the other religions have some truth in them? What does Christianity share with the other great (and by great, I mean widely practiced) religions of the world? What does this mean for evangelism? Could these truths be (in some sense) saving truths?

Three Common Characteristics and One Unique

Taking his lead from the book *The Idea of the Holy* by the German theologian Rudolf Otto, Lewis identified three characteristics common to the world religions — what he called "developed religions," for the first and second can exist without the third.[2] Each characteristic is either "a mere twist in the human mind, corresponding to nothing objective . . . [or] a direct experience of the really supernatural, to which the name Revelation might properly be given." They are sur-

1. *Mere Christianity* (Macmillan, 1960), p. 43.
2. *The Problem of Pain* (Fount, 1977), pp. 14-20.

prising and apparently inexplicable "jumps that humanity takes in its religious history." (In his book on the Narnia Chronicles, Walter Hooper showed that these three characteristics are all vested in Aslan, and the stories give Lewis's fullest illustration of developed religion.[3])

First, all these religions believe in some kind of Divine Essence, some version of "the holy." Otto called it "the Numinous," the *mysterium tremendum et fascinans,* a mystery far greater than we that holds us spellbound. Of course each religion will have a different image of the Numinous, and different ideas of how it is manifested to humanity, contingent on whether the religion is animistic, pantheistic, polytheistic, dualistic, monotheistic, or monotheistic Trinitarian. In each case, however, in the presence of the Numinous their adherents feel a sense of awe and almost irresistible attraction.[4]

Second, all of the world religions believe in some kind of absolute moral law, which people feel obliged to obey but characteristically, even habitually, break. All the religions "agree in prescribing a behavior which their adherents fail to practise." In each, all men stand under condemnation and know they are guilty.[5] In *The Abolition of Man,* Lewis called this moral law "the Tao" and showed with extensive examples how common were the basic moral principles.[6]

Third, all the developed world religions believe that the Divine Essence or Numinous is the custodian of the moral law, so that offenses against the law are offenses against the Divine Essence. Because of this, the religious adherent knows not only that he has offended against the law but that his god condemns him, and he recognizes that it is his own fault that he is estranged from the Divine.

3. Walter Hooper, *Past Watchful Dragons* (Macmillan/Collier Books, 1979), pp. 94-100.

4. Lewis, attempting to awaken in his readers a sense of this awe, reminded them of the passage in Kenneth Grahame's *Wind in the Willows* ("The Piper at the Gates of Dawn," chap. 7). In this chapter Rat and Mole find themselves on an all-night search for Portly, the young son of their friend Otter. They are led by pipe music to the very place where Portly *will* be found, but not until Rat and Mole have an encounter with Pan, the demigod and protector of animals. Their experience, as it is written by Grahame, captures, for Lewis, this awe before the Numinous. Lewis cited other examples from Genesis, Ezekiel, the Apocalypse, Aeschylus, Virgil, Malory, and Wordsworth's *Prelude. The Problem of Pain,* p. 15.

5. Ibid., p. 17.

6. *The Abolition of Man* (Macmillan, 1955), pp. 25-30 and 95-121.

(Thus, Lewis noted, religious believers cannot be accused of desiring the existence of this authority as mere wish fulfillment. If this were the case, it would be difficult to understand why believers desired the presence of one who is offended by their deficiencies.)[7]

There is a fourth characteristic peculiar to Christianity, which distinguishes it from the rest of the world religions, even Judaism. This characteristic gives a different answer than any of the other religions gives to the problem each of them recognizes. While the Christian will agree with the adherents of the other religions on the existence of a Numinous or Holy, on an absolute moral law, and on the Numinous as custodian of that moral law, he cannot agree with them on what ought to be done to fix the problem created by our failing to keep the moral law and separating ourselves from the Numinous.

Man and God (however a religion understands them) are estranged. The other world religions attempt to resolve the difficulty by developing additional moral codes. If the adherent will simply live up to the new code perfectly, he will merit some kind of peace between himself and God. The Christian looks at the problem differently. If a man could not live up to the first code, how, or by what means, will he possibly be able to live up to the new code?

Lewis believed that only God could restore what was broken in man. Nothing we can do will heal the estrangement. In the days before his own conversion to Christianity, he had reasoned his way through and out of the morass of atheism and agnosticism. He thought through the claims of the various religions of the world, and settled on theism. He thought, however, that we could no more know God personally than Hamlet could know Shakespeare.[8]

Two years later he became a Christian. He later wrote in his autobiography, *Surprised by Joy,* that he came to realize that his analogy of Hamlet and Shakespeare was a good one. Hamlet could never know Shakespeare by breaking out of the play to meet his creator. But it was possible for Shakespeare the author to write himself into the play as Shakespeare the character, thus making the meeting possible.[9] Lewis

7. *The Problem of Pain*, p. 18.
8. *Surprised by Joy* (Harcourt, Brace & World, 1955), p. 223.
9. Ibid., p. 227.

believed that an event something like this is what happened in the Incarnation, when God wrote himself into the drama of human existence and became a man.

This is a characteristic unique to Christianity, and one that makes all the difference. "All the essentials of Hinduism would, I think, remain unimpaired if you subtracted the miraculous," he wrote in *Miracles,* "and the same is almost true of Mohammedanism. But you cannot do that with Christianity. It is precisely the story of a great Miracle."[10]

Lewis understood that God must be the initiator when it comes to a relationship between God and man.

All the initiative has been on God's side; all has been free, unbounded grace. . . . Bliss is not for sale; cannot be earned. "Works" have no "merit," though of course faith, inevitably, even unconsciously, flows out into works of love at once. He is not saved because he does works of love: he does works of love because he is saved. It is faith alone that has saved him: faith bestowed by sheer gift.[11]

In this context, the other religions, to the extent that they exemplify the three characteristics, are part of "the long spiritual preparation of humanity" for the Incarnation.[12] Thus the Christian has "the double task of reconciling and converting. The activities are almost opposites, yet must go hand in hand. We have to hurl down

10. *Miracles* (Macmillan, 1960), p. 68. In a paper presented to the Socratic Club at Oxford in 1943, Lewis distinguished Christianity from the mystery religions not only by its grounding in historical events but also by its survival through history, its being both ethical and sacramental, and its creating the new or redeemed man all the religions hoped for. "If We Have Christ's Ethics Does the Rest of the Christian Faith Matter?" *Socratic Digest,* no. 1, quoted in Walter Hooper, *C. S. Lewis: Companion and Guide* (HarperCollins, 1996), pp. 330-31.

11. *English Literature in the Sixteenth Century, Excluding Drama* (Oxford University Press, 1968), p. 33.

12. *The Problem of Pain,* p. 24. Indeed, pantheism was an important movement in Lewis's own discovery of Christianity. "Wordsworthian contemplation," as he called it, was "the first and lowest form of recognition that there is something outside ourselves which demands reverence," and the man who has gotten this far "has escaped the worst arrogance of materialism; if he goes on he will be converted." "Christianity and Culture," in *Christian Reflections,* ed. Walter Hooper (Eerdmans, 1967), p. 22.

false gods and also elicit the peculiar truth preserved in the worship of each."[13]

Other religions may set the stage for the play, but the drama of redemption and reconciliation is manifest only in Christianity. For Lewis the significant difference between Christianity and the other religions was that of a historic event. God the Son became a man in order to set man right before God.

Affirming and Denying the World

In a short essay titled "Some Thoughts," Lewis clarified another distinctive that sets Christianity apart from the other religions of the world. This distinctive he called "the blessedly two-edged character of Christianity."[14] The other religions are, so to speak, one-edged.

Christianity is, with Confucianism, "one of the world-affirming religions."[15] It concerns itself with the sick and infirm, encourages culture and the arts, cares for the disenfranchised — the widow, the orphan, the poor, and others marginalized by society — celebrates sexuality and marriage, and affirms the body and all its cares and joys. But Christianity is also, with Buddhism, "one of the world-denying religions."[16] It is not *attached* to this world. It rejects the inordinate longing for temporal things, even life itself; looks forward to a life beyond mere earthly existence; and fears damnation more than death. As a result Christians can mortify the flesh, abstain from pleasures, and embrace solitude, celibacy, and the monastic life.

Lewis recognized that Christian doctrine will not give license to calling the immaterial good and the material bad, nor vice versa. Both are essentially good, though it is important to remember that their goodness is ordered, that a thing is good in its place but not out of it.

13. *The Letters of C. S. Lewis,* ed. W. H. Lewis (Harcourt Brace Jovanovich/ Harvest Books, 1966), p. 300.

14. "Some Thoughts," in *God in the Dock,* ed. Walter Hooper (Eerdmans, 1970), pp. 147-50.

15. Ibid., p. 147.

16. Ibid., p. 148.

"Because God created the Natural — invented it out of His love and artistry, it demands our reverence," he continued,

> because it is only a creature and not He, it is, from another point of view, of little account. And still more because Nature, and especially human nature, is fallen it must be corrected and the evil within it must be mortified. But its essence is good; correction is something quite different from Manichaean repudiation or Stoic superiority. Hence, in all true Christian asceticism, that respect for the thing rejected which, I think, we never find in pagan asceticism. Marriage is good, though not for me; wine is good, though I must not drink it; feasts are good, though today we fast.[17]

Since Christianity affirms the world, it stands in stark contrast with religions that are pantheistic. Pantheists never look at the universe as something that God has made, but as something that has emanated from him or is simply an illusion.[18] The world we see is therefore something less than God; indeed, something that keeps us from God. Since Christianity is also a world-denying religion, it also stands in stark contrast with religions that are polytheistic. In these, "the gods are usually the product of a universe already in existence," are essentially part of nature.[19]

Therefore, Lewis observed, "polytheism is always, in the long run, nature-worship; Pantheism always, in the long run, hostility to nature." The problem, which Christianity avoids — or rather transcends — is that neither "really leaves you free *both* to enjoy your breakfast *and* to mortify your inordinate appetites — much less to mortify appetites recognised as innocent at present lest they should become inordinate."[20] The difference is that "The Indian, looking at the material world, says, 'I am that.' I say, 'That I and I grow from one root'."[21]

17. *Letters to Malcolm: Chiefly on Prayer* (Harcourt Brace Jovanovich/Harvest Books, 1964), pp. 148-49. From this knowledge of nature follows the true enjoyment of nature, an enjoyment paganism denies. See *Miracles,* p. 66.

18. "Some Thoughts," p. 149.

19. Ibid. Polytheism, Lewis argued, naturally develops or matures into monotheism: "Behind the gods arises the One, and the gods as well as the men are only his dreams." *The Allegory of Love* (Oxford University Press, 1938), p. 57.

20. Ibid.

21. *Letters to Malcolm,* p. 79.

That Christianity has both these two edges follows from its distinctive doctrines of Creation and the Fall.[22] Though some pagan religions have some idea of a Fall, the doctrine of Creation is peculiar to Christianity (with the exception of Judaism and perhaps Islam, which some have defined as a Christian heresy), and gives the Fall its distinctive character. God created the cosmos, and therefore it is good; man's relation to the cosmos is fallen, and therefore it is a temptation and a snare. Therefore, as he wrote a friend, "One can hardly say anything either bad enough or good enough about life."[23]

One comment should be made about those religions that are neither pantheistic nor polytheistic, the nontrinitarian monotheisms of the Middle East, particularly Islam. These seek triumph over the world through regulation and law, in an attempt to achieve merit before God. Theirs is not so much the renunciation of self as it is the enlargement of self. Legalistic religion produces two kinds of people: (1) the guilty who know they cannot keep the law, and (2) the arrogant who think they can. These religions tend to produce either despair or a perfectionism that can become both rigid and domineering.

In rejecting the Incarnation, Lewis observed, Islam "will not allow that God has descended into flesh or that Manhood has been exalted into Deity. . . . It stands for all religions that are afraid of matter and afraid of mystery."[24]

---

22. "Some Thoughts," p. 149. Another difference, which we do not have room to explore in this essay, is the Christian insistence on doctrinal clarity and the willingness to live without definitions or with contradictory definitions found in other religions, as becomes clear in Lewis's comments on Hinduism in letters to Dom Bede Griffiths, a student and Roman Catholic priest living in India. In one he asked, "what do they [Hindus] deny? That has always been my trouble with Indians — to find any proposition they would pronounce false. But truth must surely involve exclusions." In the other he wrote, "the difficulty in preaching Christ in India is that there is no difficulty. One is up against true Paganism — the best sort as well as the worst — hospitable to all gods, naturally religious, ready to take any shape but able to retain none." *Letters of C. S. Lewis,* ed. W. H. Lewis (Geoffrey Bles, 1966), pp. 267 and 285. See also *Letters to an American Lady* (Eerdmans, 1971), p. 60.

23. *Letters of C. S. Lewis,* p. 266.

24. *Arthurian Torso* (Oxford University Press, 1948), p. 124.

Thou, and Not Thou

Taking a lead from his friend Charles Williams, Lewis found another support for this "blessed two-edged character." Because God created each creature separate from himself and yet is also in each creature "as the ground and root and continual supply of its reality," we must say to each thing God has created, "This also is Thou: neither is this Thou."[25] Here Lewis emphasized the mystery of the combination of God's immanence and his transcendence. Because God is present in all he has made, the Christian can say, with some religions, "This also is Thou." But because God transcends what he has made, the Christian must say, with other religions, "Neither is this Thou."

Lest I be tempted to worship the thing that motivates me to say "This also is Thou," I must remember in the same breath, "Neither is this Thou." Lest I be tempted to denigrate or exploit or abuse the things to which I say "Neither is this Thou," I must stop myself and say "This also is Thou."

The two ways of Christian spirituality have flowed from this. The first way is the way of affirmation. It worships with eyes wide open, eager not to miss any message or hint of the divine presence that God has on display in his creation. This way leads to more than mere gratitude. "Gratitude exclaims, very properly: 'How good of God to give me this.' Adoration says: 'What must be the quality of that Being whose faroff and momentary coruscations are like this!' One's mind runs back up the sunbeam to the sun."[26]

The Way of Affirmation takes its cues from data gathered empirically from the material world. It turns sights and color, smells and fragrances, textures, sounds, and even tastes ("taste and see that the Lord is good") into occasions for worship.

The second way is the Way of Negation. It worships with eyes closed. It seeks to shut out all distractions in its attempts to concentrate on God Transcendent. It remembers to say of all things made, "Neither is this Thou." It is the ascetic way.

---

25. *Letters to Malcolm*, p. 74. In Charles Williams, see *The Descent of the Dove: A Short History of the Holy Spirit in the Church* (Eerdmans, 1974), p. viii, and *The Figure of Beatrice: A Study in Dante* (Faber & Faber, 1953), p. 37.

26. *Letters to Malcolm*, p. 90.

Thus the danger of other religions is manifest more by what they lack than by what they possess. If they are right about transcendence, they are wrong about immanence, and vice versa. To the degree that they emphasize immanence without also emphasizing transcendence, they risk becoming thisworldly and self-indulgent. To the degree that they emphasize transcendence without immanence they risk becoming proud, austere, and pharisaical. The Christian is left "always fighting on at least two fronts. When one is among Pantheists one must emphasise the distinctness, and relative Independence, of the creatures. Among Deists . . . one must emphasise the divine presence in my neighbor, my dog, my cabbage-patch."[27]

Either way, isolated from the checks and balance of the other, produces a kind of idolatry, expressed in a different way. The world's religions, lacking the two edges, reshape the "both-and" into an "either-or" — as when, even among Christians, the monk condemns the married man for enjoying "the pleasures of the flesh" or the married man condemns the monk for "hiding from the real world."

The Meaning of Desire

Another, similar, way to look at Lewis's view of the relation of Christianity to the other great religions is in his treatment of desire, of the value of earthly things.

The practitioners of the Eastern religions seek to gain merit by denying all desire, by disassociating themselves from material goods and earthly pleasure. Theirs is the way of renunciation. They practice the suppression of desire and detachment from things. In *The Dhammapada* it is said that, "The disciple who is fully awakened delights only in the destruction of all desires"[28] and "Him I call Brahmin

27. Ibid., p. 74. Lewis, in defending his apologetics from the criticism of the liberal Anglican theologian Norman Pittenger, noted that he stressed the transcendence of God rather than his immanence, though he believed in both, because Deism was not a temptation to the people of his day, but "an immoral, naïve and sentimental pantheism" was. "Rejoinder to Dr. Pittenger," in *God in the Dock,* p. 181. See also *Miracles,* p. 93.

28. *The Dhammapada,* "Buddhavaggo — The Buddha (The Awakened)," 14.9, tr. Sarvepalli Radhakrishnan, 1888 (Oxford University Press, 1974), p. 121.

[enlightened or, in Christian terms, saved] for whom there is nothing before, behind, or between, who has nothing and is without attachment."[29]

Contrary to the Eastern religions, Lewis found that desire, properly followed, may lead to God. It is not a thing to be suppressed or denied, only rightly guided. He would affirm the sixteenth-century poet Thomas Traherne's remark that

> The noble inclination whereby man thirsteth after riches and dominion, is his highest virtue, when rightly guided; and carries him as a triumphant chariot, to his sovereign happiness. Men are made miserable only by abusing it. Taking a false way to satisfy it, they pursue the wind.[30]

Rather than denying the pursuit of pleasure (pursued in its proper measure and order) or suppressing desire (the desire for things worthy of desire), Lewis believed that these ought to be pursued and enjoyed. There is a desire, he believed, so characteristically human that our dignity is recovered only in following its lead till we find the very object of that desire. "It appeared to me therefore that if a man diligently followed this desire, pursuing the false objects until their falsity appeared and then resolutely abandoning them," he wrote,

> he must come out at last into the clear knowledge that the human soul was made to enjoy some object that is never fully given. . . . The only fatal error was to pretend that you had passed from desire to fruition, when, in reality, you had found either nothing, or desire itself, or the satisfaction of some different desire. The dialectic of Desire, faithfully followed, would retrieve all mistakes, head you off from all false paths, and force you not to propound, but to live through, a sort of ontological proof.[31]

So, ironically, to the degree that the religions of the world seek to suppress all desire in order to find God, their asceticism also shuts out God. In banishing desire, they renounce the path to God. As the

---

29. Ibid., "Brahmanavaggo — The Brahmin," 26.28, p. 184.
30. Thomas Traherne, *Centuries* (Faith Press, 1923), p. 12.
31. *The Pilgrim's Regress* (Eerdmans, 1981), pp. 204-5.

Psalmist wrote, "Thou wilt make known to me the path of life: in thy Presence is fulness of joy; at thy right hand there are pleasures forever" (Psalm 16:11). As in St. Augustine's famous words from his *Confessions,* "Our hearts are restless until they find their rest in Thee."

The Hope of Those Who Follow Other Religions

This leaves the question of what Lewis thought about the eternal destiny of the followers of the other religions, who have seen something of the truth but not the central and crucial truth that Jesus is the Son of God who died for our sins and rose again. Lewis was not a universalist. Unlike his mentor George MacDonald,[32] he did not believe that all will be saved, but he did speculate that the door to Heaven may be opened for some who follow other religions, that they may find themselves in Heaven after death.

The most alarming presentation of his position meets us in *The Last Battle,* the seventh and final book of his Chronicles of Narnia. Emeth, a Calormene warrior and follower of the false god Tash, dies in battle and finds himself, to his great surprise, in Narnian Heaven. Emeth tells others the story of his encounter with Aslan, the Christ figure of Narnia. Aslan welcomes him, but Emeth, an honest man (his name means faithful or true in Hebrew), admits that he was a follower of Tash. Aslan responds: "Child, all the service thou hast done to Tash, I account as service done to me." Emeth then asks if Aslan and Tash are really the same, and Aslan

> growled so that the earth shook (but his wrath was not against me) and said, It is false. Not because he and I are one, but because we are opposites, I take to me the services which thou hast done to him, for I and he are of such different kinds that no service which is vile can be done to me, and none which is not vile can be done to him.

---

32. MacDonald *was* a universalist, although Lewis said of him that "He hopes, indeed, that all men will be saved; but that is because he hopes that all will repent. He knows (none better) that even Omnipotence cannot save the unconverted. He never trifles with eternal impossibilities." *George MacDonald: An Anthology,* ed. with an intro. by C. S. Lewis (Geoffrey Bles, 1970), p. 20.

Aslan explains that all good deeds are done for him, whether or not the doer knows it, and all evil deeds done for Tash. Then Emeth admits he had been looking for Tash all his life, and Aslan, the "Glorious One," answers him: "Beloved . . . thy desire had been for me thou wouldst not have sought so long and so truly. For all find what they truly seek."[33]

Some, to be sure, have thought that Lewis went too far in this passage. They wonder if he did not flirt with universalism. An earlier scene in *The Last Battle* shows that this is not the case. At the climax of Narnian history a long queue forms before an open Door. Aslan stands at the Door, and all the citizens of Narnia must come up and face him. In that moment, they either turn and enter through the Door to be with Aslan or they turn away, preferring eternal darkness and death to life with the Lion. Choices are made, and they have eternal consequences.

Lewis was certainly not a universalist. The story of Emeth is nothing more than Lewis's imagination engaged in hopeful theological speculation — though it was perhaps an unfortunate choice to speculate on the *ordo salutis* in a children's book. Lewis, to a lesser degree, and MacDonald, to a greater degree, trifled with eternal possibilities. MacDonald believed that, no matter how long or how much suffering it might take, eventually everyone would make it into Heaven. Lewis left open the possibility that some, who have begun the process in this life, might complete the process of conversion in the next life.

If regenerate souls still unconverted could die before conversion, could they be given an opportunity to complete in the next life what God had begun in them in this life? Some would object that God could certainly so superintend the life of the regenerate, keeping them from death until they completed the process leading to conversion. While the objection is a strong and a worthy one, Lewis appeared to be proposing nonetheless that if a person in such a process did die before completing that process there still is hope for him.[34] I think this is the meaning of the story of Emeth.

33. *The Last Battle* (Macmillan/Collier Books, 1970), pp. 164-65.

34. Lewis maintained a similar hope for the Egyptian pharaoh and monotheist Akhenaten, as well as for Virgil and Plato. *Reflections on the Psalms* (Geoffrey Bles, 1958), pp. 89 and 108.

It might well be argued that a children's book is not a good place to do speculative theology. On the other hand, perhaps it is legitimate to begin, as early as childhood, recognizing that there are elements of our faith that are shrouded in mystery. The best we can say is that we do not know for sure. Moses reminds us that, "The secret things belong to God, but the things revealed belong to us and to our children forever" (Deuteronomy 29:29).

There may be some element of mystery surrounding the eternal destiny of some followers of other faiths. Two things appear certain from Scripture: (1) no one gets into Heaven apart from faith in God's provision for sin in the finished work of Jesus Christ; and (2) some do not make it.

So what comes of the faithful and sincere follower of another religion? Lewis told a group of seminarians, "Woe to you if you do not evangelize," for "you exist in the long run for no other purpose."[35] Since Lewis believed that people could be damned — and in *The Last Battle, The Great Divorce,* and *That Hideous Strength* are damned — he thought it necessary to be zealous in his evangelistic endeavors. God has said it is the responsibility of those who know to tell those who have not yet heard. Whether it be apostate Westerners or errant Easterners, all need to hear clearly the claims of Christ, which have

> no parallel in other religions. If you had gone to Buddha and asked him, "Are you the son of Brahma?" he would have said, "My son, you are still in the vale of illusion." If you had gone to Socrates and asked, "Are you Zeus?" he would have laughed at you. If you had gone to Mohammed and asked, "Are you Allah?" he would first have rent his clothes and then cut your head off. If you had asked Confucius, "Are you Heaven?" I think he would have probably replied, "Remarks which are not in accordance with nature are in bad taste."

Jesus was either the Son of God, and the fulfillment of all that is true in the great religions, or he was a lunatic or a liar and the denial of all that is true in the great world religions. And indeed no one who met him in the flesh thought of him as "a mere moral teacher. He

35. "Modern Theology and Biblical Criticism," in *Christian Reflections,* p. 152. In *Mere Christianity* Lewis remarked that God has not told us the end of those who never hear of him and made this an argument for conversion (p. 65). See also John 10:16.

did not produce that effect on any of the people who actually met
Him. He produced mainly three effects: Hatred — Terror — Adoration. There was no trace of people expressing mild approval."[36]

Final Observations

Lewis did not write a formal philosophy of religion. Nor did he
provide for his readers an exhaustive comparison of the world religions. Nevertheless, from his writings it is possible to glean some
valuable insight into understanding how Christianity relates to other
religions. Though sharing the three common elements he identified
in all religions, Christianity yet provided more substance than could
be found in the others. It did so because of the historic element, the
Incarnation.

Thus the Numinous becomes articulate in Christ, "the Word
made flesh." It is not just an Essence, it is a Person, or rather a Trinity
of Persons. In the doctrine of the Trinity, God "is revealed to us as
super-personal, which is very different from being *im*-personal."[37]

The absolute moral law also finds a clearer expression in Christianity. The demands of the Tao are made more specific, in fact made
more intense and demanding — as when Jesus declares that lust is an
act of adultery and hate an act of murder. Christianity also declares
not only that we are guilty of violating this law, but that we can do
nothing to remove our guilt. With the appearance of Christ in the
Incarnation, there is the bold affirmation that the Law is true and its
demands must be fulfilled.

The Numinous as the guardian of morality also finds its clearest
expression in Christ. Christianity acknowledges the authority that
condemns, and it provides hope in the face of the guilt that prohibits
access to the presence of God. The religions of the world acknowledge
the inability of man to meet the demands of their various moral and
ethical codes. They admit the distance that separates them from the
Numinous. But what then? In a letter to Sheldon Vanauken, Lewis
wrote, "Have you read the *Analects* of Confucius? He ends up by

36. "What Are We to Make of Jesus Christ?" in *God in the Dock,* pp. 157-58.
37. *Letters of C. S. Lewis,* p. 305.

saying 'This is the Tao. I do not know if anyone has ever kept it.' That's significant. One can really go direct from there to the *Epistle to the Romans.*"[38]

And this leads to the Incarnation, that peculiar and most significant feature that separates Christianity from the other religions. What Jesus says, wrote Lewis, is

> very different from what any other teacher has said. Others say, "This is the truth about the Universe. This is the way you ought to go," but He says, "I am the Truth, and the Way, and the Life." He says, "No man can reach absolute reality, except through Me. . . . Your sins, all of them, are wiped out, I can do that. I am Re-birth, I am Life. Eat Me, drink Me, I am your Food. And finally, do not be afraid, I have overcome the whole Universe."[39]

The existence of the other religions does not mean that God has somehow lost sovereign control of some corners of the universe. Other religions are not an affront to his power and purposes. He still works all things after the counsel of his own will. In his Latin letters, Lewis wrote,

> Satan is without doubt nothing else than a hammer in the hand of a benevolent and severe God. For all, either willingly or unwillingly, do the will of God: Judas and Satan as tools or instruments, John and Peter as Sons.[40]

While Lewis saw the inadequacies of rival religions, he also understood that they have seen some things (not everything, and not the most important things) truly, and that they too can be tools by which God will accomplish his purposes and plans.

---

38. Sheldon Vanauken, *A Severe Mercy* (Harper & Row, 1977), p. 90.

39. *God in the Dock,* p. 160.

40. *Letters: C. S. Lewis and Don Giovanni Calabria,* tr. and ed. Martin Moynihan (Servant Publications, 1988), pp. 33-35.

Nothingness and Human Destiny: Hell in the Thought of C. S. Lewis

KENDALL HARMON

IN THE LATE nineteenth century Lewis Carroll (the Rev. Charles Dodgson) wrote an essay he intended to be the first in a book on religious difficulties that "tend to affect life." The first subject he chose was "Eternal Punishment."[1] In this century, however, the subject of Hell and the eternal significance of human decisions virtually disappeared from Christian discourse. Yet it plays a vital role in C. S. Lewis's thought in a manner unusual for a modern apologist and highly unfashionable in the academic circles in which he lived and worked. Preaching in Oxford in 1939, he observed that

> to a Christian the true tragedy of Nero must be not that he fiddled while the city was on fire but that he fiddled on the brink of Hell. You must forgive me for that crude monosyllable. I know that many wiser and better Christians than I in these days do not like to mention heaven and hell even in a pulpit. I know, too, that nearly all the references to this subject in the New Testament come from a single source. But then that source is Our Lord Himself. People will tell you it is St. Paul, but that is untrue. These overwhelming doctrines are dominical. They are not really removable from the teaching of Christ or of His Church. If we do not believe them, our presence in this church is great tomfoolery. If we do, we must sometime overcome our spiritual prudery and mention them.[2]

1. Stuart D. Collingwood, *The Life and Letters of Lewis Carroll* (T. Fisher Unwin, 1898), p. 327.
2. "Learning in War-Time," in *The Weight of Glory and Other Addresses,* ed. Walter Hooper (rev. ed., Macmillan, 1980), pp. 20-21.

Lewis's creation of new images of Hell, at a time when even Christians were shy of acknowledging the doctrine at all, illustrates not only his boldness as an apologist but his genius as a remythologizer. He took ancient (God-given) truths and reclothed them in accessible and intelligible and revealing images. Those who criticize him for not being a theologian — by which they mean a theologian of a specific, academic, sort — miss the way he is doing theology. Who else could have invented *The Great Divorce* and *The Screwtape Letters?* In my research I found his work, and especially *The Great Divorce,* quoted everywhere, even by the most scholarly of German theologians.

With the exception of a few letters and the sermon just quoted, Lewis's only directly theological reflections on Hell come in a very short essay entitled "The Trouble with 'X' . . ." (1948) and a brief chapter in *The Problem of Pain* (1940).[3] But he has much to say about Hell, and about the way men and women get there, in his imaginative works, especially *The Pilgrim's Regress* (1933), *The Screwtape Letters* (1942), and *The Great Divorce* (1945).[4]

Sin as Radical Self-cleaving

Lewis's theology of sin was thoroughly Augustinian. For Augustine the original act of transgression — the eating of the fruit — was preceded by Adam and Eve's decision to seek satisfaction in themselves and not in their Maker. Sin is man curved in upon himself, an "act of self-will on the part of the creature, which constitutes an utter falseness to its true creaturely position," as Lewis put it in *The Problem of Pain.*[5] Lewis saw that this choice of self against God begins with minute, almost unnoticeable, apparently insignificant acts. A radical crime such as treachery starts very small: with taking pride in oneself, then forgetting one's duties and one's position of dependence, then

3. *God in the Dock,* ed. Walter Hooper (Eerdmans, 1970), pp. 151-55; *The Problem of Pain* (Fount Paperback, 1977), pp. 106-16.
4. *The Pilgrim's Regress* (Geoffrey Bles, 1943); *The Screwtape Letters & Screwtape Proposes a Toast* (Geoffrey Bles, 1960); *The Great Divorce* (Geoffrey Bles, 1945).
5. *The Problem of Pain,* pp. 68-69.

ever widening self-deception as one transforms self-interest into self-worship.

In *The Great Divorce* George MacDonald tells Lewis that sin "begins with a grumbling mood, and yourself still distinct from it: perhaps criticizing it. And yourself, in a dark hour, may will that mood, embrace it. You can repent and come out of it again. But there may come a day when you can do that no longer."[6] Edmund's movement in *The Lion, the Witch and the Wardrobe* from greed and deception (of himself as well as others) to the betrayal, perhaps to their deaths, of his brother and sisters is an example.

Lewis's understanding of character is also Thomistic. Thomas Aquinas taught that individuals make choices that become habits over time, and are therefore increasingly difficult to alter. Nevertheless, one can change, for good or ill, until death, when one's end is finally chosen. (Although Lewis seemed to endorse the possibility of conversion after death in *The Great Divorce,* he meant that if people leave the grey town for Heaven, then it was for them Purgatory, the place where they are cleansed and purged from sin in preparation for the life in Heaven — he believed in Purgatory, as we shall see — whereas if they remain there it is Hell.)[7]

What would a person be like if he kept persistently going in the Hellish direction? Consider the dwarfs in *The Last Battle.* In the last days of Narnia an ape named Shift creates an imitation Aslan, who is nothing more than the donkey Puzzle dressed up in a poorly fitting lion's skin. Shift only shows him a dark stable door, and does not let him speak. The Narnians begin to believe that he is the real Aslan and Shift his spokesman — even though his appearance and Shift's words violate what Aslan had said and done in the past. Shift forms an alliance with the Calormene army and announces that Aslan is really the same as the Calormen god Tash. He combines the two names as Tashlan.

Shift captures the good king Tirian, who calls out to Aslan for assistance, and Jill and Eustace arrive from our world to rescue him, Puzzle, and others. They meet a large group of dwarfs being taken

---

6. *The Great Divorce,* p. 69. For a longer description of this process, see *Mere Christianity* (Macmillan, 1960), pp. 86-87.

7. Ibid., p. 61.

away as slaves by Calormene soldiers. Tirian explains to them how they have been taken in by the ape, and shows them Puzzle and the lionskin he was wearing. After defeating the Calormene warriors, Tirian proudly tells the dwarfs that they are free and calls them to cheer for Aslan.

The dwarfs' responses surprise all: sulky growls, some mutterings, and silence. Having been taken in once by an imitation Aslan, they will not risk being taken in again. They demand that the real Aslan be shown; their suspicion is only reinforced when he cannot be. One dwarf then utters these words from Hell: "We're going to look after ourselves from now on and touch our caps to nobody. See?" The others agree: "'That's right. . . . We're on our own now. No more Aslan, no more kings, no more silly stories about other worlds. *The dwarfs are for the dwarfs.*'" Then they march away. (Their response is anticipated in *Prince Caspian* in the dwarf Nikabrik, who has let a sense of resentment that — as he thinks, wrongly — the dwarfs are asked to do more than anyone else to grow into treachery and treason against the king and even into consorting with witches and werewolves.)

Four more times in the remainder of the book this Satanic liturgical chorus recurs: the dwarfs are for the dwarfs. They interpret everything through their self-interest and suspicion and as a result radically distort what occurs. Eustace tells them they should be thankful for being saved from the salt mines. No, they reply, you just rescued us so you can use us. In the final battle they murder the talking horses, who were fighting for the side that had rescued them. This infuriates Eustace, but the dwarfs jeer at him: "'That was a surprise for you, little boy, eh? Thought we were on your side, did you? No fear. We don't want any Talking Horses. We don't want you to win any more than the other gang. You can't take us in. *The dwarfs are for the dwarfs.*'"

A little later, even sitting on the doorstep of Heaven, with the light of the world standing right in front of them, the dwarfs think they live in a "pitch-black, poky, smelly little hole of a stable." They finally reap what they have sown. Unwilling to be helped, they no longer can be helped; unwilling to be thankful, they no longer have anything to be thankful for; looking out only for themselves, they are left looking out only from the prison of their own minds; unwilling to be taken in, they are left out, never to be taken out of the dungeon of their own egos.

The dwarfs have become a lie; they believe their own propaganda; they have manufactured their own Hell, continuing their choice unabated all the way to the blackest darkness. They illustrate the terrifyingly close relation between the self-enclosing power of sin and its final end, if unrepented, in Hell.

Hell the Final Refusal

The theology of *The Problem of Pain* is the basis for all Lewis's fiction. He began with the Augustinian sequence of creation-Fall-sin-redemption and stressed that God chose to create free beings who can rebel against him by choosing their own wills over his. As he noted in "The Trouble with 'X'," we do not know why God created free beings, "But apparently he thinks it worth doing. He would rather have a world of free beings, with all its risks, than a world of people who did right like machines because they couldn't do anything else."[8]

Once man rebelled, God paid the outrageous price of his own death at Calvary, but even this is a gift that calls for a response. "Where that heroic remedy fails," God "seems unwilling, or even unable, to arrest the ruin by an act of mere power."[9] The brutal fact must therefore be confronted: "Some will not be redeemed. There is no doctrine which I would more willingly remove from Christianity than this."[10]

He did not remove it for two reasons. First, final punishment is biblical and taught by Jesus himself. Second, the universal sense that choices matter, that freely made decisions have consequences, requires a Hell for people who choose against God.

> If the happiness of a creature lies in self-surrender, no one can make that surrender but himself . . . and he may refuse. I would pay any price to be able to say truthfully "All will be saved." But my reason retorts, "Without their will, or with it?" If I say "Without their will"

8. "The Trouble with 'X'," in *God in the Dock,* p. 153.

9. *The Problem of Pain,* p. 108. John Hick calls Lewis's discussion "one of the most eloquent recent presentations of the traditional conception of a temporal fall of man." *Evil and the God of Love* (Macmillan, 1966), p. 284n.1.

10. *The Problem of Pain,* p. 106.

I at once perceive a contradiction; how can the supremely voluntary act of self-surrender be involuntary? If I say "With their will," my reason replies "How if they *will not* give in?"[11]

Hell is thus a risk inherent in creation itself, and one that God took knowing the consequences for himself. "What you call defeat [of God's mercy], I call miracle: for to make things which are not Itself, and thus to become, in a sense, capable of being resisted, is the most astonishing and unimaginable of all the feats we attribute to the Deity." The damned are "successful rebels to the end." God cannot forgive them because they will not be forgiven, and so "they enjoy forever the horrible freedom they have demanded."[12] God does not send us to Hell, but "In each one of us there is something growing up which will itself be Hell unless it is nipped in the bud."[13]

As he suggested in a letter, perhaps God "knows that if you can't learn the way in 60 or 70 years on this planet (a place probably constructed by Divine skill for the very purpose of teaching you) then you will never learn it anywhere."[14]

The Images of Hell

It was not, however, in his belief in Hell that Lewis's originality is found — unusual and courageous as that was in his circles — but in his creation of new images for Hell. He did not think that belief in the reality of Hell committed Christians to the traditional images of torture and punishment. The word for punishment was used only once in the New Testament, whose "regular emphasis is on the *finality* of rejection or exclusion." In Jesus' words, "the dust-bin . . . image is perhaps more prominent than the prison image. . . . the poetic image which simply seizes the moment of 'Come inside' or 'Go away.' "[15]

11. Ibid., pp. 106-7.
12. Ibid., pp. 115-16.
13. "The Trouble with 'X'," pp. 154-55.
14. *They Stand Together: The Letters of C. S. Lewis to Arthur Greeves (1914-1963),* ed. Walter Hooper (Collins, 1979), p. 465.
15. A personal letter, previously unpublished, lent to me by its recipient, the Rev. Alan Fairhurst.

The three images used in the New Testament to portray Hell — punishment, destruction, and "privation, exclusion or banishment" — are all "intended to suggest something unspeakably horrid" and all point in a single direction:

> To enter Heaven is to become more human than you ever succeeded in being on earth; to enter Hell, is to be banished from humanity. What is cast (or casts itself) into Hell is not a man: it is "remains." To be a complete man means to have the passions obedient to the will and the will offered to God: to *have been* a man — to be an ex-man or "damned ghost" — would presumably mean to consist of a will utterly centred in its self and passions uncontrolled by the will.[16]

Our everyday lives are thus tremendously serious, they present us an unavoidable "either-or": "If we insist on keeping Hell (or even earth) we shall not see Heaven: if we accept Heaven we shall not be able to retain even the smallest and most intimate souvenirs of Hell."[17]

This quick sketch of Lewis's theology of Hell may now be supplemented by examining some of his imaginative works. In *The Pilgrim's Regress* Lewis showed Hell from God's point of view, in *The Screwtape Letters,* from Hell's, and in *The Great Divorce,* from ours.

The Pilgrim's Regress

In *The Pilgrim's Regress,* Lewis's autobiography in narrative form, written just after his conversion, a boy named John, born in the land of Puritania, thinks of God as a kind of cosmic torturer. He goes around the world and is converted, and with his companion Vertue is led by a new Guide back the way they came, but he now sees the places they had visited before from an entirely new perspective.

In this book Lewis introduces a belief in Limbo, which sits on the "twilit porches of the black hole" (Hell). The Guide brings them to Limbo, which before his conversion John thought the Valley of Wisdom. John asks who lives there and what their suffering is, and the Guide responds that the few who live there

16. *The Problem of Pain,* pp. 113-14.
17. *The Great Divorce,* pp. 7-8.

are all men like old Mr. Wisdom — men who have kept alive and pure the deep desire of the soul but through some fatal flaw, of pride or sloth or, it may be, timidity, have refused till the end the only means to its fulfilment; taking huge pains, often, to prove to themselves that the fulfilment is impossible. . . . As for their sufferings, it is their doom to live for ever in desire without hope.

But, John asks, is it not harsh that the Landlord makes them suffer at all? The Landlord did not condemn them to live without hope, the Guide responds, they have done that to themselves.

The Landlord's interference is all on the other side. Left to itself, the desire without the hope would soon fall back to spurious satisfactions, and these souls would follow it of their own free will into far darker regions at the very bottom of the black hole. What the Landlord has done is to fix it forever, and by his art, though unfulfilled, it is uncorrupted.

Limbo is not a literary device, for Lewis believed in it. In a letter written in 1939, he wrote that it

is compatible with "perishing everlastingly," and you'll find it quite jolly, for whereas Heaven is an acquired taste, Limbo is a place of "perfect natural happiness." In fact you may be able to realize your wish "of attending with one's whole mind to the history of the human spirit." There are grand libraries in Limbo, endless discussions, and no colds. There will be a faint melancholy because you'll all know that you have missed the bus, but that will provide a subject for poetry.[18]

Though not Heaven, Limbo is still a place where God exercises his mercy to those who will not consciously accept it. Even existing forever "in desire without hope" is better than not existing at all, since existence itself derives from the Creator's goodness. True, it is painful to live with unfulfilled desire, but this pain is still a function of a God-given capacity to think and feel, and more importantly, God has graciously ensured that they will not follow these desires deeper into degradation and suffering, as they would without his restraint.

18. *Letters of C. S. Lewis,* ed. W. H. Lewis (Harcourt Brace, 1966), p. 164.

The Fixed Pains of Hell

Then, as the Guide leads John and Vertue toward the Black Hole, he sings a song beginning with the surprising words "God in His mercy made/The fixed pains of Hell." John raises the problem of the Landlord's cruelty in making such a place as Hell, and the Guide responds that having given his tenants freedom he cannot make

> it impossible for them to go into forbidden places and eat forbidden fruits. Up to a certain point he can doctor them even when they have done so, and break them off the habit. But beyond that point — you can see for yourself. A man can go on eating mountain-apple so long that *nothing* will cure his craving for it: and the very worms it breeds inside him will make him more certain to eat more. You must not try to fix the point after which a return is impossible, but you can see that there will be such a point somewhere.

But surely, John protests, the Landlord can do anything he wants to? "He cannot do what is contradictory," the Guide says. A meaningless sentence will not become meaningful simply because someone chooses to prefix to it the words "the Landlord can." It is meaningless to talk of forcing a man to do freely what a man has freely made impossible for himself.

John is still not satisfied. Since the creatures are already unhappy, why add a black hole to their misery? The Guide says that the creatures' self-will created the blackness, but that God created the hole, as he created Limbo, as an act of mercy. A hole has limits and "A black hole is blackness enclosed, limited." By making the black hole, God

> has put into the world a Worst Thing. But evil of itself would never reach a worst: for evil is fissiparous and could never in a thousand eternities find any way to arrest its own reproduction. If it could, it would no longer be evil: for Form and Limit belong to the good. The walls of the black hole are the tourniquet on the wound through which the lost soul else would bleed to a death she never reached. It is the Landlord's last service to those who will let him do nothing better for them.

Like Augustine before him, Lewis saw Hell as a consequence of creation and the gift of human freedom. Free tenants may choose wrongly and form habits that grow into characteristics that become permanent and unchangeable. Not even the Landlord can coerce a man to do something freely if the man has made himself into someone for whom such a choice is impossible.

Yet even these people are not left without mercy, which God shows them in the same way he showed mercy to the souls in Limbo. "By keeping the damned from doing further evil . . . [God] prevents their further disintegration, their further loss of goodness and being," in the words of one scholar commenting on Dante's *Divine Comedy*. "He cannot increase or fulfill the being of the damned; but by putting restraints on the evil they can do, he can maximize their being by keeping them from additional decay. In this way . . . he shows love . . . for the damned."[19]

The Screwtape Letters

If *The Pilgrim's Regress* helps us understand Hell from God's perspective, *The Screwtape Letters* seeks to portray Hell from the inside. It is a series of letters from Screwtape, undersecretary to the ruler of the infernal domain, to his nephew Wormwood, an apprentice tempter who has been given charge of a man close to becoming a Christian. Screwtape's letters show that the means of the demons' war on human souls will vary with the victim, but the method is always the same. Screwtape exhorts Wormwood not to fall prey to the temptation to try to get his victim to stumble into "spectacular wickedness." There is a better way:

> It does not matter how small the sins are provided that their cumulative effect is to edge the man away from the Light and out into the

19. Eleonore Stump, "Dante's Hell, Aquinas's Moral Theory, and the Love of God," *Canadian Journal of Philosophy* 16.2 (1986): 196-97. Aquinas wrote that "God, for His own part, has mercy on all. Since, however, His mercy is ruled by the order of His wisdom, the result is that it does not reach to certain people who render themselves unworthy of that mercy, as do the demons and the damned who are obstinate in wickedness. And yet we may say that even in them His mercy finds a place, in so far as they are punished less than they deserve . . ." (*Summa Theologica*, Supplement q. 99, art. 2, reply obj. 1, English Dominican tr., vol. 19, p. 206).

Nothing. Murder is no better than cards if cards can do the trick. Indeed the safest road to Hell is the gradual one — the gentle slope, soft underfoot, without sudden turnings, without milestones, without signposts.

A victim so deceived is, "however slowly, heading away from the sun on a line which will carry him into the cold and dark of utmost space."

Although this process may begin with a step that seems both innocent and appealing to the one tempted, the nature of human character is such that even small choices for evil both place one on a path, at first an easy path sloping imperceptibly downward, and are hard (and become harder) to retract or undo. If they are not retracted and another path chosen, the path will someday become a downward spiral so severe that the small choices of sin become the final rejection of God himself.

Philosopher John Finnis noted that it is easy to imagine "the constitution by free choices of a character that would be described simply as repudiating all friendship with God," which condition some have called Hell. "No-one who has thought seriously about ethics, and about his own character, will be inclined to shrug off the possibility that that is the situation he is heading for because he has already, implicitly, chosen it, or might tomorrow do so."[20]

As a portrait of the strategy that seeks to cause someone to go through exactly this process of being edged far enough from God so as to be entombed in one's own ego, *The Screwtape Letters* shows that Hellish character develops from the choice of self against others and against God, which is always plausible and seductive. As Lewis wrote in *The Four Loves,* to love anything means that your heart may well be broken. To protect it,

> you must give your heart to no one, not even to an animal. Wrap it carefully round with hobbies and little luxuries; avoid all entanglements; lock it up safe in the casket or coffin of your selfishness. But in that casket — safe, dark, motionless, airless — it will change. It will not be broken; it will become unbreakable, impenetrable, irredeemable. The alternative to tragedy, or at least to the risk of tragedy,

20. John Finnis, *Fundamentals of Ethics* (Georgetown University Press, 1983), p. 183.

is damnation. The only place outside Heaven where you can be perfectly safe from all the dangers and perturbations of love is Hell.[21]

Thus Screwtape's message is always the same: create an invulnerable self.

Four other aspects of Hell in *The Screwtape Letters* should be noted. First, Hell is deeply competitive. Screwtape says "the whole philosophy of Hell [is]. . . . My good is my good and your good is yours. What one gains another loses." Second, it is a place of voracious appetites. Hell needs food — at the most basic level, the food of information, which is the reason for Wormwood's constant progress reports, but at the deepest Hellish appetite, the spiritual hunger to possess others in either the human or the demonic realm. In Hell one wants "to dominate, almost to digest, one's fellow; to make his whole intellectual and emotional life merely an extension of one's own — to hate one's hatreds and resent one's grievances and indulge one's egotism through him as well as through oneself."

Third, Hell is a place without love. In Hell one may have alliances but never friends. "You will soon find," Screwtape tells the bumbling Wormwood, "that the justice of Hell is realistic, and concerned only with results. Bring us back food, or be food yourself." Finally, Hell is a place of lies because it is a place that hates reality. In his original preface Lewis warned that "the devil is a liar. Not everything that Screwtape says should be assumed to be true even from his own angle."[22] In the simple phrase of Charles Williams that Lewis cited in *A Preface to "Paradise Lost,"* "Hell is inaccurate."[23] Hell is the place where the prayer of Milton's Satan, "nonsense, be thou my sense," is answered.

The Great Divorce

In *The Great Divorce* we see Hell from the human point of view. It is Lewis's most adventuresome attempt to describe what Heaven and

---

21. *The Four Loves* (Geoffrey Bles, 1960), pp. 138-39.
22. *The Screwtape Letters & Screwtape Proposes a Toast,* p. 9.
23. *A Preface to "Paradise Lost"* (Oxford University Press, 1960), p. 97.

Hell might be like, which even A. N. Wilson called "something approaching a masterpiece."[24] The book illustrates two principles: that God, though he longs to change us, will not coerce us since he has given us freedom; and that everyone has something in himself that could grow into Hell unless he willfully sacrifices it to gain Heaven.

The Great Divorce illustrates these two principles in a beguilingly simple story. People come by bus from a grey city to the gate of Heaven. After they leave the bus, they find themselves almost fully transparent. In fact, they are ghosts who are so frail that they cannot pick up a leaf and the grass does not bend when they walk on it. The people coming to meet them are bright and solid, ageless, and full of grandeur.

Every ghost is asked to give up a Hellish part of his or her character. If they consent, they receive a painful purgation and then deliverance. But if they refuse, they remain ghosts and flee Heaven (by their own choice) to return to the grey town of near-nothingness. The narrator, Lewis, observes several of these encounters and meets George MacDonald, who serves as his guide and interpreter.

Early in the story an episcopal ghost who has turned intellectual inquiry into an end in itself meets a bright person, a former schoolmate. The ghost, always genial, insists that his opinions were formed not only honestly but bravely. When the Resurrection of Jesus "ceased to commend itself" to his intellect, he openly rejected it in a tremendous act of risk and courage. But the bright person has a different interpretation: the bishop's radicalism could hardly be called risky or courageous since it led to fame, wealth, and his elevation to the episcopate. Had this not all begun in college when both of them wrote "the kind of essays that got good marks and saying the kind of things that won applause?"

But the episcopal ghost maintains that his views were always sincerely and honestly held, and as they talk it becomes plain that this self-image, of a bold and fearless yet humble seeker after truth, is what most matters to him. Even when he is offered the opportunity to see the face of God, he refuses because (he thinks) there is no such thing as a final answer. "The free wind of inquiry must always continue to blow through the mind, must it not?"

24. A. N. Wilson, *C. S. Lewis: A Biography* (W. W. Norton, 1990), p. 202.

Even a theological rebuttal, of the sort he seems to be asking for, does not move him. The bright person says that the thirst for truth implies a truthful destination, but the ghost clings to his idol: "Will you leave me the free play of Mind . . . ? I must insist on that, you know." Eventually he returns to the grey town to continue his inquiries about the nature of God and of Truth in a Theological Society there — inquiries about the reality he has refused a chance to see.

Refusing Consent to Love God

The saddest stories in *The Great Divorce* involve distorted human relationships. In one meeting the narrator witnesses, a woman encounters her brother, who asks her to let go of the worship of the memory of her dead son. For ten years she has kept his room exactly as he left it, celebrated his birthday, and refused to move to another home although his father and sister desperately wanted to go. Her brother issues a simple invitation: let go of your obsessive devotion to your son and consent to love God. No, she says, maternal love is "the highest and holiest feeling in human nature"; if she and her son lived together forever they would still be happy.

But this is a false god, the brother pleads, and asks her to look honestly at what it has done. She has neglected her husband and daughter and never thought of her own mother. Her maternal love was "uncontrolled and fierce and monomaniac." He tries to convince her by describing another family in Hell where natural affection became perverted and created nothing but misery. But they were different, the mother insists. Her son will make *her* content. She has a right to him, she says, and demands that he be returned to her (which means removed from Heaven).

> Give me my boy. Do you hear? I don't care about all your rules and regulations. I don't believe in a God who keeps mother and son apart. I believe in a God of love. No one has a right to come between me and my son. Not even God. Tell Him that to His face. I want my boy, and I mean to have him. He is mine, do you understand? Mine, mine, mine, for ever and ever.

Even though her son now enjoys the presence of God in Heaven, she demands to take him back with her to Hell. If she cannot have him, she will continue to worship in the shrine of his empty room in (though she does not see this) Hell.

Though most of the ghosts had grown too Hellish to choose Heaven, one does. As Lewis is talking with MacDonald, he sees a ghost speaking with someone so bright he can hardly bear to look at him. On the ghost's shoulder is a lizard whispering to him. The lizard is a creature of lust who provides "really nice dreams — all sweet and fresh and almost innocent." The radiant being, an angel, requests permission to quiet the lizard. The man readily agrees. "Then I will kill him," the angel says, taking a step forward.

The ghost is frightened and changes his mind, but again and again the angel asks, "May I kill it?" The lizard panics and chatters away about how unnatural life would be without him. Finally the ghost bellows, "Get it over. Do what you like." When the angel grabs the lizard, the ghost screams, but then becomes a solid, bright man whose face flows with tears, while the broken lizard is transformed into a great stallion. Together they ride off toward the blue mountains of deep Heaven, "into the rosebrightness of that everlasting morning."

This ghost sacrifices his idol and enters Heaven, whereas the others cling to the love of something worldly that has grown up into Hell. In the end, a choice has to be made; finally there really will be a divorce. MacDonald summarizes the book's theme:

> There are only two kinds of people in the end: those who say to God, "Thy will be done," and those to whom God says, in the end, "Thy will be done." All that are in Hell, choose it. Without that self-choice there could be no Hell. No soul that seriously and constantly desires joy will ever miss it. Those who seek find. To those who knock it is opened.

Lewis's View of Hell

Together, *The Pilgrim's Regress, The Screwtape Letters,* and *The Great Divorce* illustrate Lewis's view of Hell and human destiny and his attempt to remythologize Hell for people who could not or would not accept it. Several aspects of this project may be noted in summary.

First and most fundamentally, Hell is the result of humanity's final refusal of God rather than God's final rejection of humanity. The creature, not his Creator, bears responsibility. God has done all he can, even to the Incarnation and the sacrificial death of his own Son, to convince free creatures to choose him.

Second, Hell is much more the absence of meaning than the suffering of divine punishment, and thus better conceived as a state than a place. As MacDonald tells Lewis in *The Great Divorce:* "Hell is a state of mind. . . . And every state of mind, left to itself, every shutting up of the creature within the dungeon of its own mind — is, in the end, Hell." As Aslan says about the dwarfs in *The Last Battle:* "They have chosen cunning instead of belief. Their prison is only in their own minds, yet they are in that prison, and so afraid of being taken in that they cannot be taken out."

"All I have ever said is that the N.T. plainly implies the possibility of some being finally left in 'the outer darkness'," Lewis wrote his childhood friend Arthur Greeves in 1946.

> Whether this means (horror of horror) being left to a purely *mental* existence, left with nothing at all but one's own envy, prurience, resentment, loneliness & self conceit, or whether there is still some sort of environment, something you cd. call a world or reality, I wd. never pretend to know.

But even if Hell is "purely mental," he continued, "when there is nothing for you but your own mind (no body to sleep, no books or landscape, no sounds, no drugs) it will be as actual as — as — well, as a coffin is actual to a man buried alive."[25]

Third, even to the damned God shows mercy. If they have turned against God, God has not turned against them. He has set limits on the harm they can do themselves. Even Hell, he wrote in *The Great Divorce,* is "is the Landlord's last service to those who will let him do nothing better for them."

Fourth, when men and women reject God, they reject reality. In

---

25. *They Stand Together,* p. 508.

an essay analyzing the meaning of Heaven and Hell, the writer (and Lewis's friend) Dorothy Sayers made this perceptive comment, which may be taken as a summary of Lewis's view:

> If we refuse assent to reality, if we rebel against the nature of things and choose to think that what we at the moment want is the centre of the universe to which everything else ought to accommodate itself, the first effect on us will be that the whole universe will seem to be filled with an implacable and inexplicable hostility. We shall begin to feel that everything has a down on us, and that, being so badly treated, we have a just grievance against things in general. That is the knowledge of good and evil and the fall into illusion.[26]

Lewis showed this process at work most frighteningly in the agnostic bishop and the possessive mother in *The Great Divorce* and the dwarfs in *The Last Battle*. Heaven is (literally) right in front of them all, but absorbed in themselves they cannot see it.

Fifth, while pessimistic about fallen human nature, Lewis was hopeful about our ability (through grace) to change. All may be saved if they choose, and Lewis suggested in *The Great Divorce* that the choices we make in this life reach final fruition only in the next world. Sadly, however, although all from the grey town can make the journey to Heaven, "most of the silly creatures don't." Of the few that do, most return. Yet it takes only the smallest choice for good and against evil to turn the soul to God. "If there's one wee spark in all those ashes," says MacDonald, "we'll blow it till the whole pile is red and clear."

Sixth, Lewis believed in Purgatory and, though he mentioned it less often, Limbo. Belief in Purgatory appears all through his personal correspondence. In *Letters to Malcolm* he very strongly rejected the idea that it is some kind of "temporary Hell." Our souls will demand a cleansing and purgation before God, even if it hurts. He offered his friend Malcolm an image from the dentist's chair. "I hope that when the tooth of life is drawn and I am 'coming round,' a voice will say 'rinse your mouth out with this.' This will be Purgatory. The rinsing may take longer than I can now imagine. The taste of this may be

---

26. Dorothy Sayers, *Introductory Papers on Dante* (Methuen, 1954), p. 62.

more fiery and astringent than my present sensibility could endure. But . . . it will [not] be disgusting and unhallowed."[27]

Seventh, Lewis rejected the "abominable fancy," the idea that the sight of a person in Hell might enhance the joy of the saved. This idea was later transformed, through changing cultural attitudes toward the sufferings of others, into a major objection against the doctrine of Hell. Would not the loss of a person one cared for ruin the joy of the saved? This ruination may be the desire of the damned, but Mac-Donald tells Lewis that this is a "demand that they [the damned] should be allowed to blackmail the universe," that until "they consent to be happy (on their own terms) no one else shall taste joy." Those in Hell insist "that theirs should be the final power, that Hell should be able to veto Heaven." This is obviously not allowable.

Eighth, Lewis is not a universalist. No one who has considered all of his works and his various attempts to depict damnation could say otherwise. In case there is any doubt, however, there is a previously unpublished letter for corroboration. The Rev. Alan Fairhurst, knowing of Lewis's respect for MacDonald, asked him why he did not agree with MacDonald's universalism. "I parted company from MacDonald on that point because a higher authority — the Dominical utterances themselves — seemed to me irreconcilable with universalism," Lewis replied in 1959.

> The finality of the *Either-Or,* the Sheep and Goats, the Wise and Foolish Virgins — is so emphatic and reiterated in our Lord's teaching that, in my opinion, it simply cannot be evaded. If we do not know that he said that, then we do not know what he said about anything. And this is my *sole* reason. . . . Need I add that I shd. v. much prefer to follow G.M. on this point if I could?[28]

Finally, because "The whole difficulty of understanding Hell is that the thing to be understood is *so nearly Nothing*," as George Mac-

---

27. *Letters to Malcolm: Chiefly on Prayer* (Harcourt Brace Jovanovich/Harvest Books, 1964), pp. 108-9. For an understanding of Lewis's view of Purgatory, see Gilbert Meilaender's *The Taste for the Other* (Eerdmans, 1978), pp. 110-17. Lewis gave a correspondent a humorous picture in *Letters to an American Lady* (Eerdmans, 1971), pp. 105, 107.

28. Personal letter, September 6, 1959.

Donald says in *The Great Divorce,* different and apparently contradictory images must be used to depict it. In *The Problem of Pain,* Lewis
argued both that "destruction" is an image for damnation and "that
the lost soul is eternally fixed in its diabolical attitude we cannot
doubt."[29] In Hell the sinner receives her own punishment by being
who she is, not nothing but nearly nothing, and thus Hell is not
destruction but it is like destruction. Perhaps the closest we can get
to an image of Hell is the ghost town in *The Great Divorce.*

Lewis's Chief Strengths

What are the chief strengths of Lewis's understanding of Hell? First,
it is imaginative and original, combining scriptural insight with creative images. He helps us conceive the inconceivable. But most important, his idea of Hell as ultimate and self-willed dehumanization
enables us to connect the real possibility of damnation with our own
lives. He emphasized what we often forget, that choices for Heaven
or Hell are made constantly, in the smallest and apparently most
insignificant decisions, that we make a choice for Hell whenever we
seek satisfaction in ourselves and refuse self-surrender to God.

Lewis's books provide a vocabulary in which the symbol of damnation becomes ominous enough to carry the gravity of the situation
of personal decision for or against God. Through his images of Hell
we really see that what happens to Weston in *Perelandra* (and to the
dwarfs in *The Last Battle*) may happen to us:

> The forces which had begun, perhaps years ago, to eat away his
> humanity had now completed their work. The intoxicated will which
> had been slowly poisoning the intelligence and the affections had
> now at last poisoned itself and the whole psychic organism had fallen
> to pieces. Only a ghost was left — an everlasting unrest, a crumbling,
> a ruin, an odour of decay.[30]

29. *The Problem of Pain,* pp. 112, 115.
30. *Perelandra* (Macmillan, 1944), p. 130.

Appendices

A Reader's Guide to Books about
C. S. Lewis, and Other Resources

DIANA PAVLAC GLYER

C. S. LEWIS WROTE nearly forty books in his lifetime, and his posthumously collected essays, papers, and letters fill volumes more. Not to be outdone, fans and scholars alike have written more than a hundred books about him. And there are hundreds of others that include significant discussion of him, plus individual articles and essays that describe him and analyze his achievements.

This article focuses solely on book-length works that have been written about C. S. Lewis. It begins with an essay that discusses significant titles, grouping them by topic, and it ends with an alphabetical list of books, giving a brief description of each one.

Biographies

Lewis was born in 1898 just outside Belfast, Ireland; he lived most of his life in Oxford, England; he died on November 22, 1963, the same day President John F. Kennedy was assassinated.

Although most Lewis scholars say that the definitive biography of C. S. Lewis has yet to be written, there is widespread agreement that the best so far is *Jack: C. S. Lewis and His Times*. The author, George Sayer, studied under Lewis at Oxford, and the two men became lifelong friends. This biography is warm and personal, honest and balanced. It does a particularly good job of connecting the events of his life and the books he has written.

In contrast, one of the most controversial biographies of Lewis is *C. S. Lewis: A Biography.* A. N. Wilson's book, while certainly lively, is rife with careless errors and questionable interpretations. Several scholars have published critiques and corrections; see, for example, Kathryn Lindskoog's *Light in the Shadowlands,* and the preface to the second edition of Sayer's *Jack.*

I have learned the most about Lewis through the reflections of those who knew him well. G. B. Tennyson has collected remembrances by Owen Barfield, one of Lewis's closest friends, in *Owen Barfield on C. S. Lewis.* Walter Hooper and Roger Lancelyn Green have written *C. S. Lewis: A Biography,* an early work first published in 1974 and recently revised. It is largely descriptive rather than analytical, and that is its key strength — Hooper and Green simply tell us about the Lewis they knew. An autobiography entitled *Lenten Lands,* written by Lewis's stepson Douglas Gresham, is another particularly good first-hand account. Part of the appeal of this book is its insight into British culture, specifically the culture of Oxford in the 1950s, seen through the eyes of an American boy.

In addition, a number of books collect short biographical essays and remembrances. My favorite by far is James Como's *C. S. Lewis at the Breakfast Table,* in which Leo Baker, Dom Bede Griffiths, A. C. Harwood, Austin Farrer, and others offer personal reflections on Lewis's life and character. As the title suggests, reading this book is like sitting down with a friend and asking, "What do you remember about Lewis? What was he like?" I recommend it more often than any other book about Lewis because I think it gives the most well-rounded perspective of him. Two similar collections are Stephen Schofield's *In Search of C. S. Lewis* and Jocelyn Gibb's *Light on C. S. Lewis.*

I also recommend Humphrey Carpenter's *The Inklings.* It presents Lewis in the context of his closest friends at Oxford, a group of writers who called themselves the Inklings. The group included J. R. R. Tolkien, Charles Williams, Owen Barfield, and Warren Lewis. They met every week for many years, reading works-in-progress and responding to one another with lively conversation, sincere encouragement, and bracing criticism.

Perhaps the most significant source of information and insight into Lewis's life is the diary kept by his older brother, Warren Hamilton Lewis. Excerpts from this remarkable diary have been edited by

Clyde S. Kilby and Marjorie Lamp Mead and published under the title *Brothers and Friends*.

The Shadowlands

The movie *Shadowlands* has created a great deal of interest in Lewis and his wife, Joy Davidman. It is an extraordinary love story, their happy marriage cut short by the devastation of cancer. While the script takes liberties with the facts of Lewis's life, it is a fascinating, creative work. Wayne Martindale's essay in *Lightbearer in the Shadowlands* assesses the accuracy and impact of the movie *Shadowlands* and is sure to become the definitive treatment of this much-debated issue.

Lyle Dorsett's *Joy and C. S. Lewis* is a complete biography of Joy Davidman, a Jewish American who became an atheist, then a committed communist, then a devoted follower of Christ. Brian Sibley's *Through the Shadowlands* is also good. It takes a more narrative approach, and focuses on Davidman's marriage to Lewis rather than illuminating her entire life and accomplishments, as Dorsett does.

While I quibble with the facts of the film, I appreciate the way it handles thought-provoking issues like the problem of pain and the nature of love. Peter Kreeft has compiled an anthology called *The Shadow-lands of C. S. Lewis: The Man behind the Movie.* It covers topics like Heaven and grief and marriage in Lewis's own words. In some ways, it is a good antidote to the inaccuracies of the film.

Of course, the best antidote of all is to read Lewis's own account of the loss of his wife. He kept a journal following her death, and published it (pseudonymously) under the title *A Grief Observed.* And there is much to be learned from Lewis's book *The Four Loves,* written during the years Jack and Joy were married, and published the year that Joy died.

Lewis's Fiction

Lewis began writing fiction as a child. He created a fantasy world called Animal-land, filling composition books with stories of talking animals and illustrating them with maps and watercolor pictures. Lewis's best-known and best-selling books continue to be his works of fiction, especially *Out of the Silent Planet, Perelandra, The Screwtape Letters,* the Chronicles of Narnia, *The Great Divorce, The Pilgrim's Regress,* and *Till We Have Faces.* A number of good books explain Lewis's accomplishments as a fiction writer.

Thomas Howard's *The Achievement of C. S. Lewis: A Reading of His Fiction* is full of spiritual as well as literary insight. Howard is a particularly good writer — clear, graceful, and artistic. Colin Manlove, a British scholar, has written extensively on imaginative literature, and *C. S. Lewis: His Literary Achievement* is a substantial and intelligent analysis of Lewis as an imaginative writer.

Evan K. Gibson's *C. S. Lewis: Spinner of Tales,* though somewhat less perceptive, is still an accurate, readable introduction to Lewis's work. Another excellent source is Chad Walsh's *The Literary Legacy of C. S. Lewis,* largely an assessment of strengths and weaknesses in Lewis's creative work, as well as a prediction (published twenty years ago!) that Lewis is destined to be remembered primarily as a writer of fantasy fiction.

The books I have just listed survey all of Lewis's fiction in a single volume. There are also a number of books that address individual works in more depth.

Till We Have Faces. In *Reason and Imagination in C. S. Lewis,* Peter Schakel analyzes Lewis's last fictional work brilliantly, chapter by chapter, then surveys Lewis's earlier fiction to demonstrate that the characters, themes, and images of *Till We Have Faces* are all consistent with Lewis's prior work.

The Space Trilogy. David Downing's *Planets in Peril* describes the biographical and theological backgrounds of the Space Trilogy, and offers a careful critical assessment. Martha Sammons's *A Guide through C. S. Lewis' Space Trilogy* emphasizes the sources Lewis uses for his imagery in these three novels.

The Pilgrim's Regress. Readers of Lewis's allegorical autobiography *The Pilgrim's Regress* will benefit from Kathryn Lindskoog's *Finding the Landlord.* She wrote it to renew appreciation for *The Pilgrim's Regress,* but her most important accomplishment is the clear guidance she offers through one of Lewis's toughest texts. As Lewis admitted to one reader, "I don't wonder that you got fogged in *Pilgrim's Regress.* It was my first religious book and I didn't then know how to make things easy. I was not even trying to."

The Chronicles of Narnia. Those interested in knowing more about the origin and meaning of Narnia have a number of good books to choose from, including Paul Ford's *Companion to Narnia,* Colin Manlove's *The Chronicles of Narnia: The Patterning of a Fantastic World,* Kathryn Lindskoog's *Journey to Narnia,* and Peter Schakel's *Reading with the Heart: The Way into Narnia.* Walter Hooper's *Past Watchful Dragons* offers background information on how Lewis came to create Narnia. He includes some fragments of early drafts, interesting to anyone who is curious to know more about how Lewis worked as a writer.

The Lay Theologian

Lewis was thirty-one when he first "admitted God was God, and knelt and prayed," describing himself as "the most dejected and reluctant convert in all England." All in all, it was a humble beginning for a man who became one of the most important Christian apologists of the century, writing such solid and persuasive books as *Mere Christianity, The Problem of Pain,* and *Miracles.*

Lewis's beliefs are carefully described by Richard Purtill in *C. S. Lewis' Case for the Christian Faith.* He gives an evenhanded overview of Lewis's thought on the nature of God, the divinity of Christ, the challenge of faith, the meaning of death, and the reality of miracles in under 150 pages. Other treatments of Lewis as a lay theologian include Richard Cunningham's *C. S. Lewis: Defender of the Faith,* Clyde S. Kilby's *The Christian World of C. S. Lewis,* Kathryn Lindskoog's *C. S. Lewis: Mere Christian,* Chad Walsh's *C. S. Lewis: Apostle to the Skeptics,* and John Randolph Willis's *Pleasures Forevermore: The Theology of C. S. Lewis.*

Readers who are interested in a sustained and substantial treatment of Lewis's contribution to lay theology will appreciate Gilbert Meilander's *The Taste for the Other: The Social and Ethical Thought of C. S. Lewis.* Meilander's focus is Lewis's vision of Christian community, but he sheds significant light on the much broader question of Lewis's whole manner of approaching theological issues.

Lewis's own spiritual life and practice are the subject of two new books. In *C. S. Lewis: Life at the Center,* Perry Bramlett writes a general introduction in a comfortable, devotional style. Terry Glaspey's *Not a Tame Lion: The Spiritual Legacy of C. S. Lewis,* made up of fifty-seven very, very short and remarkably lucid chapters, serves as an excellent introduction to Lewis as a Christian.

The Literary Critic

Lewis was featured on the cover of *Time* magazine and hailed as a world renowned fiction writer and lay theologian. All this acclaim makes it hard to remember that Lewis earned his living as a college teacher, giving tutorials, delivering lectures, and writing academic articles and books. Most of his academic writing focused on the literature of the medieval and Renaissance periods, including *English Literature in the Sixteenth Century, Preface to "Paradise Lost," The Allegory of Love,* and *The Discarded Image.*

One book that addresses this often neglected aspect of Lewis is *Critical Essays on C. S. Lewis* edited by George Watson, who observed that "Reviewers found Lewis' critical writings unfashionable, quirky and uncompromising. . . ." These forty-six reviews are interesting for their insight into Lewis as a literary scholar, and for the glimpse they give us into how Lewis's books were received when they were first published.

In addition to writing books about specific works of literature, Lewis also contributed significant insight into the philosophical debate about how literary texts should be read, particularly in his book *An Experiment in Criticism.* Lewis's importance as a literary critic is the subject of Bruce Edwards's *A Rhetoric of Reading: C. S. Lewis' Defense of Western Literacy.* Doris Myers covers similar territory in *C. S. Lewis in Context.* Both are well written and thought-provoking.

There are also a number of essay collections that deal with this important subject. Bruce Edwards has edited *The Taste of the Pineapple: Essays on C. S. Lewis as Reader, Critic, and Imaginative Writer.* Peter Schakel and Charles A. Huttar have edited *Word and Story in C. S. Lewis,* essays that consider Lewis as a scholar of language and literature.

If this aspect of Lewis is unfamiliar to you, a brand new book offers an excellent introduction. Thomas Martin has edited a collection of interesting and accessible essays entitled *Reading Literature with C. S. Lewis.*

General Reference Books

A number of reference books offer a comprehensive look at Lewis. Walter Hooper's *C. S. Lewis: Companion and Guide* is nearly a thousand pages long and packed with concrete, specific, reliable information. This book sits at my right hand for most of the Lewis scholarship I do. Hooper discusses each of Lewis's books, giving its history, summarizing its content, and excerpting its reviewers. The book opens with an informative biography, and ends with three brief dictionaries: "Key Ideas," "Who's Who," and "What's What."

C. S. Lewis: A Reader's Encyclopedia, edited by Jeffrey Schultz, reflects the insights of an impressive team of scholars. The encyclopedia is a valuable complement to Hooper's *Companion and Guide:* while Hooper *describes* Lewis's books, Schultz and his group *analyze* them. And the encyclopedia covers Lewis's essays, sermons, and other short pieces as well as his book-length texts.

Another important reference book, one I constantly recommend for preachers and teachers, is *The Quotable Lewis* by Wayne Martindale and Jerry Root, a compilation of 1,565 quotations taken from his published works. It gives a comprehensive overview of Lewis's thought and is a genuinely useful way to investigate his views. It is also an easy way to find the right Lewis quotation for a sermon, a paper, a newsletter, or a talk.

Three other books are absolutely indispensable for the Lewis scholar. Janine Goffar's *C. S. Lewis Index,* a detailed index to Lewis's fifteen theological books, is a remarkable, essential reference book. Joe Christopher and Joan Ostling's *C. S. Lewis: An Annotated Checklist of Writings about Him and His Works* (covering his works until 1972) and Susan Lowenberg's *C. S. Lewis: A Reference Guide, 1972-1988* are excellent sources of comment on Lewis.

Conclusion

Given such a wealth of resources, is there anything left to say about C. S. Lewis? One area of renewed interest is Lewis as a poet. Watch for several new studies that examine the volumes of poetry, narrative and lyric, that Lewis produced in his lifetime. Future scholars might also help us to assess Lewis's work as an autobiographer, considering *Surprised by Joy,* for example, as well as his collected letters and diaries.

Of all the books I have mentioned in this article, there are three that I most highly recommend: George Sayer's *Jack* is the best biography; Walter Hooper's *C. S. Lewis: Companion and Guide* is the best reference book; and James Como's *C. S. Lewis at the Breakfast Table* gives the most well-rounded and interesting portrait. For insight into Lewis's thought, I recommend anything by Chad Walsh, Peter Schakel, Thomas Howard, or Peter Kreeft. And *C. S. Lewis: A Reader's Encyclopedia* will prove a thoughtful, faithful, and helpful guide.

All in all, an impressive number of resources for the study of Lewis are available. Many of them not only offer insight into Lewis, but also enrich our understanding of the things that he cared about. But there is simply nothing to compare with reading Lewis firsthand.

If you are reading Lewis for the very first time, I recommend Lyle Dorsett's anthology, *The Essential C. S. Lewis.* Dorsett included *The Lion, the Witch and the Wardrobe, Perelandra, The Abolition of Man,* and some of Lewis's best essays, poems, letters, and more. The book includes a brief biographical introduction and helpful notes throughout.

Several other Lewis works make particularly good starting places. *The Four Loves* and *Letters to Malcolm: Chiefly on Prayer,* books he wrote late in life, are especially readable and spiritually nourishing. *Reflections on the Psalms* is another good one, a book full of insight into Scripture and Lewis's perspective on the Word of God. I am very fond of Lewis's collected letters, especially *The Letters of C. S. Lewis* and the shorter *Letters to an American Lady.* So much has been written about Lewis; in these letters we come as close as we can to hearing him speak in his most authentic voice.

Other Resources

Journals that deal with Lewis include *The Lamp-post* of the Southern California C. S. Lewis Society (1212 W. 162nd Street, Gardena, CA 90247), *CSL: The Bulletin of the New York C. S. Lewis Society* (84-23 77th Avenue, Glendale, NY 11385), and *The Canadian C. S. Lewis Journal* (Western Pentecostal Bible College, P.O. Box 1700, Abbotsford, B.C. V2S 7E7 Canada). Two journals — *Seven,* published by Wheaton College's Wade Center (Wheaton, IL 60187), and *Mythlore,* published by the Mythopoeic Society (P.O. Box 6707, Altadena, CA 91001) — address Lewis and others, including fellow Inklings J. R. R. Tolkien and Charles Williams.

The Marion E. Wade Center at Wheaton College is an unparalleled resource for Lewis studies. In addition to books by and about Lewis, they also have most of his letters, many books from his own library, a number of his manuscripts, and assorted personal belongings, including a table, a tea mug, and a large wooden wardrobe. The Bodleian Library at Oxford University in England has many of his books, letters, and manuscripts as well.

There are quite a number of websites dedicated to C. S. Lewis. A newsgroup (alt.books.cs_lewis) and listerve (Merelewis) link more than a thousand Lewis fans internationally. A links page (www.tesm.edu/Inklings) has extensive links not only to the Inklings but also to G. K. Chesterton, Dorothy Sayers, and others, including their contemporary disciples. It also includes links to important articles on specific subjects in apologetics. Also good are the C. S. Lewis and the Inklings Page maintained by Bruce Edwards, the Mythopoeic Society Page maintained by Eleanor Farrell, and the Lewis Centenary Group (Ulster) maintained by James O'Fee. My web page includes an expanded version of this bibliographic article, and it will be updated as new books continue to be published.

The best way to access these and other Lewis sources on the internet is *Into the Wardrobe,* a web page maintained by John Visser. The address is www.cache.net/~john/cslewis/index.html.

Selected Bibliography

Adey, Lionel, *C. S. Lewis: Writer, Dreamer, and Mentor* (Eerdmans, 1998). An illuminating, scholarly treatment of Lewis's writing, drawing out his sources and including much on his relationship with Owen Barfield.

Aeschliman, Michael, *The Restitution of Man: C. S. Lewis and the Case against Scientism* (Eerdmans, 1998; first published in 1983). Elaborates the debate between the metaphysical tradition (Plato, Augustine,

Aquinas, and Lewis) and materialistic scientism (Bacon, Huxley, Nietzsche, and Skinner), explaining what each idea does to man.

Barfield, Owen, *Owen Barfield on C. S. Lewis,* edited by G. B. Tennyson (Wesleyan University Press, 1989). Includes addresses, essays, and interviews on Lewis by his close friend, as well as a portrait of Lewis as he appears in one of Barfield's novels.

Beversluis, John, *C. S. Lewis and the Search for Rational Religion* (Eerdmans, 1985). A poorly written, poorly argued attack on Lewis's use of logic and argumentation. To be avoided.

Bramlett, Perry, *C. S. Lewis: Life at the Center* (Peak Road, 1996). A biographical essay that describes Lewis's spiritual practice.

Burson, Scott and Jerry Walls, *C. S. Lewis and Francis Schaeffer* (InterVarsity Press, 1998). A comparison of Lewis's apologetic work with the Calvinist Francis Schaeffer's, drawing lessons from their examples for apologetics today.

Carnell, Corbin Scott, *Bright Shadow of Reality: C. S. Lewis and the Feeling Intellect* (Eerdmans, 1974). One of the most insightful and best-written studies of Lewis, this classic explores Lewis's concept of *sehnsucht* or "longing."

Carpenter, Humphrey, *The Inklings: C. S. Lewis, J. R. R. Tolkien, Charles Williams and Their Friends* (Houghton Mifflin, 1979). A good collective biography of this writers' group, though Carpenter persistently underestimates the mutual influence of the group.

Christopher, Joe R., *C. S. Lewis* (Twayne, 1987). An excellent, accurate overview of Lewis as autobiographer, literary critic, moral philosopher, apologist, and romancer, with a good annotated bibliography of secondary sources. Recommended.

Christopher, Joe R. and Joan K. Ostling, compilers, *C. S. Lewis: An Annotated Checklist of Writings about Him and His Works* (Kent State University Press, 1974). A detailed annotated bibliography, this is *the* reference for finding and evaluating works about Lewis. Susan Lowenberg's *C. S. Lewis: A Reference Guide, 1972-1988* (Maxwell Macmillan International, 1993) picks up where Christopher and Ostling leave off.

Como, James T., *Branches to Heaven: The Geniuses of C. S. Lewis* (Spence, 1998). A provocative study of the relationship of Lewis's rhetoric to his inner life. Dr. Como is a professor of rhetoric and has led the New York C. S. Lewis Society since its founding.

————, ed., *C. S. Lewis at the Breakfast Table and Other Reminiscences* (Macmillan, 1979). Twenty-four essays, mostly by people who knew Lewis well, including poet John Wain, his friend George Sayer, theologian Austin Farrer, and his doctor R. E. Havard. One of my very favorite books about Lewis. Highly recommended.

Coren, Michael, *The Man Who Created Narnia: The Story of C. S. Lewis* (Eerdmans, 1994). A new biography of Lewis for children, attractively packaged with a pleasing layout and good photographs, but marred by many small errors of fact and interpretation.

Cunningham, Richard B., *C. S. Lewis: Defender of the Faith* (Westminster, 1967). Analyzes Lewis as apologist, including discussion of his epistemology, eschatology, theology, and hermeneutics.

Dorsett, Lyle, *Joy and C. S. Lewis* (HarperCollins, 1988 and 1994). A wonderful biography of Joy Davidman Lewis, rich in specific information about this amazing woman. A reprint of *And God Came In* (Macmillan, 1983). Highly recommended.

————, *The Essential C. S. Lewis* (Macmillan, 1988). This anthology is a good starting place for those completely unfamiliar with Lewis. Contains *The Lion, the Witch and the Wardrobe, Perelandra, The Abolition of Man,* and selected letters, essays, and poems.

Downing, David, *Planets in Peril* (University of Massachusetts Press, 1992). An in-depth study of Lewis's space trilogy, well written and insightful. Recommended.

Duriez, Colin, *The C. S. Lewis Handbook: A Comprehensive Guide to His Life, Thought, and Writings* (Baker Book House, 1990). An enjoyable collection of brief articles on the life and work of Lewis, though superseded by Hooper's *C. S. Lewis: Companion and Guide.*

Edwards, Bruce L., Jr., *A Rhetoric of Reading: C. S. Lewis' Defense of Western Literacy* (Brigham Young University, 1986). An in-depth look at Lewis as literary critic.

————, ed., *The Taste of the Pineapple: Essays on C. S. Lewis as Reader, Critic, and Imaginative Writer* (Bowling Green State University Popular Press, 1988). Fourteen essays of outstanding quality on this important aspect of Lewis. Contributors include Kath Filmer, Joe McClatchey, Alzina Stone Dale, Margaret Hannay, and Kathryn Lindskoog.

Ford, Paul, *A Companion to Narnia* (Harper & Row, 1980). An ency-

clopedia of brief articles that describe and clarify all aspects of
Narnia. Specific, insightful, and even entertaining.

Gibb, Jocelyn, ed., *Light on C. S. Lewis* (Geoffrey Bles, 1965). Seven
biographical essays by Lewis's friends, including Barfield, Farrer,
Nevill Coghill, Stella Gibbons (author of *Cold Comfort Farm*),
Chad Walsh, and Walter Hooper.

Gibson, Evan K., *C. S. Lewis: Spinner of Tales: A Guide to His Fiction*
(Eerdmans, 1980). A good starting place for those interested in an
general overview of characters, ideas, and Christian themes in
Lewis's fiction.

Gilbert, Douglas and Clyde Kilby, *C. S. Lewis: Images of His World*
(Eerdmans, 1973). A book of artistic photographs of people and
places important to Lewis.

Glaspey, Terry, *Not a Tame Lion: The Spiritual Legacy of C. S. Lewis*
(Highland Books, 1996). Called "lively, concise, and lucid" for
good reason. An excellent short introduction to Lewis's life and
thought. Recommended.

Glover, Donald F., *C. S. Lewis: The Art of Enchantment* (Ohio University Press, 1981). Glover uses Lewis's own critical method as
described in *An Experiment in Criticism* to discuss Lewis's fiction.

Gormley, Beatrice, *C. S. Lewis: Christian and Storyteller* (Eerdmans,
1998). A good biography written for young people.

Green, Roger Lancelyn and Walter Hooper, *C. S. Lewis: A Biography*
(Harcourt Brace Jovanovich, 1974). This authorized biography features many personal stories by these two important friends of Lewis.
Especially good are Green's accounts of the creation of Narnia and
his insight into the relationship of Joy Davidman and C. S. Lewis.

Gresham, Douglas, *Lenten Lands: My Childhood with Joy Davidman and
C. S. Lewis* (Macmillan, 1988). An appealing autobiography by
Lewis's stepson, Douglas Gresham. Especially useful for those who
are interested in knowing more about Lewis's marriage to Joy
Davidman and a bit more about what happened after her death.

Goffar, Janine, ed., *C. S. Lewis Index: Rumours from the Sculptor's Shop*
(La Sierra University Press, 1995). A terrific detailed index to
fifteen of Lewis's theological works. Highly recommended.

Griffin, William. *Clive Staples Lewis: A Dramatic Life* (Harper & Row,
1986). Griffin takes you year by year through Lewis's life in a
series of dramatic vignettes. Inventive.

Holbrook, David, *Skeleton in the Wardrobe: C. S. Lewis' Fantasies: A Phenomenological Study* (Associated University Presses, 1991). A truly dreadful book that interprets all of Lewis's fiction as indicators of personality disorders and advanced neurosis. To be avoided.

Hooper, Walter, *C. S. Lewis: A Companion and Guide* (HarperSanFrancisco, 1996). What a book! Hooper offers summaries of Lewis's books, and encyclopedic articles about important people, places, and ideas. Packed with facts. Highly recommended.

————, *Past Watchful Dragons: The Narnian Chronicles of C. S. Lewis* (Collier Books, 1979). A good introduction to the Narnia series, containing some early drafts that shed light on Lewis's creative process.

————, *Through Joy and Beyond: A Pictorial Biography of C. S. Lewis* (Macmillan, 1982). Contains many (mostly black and white) photographs of Lewis's homes and friends. This book is the companion to the one-hour documentary film by the same name.

Howard, Thomas, *C. S. Lewis: Man of Letters* (Ignatius, 1994). Beautifully written, spiritually rich discussion of Lewis as a fiction writer. A reprint of *The Achievement of C. S. Lewis* (Harold Shaw, 1980). Highly recommended.

Keefe, Carolyn, ed., *C. S. Lewis: Speaker and Teacher* (Zondervan, 1971). Seven essays that fill an important gap, exploring Lewis as an oral communicator — teacher, lecturer, debater, and radio broadcaster. Contributors include Clyde Kilby, Walter Hooper, and Owen Barfield.

Kilby, Clyde S., *The Christian World of C. S. Lewis* (Eerdmans, 1996; first published in 1964). A light and appreciative discussion of Christian themes in Lewis's works.

Kreeft, Peter, *C. S. Lewis: A Critical Essay* (Eerdmans, 1969). Perhaps the ideal introduction to Lewis for those unfamiliar with his work: it avoids unnecessary summaries, uses lots of direct quotations, accurately describes Lewis's life and work, and is only sixty-eight pages long.

————, *C. S. Lewis for the Third Millennium: Six Essays on The Abolition of Man* (Ignatius, 1994). Kreeft explains and defends Lewis's idea of natural law, and applies it to the challenges of contemporary culture.

————, ed., *The Shadow-lands of C. S. Lewis: The Man behind the Movie*

(Ignatius, 1994). Recommended for those who were intrigued by the *Shadowlands* movie and want to read (in excerpts) what Lewis *really* said about love, grief, faith, and pain.

Lewis, Warren Hamilton, *Brothers and Friends: The Diaries of Major Warren Hamilton Lewis,* edited by Clyde S. Kilby and Marjorie Lamp Mead (Harper & Row, 1982). Lewis enjoyed a close friendship with his brother Warren, and these diaries remain one of the most important sources of information about him. The excerpts are well chosen and helpfully annotated.

Lindskoog, Kathryn, *C. S. Lewis: Mere Christian* (Cornerstone Press, 4th ed. 1997). A series of essays that summarize Lewis's thoughts on such topics as nature, God, and education.

————, *Finding the Landlord: A Guidebook to C. S. Lewis' Pilgrim's Regress* (Cornerstone Press, 1995). A well-written and helpful guide to the allegory in *Pilgrim's Regress*.

————, *Journey into Narnia* (Hope Publishing House, 1997). An updated version of *The Lion of Judah in Never-Never Land* with seven new chapters reflecting on each of the Chronicles. Lewis himself read an early version of this study and praised it highly.

Lindvall, Terry, *Surprised by Laughter* (Thomas Nelson, 1996). Short chapters and copious examples: this functions as a catalogue of funny moments in Lewis's writing.

Macdonald, Michael and Andrew A. Tadie, eds., *G. K. Chesterton and C. S. Lewis: The Riddle of Joy* (Eerdmans, 1989). Includes papers on Lewis by Thomas Howard, Walter Hooper, Peter Kreeft, James Houston, and others.

Martin, Thomas, ed., *Reading Literature with C. S. Lewis* (Baker, forthcoming). A collection of essays by Charles Huttar, Doris T. Myers, David Downing, Joe R. Christopher, and others that describe Lewis's habits as a reader and responder to good books.

Martindale, Wayne and Jerry Root, eds., *The Quotable Lewis* (Tyndale House, 1989). Interesting for browsing, indispensable for research. Martindale and Root provide an alphabetized list of 1,565 quotable Lewis quotes. Highly recommended.

Manlove, Colin, *C. S. Lewis: His Literary Achievement* (St. Martin's Press, 1987). A thorough analysis of Lewis's fiction in terms of its literary technique (rather than its mythic structure or moral values or Christian symbolism).

————, *The Chronicles of Narnia: The Patterning of a Fantastic World* (Twayne Publishers, 1993). In just over a hundred pages, Manlove offers historical context, critical reception, a careful reading, and notes on teaching the seven books, and does so with remarkable accuracy and grace. Impressive.

Meilander, Gilbert, *The Taste for the Other: The Social and Ethical Thought of C. S. Lewis* (Eerdmans, 1998; first published in 1978). Thoughtful discussion of Lewis's view of the Christian's place in society, offering particularly good insight on the nature of love. Scholarly, wise, and often moving.

Milward, Peter, S.J. *A Challenge to C. S. Lewis* (Fairleigh Dickinson University Press, 1995). A thoughtful critique of Lewis.

Menuge, Angus, ed., *Lightbearer in the Shadowlands: The Evangelistic Vision of C. S. Lewis* (Crossway Books, 1997). One of the best new books about Lewis, it contains sixteen essays by Wayne Martindale, Corbin Scott Carnell, Michael Ward, George Musacchio, Christopher Mitchell, Jerry Root, Gene Edward Veith, and others, with a focus on evangelism. Recommended.

Myers, Doris, *C. S. Lewis in Context* (Kent State University Press, 1994). Myers is an able guide through the tough terrain of metaphor, literary criticism, genre studies, myth, and historical studies as she examines Lewis's work in the context of his intellectual contemporaries. Substantial and thought-provoking.

Patrick, James, *The Magdalen Metaphysicals: Idealism and Orthodoxy at Oxford 1901-1945* (Mercer University Press, 1985). A close study C. S. Lewis and his philosophical peers at Oxford in the 1930s and 1940s and their battle against relativism and other philosophical challenges. For those with some background in philosophy.

Peters, Thomas, *Simply C. S. Lewis: A Beginner's Guide to His Life and Works* (Crossway Books, 1997). A new general introduction to Lewis. Peters admits that Lewis can be daunting, and has written this overview to give the beginner "a broad view of the field, as well as some basic helps in understanding certain of Lewis's books."

Purtill, Richard, *C. S. Lewis' Case for the Christian Faith* (Harper & Row, 1981). A clear, comprehensive description of Lewis's Christianity from a philosophical perspective.

————, *The Lord of the Elves and Eldils: Fantasy and Philosophy in C. S.*

Lewis and J. R. R. Tolkien (Eerdmans, 1974). A brief book, helpful in its insights into fantasy as a vehicle for expressing ethical and religious ideas.

Sammons, Martha C., *A Guide through C. S. Lewis' Space Trilogy* (Cornerstone Books, 1980). A useful guide to the biblical, Arthurian, medieval, historical background used by Lewis in the space trilogy.

Sayer, George, *Jack: C. S. Lewis and His Times* (Harper and Row, 1988). Considered by most to be the very best biography of Lewis. Highly recommended.

Schakel, Peter, *Reading with the Heart: The Way into Narnia* (Eerdmans, 1979). Probably the most insightful and thorough of the studies of the Chronicles. Schakel's writing style is a pleasure. Recommended.

————, *Reason and Imagination in C. S. Lewis: A Study in Till We Have Faces* (Eerdmans, 1984). An utterly brilliant study.

————, ed., *The Longing for a Form: Essays on the Fiction of C. S. Lewis* (Kent State University Press, 1977). One of the earliest and best literary studies of Lewis. Fourteen essays by a who's who of Lewis scholars.

Schakel, Peter J. and Charles A. Huttar, eds., *Word and Story in C. S. Lewis* (University of Missouri Press, 1991). One of the best collections of scholarly papers about Lewis, clearly organized and carefully edited, with essays by Meilaender, Glover, Manlove, and others. Recommended.

Schofield, Stephen, ed., *In Search of C. S. Lewis* (Bridge Publishing, 1983). Contains twenty-five essays, interviews, and letters, most reprinted from *The Canadian C. S. Lewis Journal*. An interesting assortment.

Schultz, Jeffrey D., John G. West Jr., and Mike Perry, eds., *C. S. Lewis: A Readers' Encyclopedia* (Zondervan Publishing House, 1998). A new and noteworthy reference book, offering interpretative essays on every book and article published by Lewis, plus entries on important people, places, and concepts. It also contains useful lists of publications and organizations devoted to Lewis studies. The writers include Christopher Mitchell, director of the Wade Collection, and Edwards. Highly recommended.

Sibley, Brian, *C. S. Lewis through the Shadowlands* (Revell, 1985).

Light and interesting, Sibley tells the story of Lewis's marriage to Joy Davidman.

Walker, Andrew and James Patrick, eds., *A Christian for All Christians: Essays in Honour of C. S. Lewis* (Regnery Gateway, 1992). Thirteen fairly short essays on Lewis by the editors, Purtill, Schakel, Dorsett, Christopher, Aidan Mackey, and others.

Walsh, Chad, *C. S. Lewis: Apostle to the Skeptics* (Macmillan, 1949). Walsh was one of the earliest Lewis scholars and remains one of the most insightful and reliable. This is the first full-length study written about Lewis's life and work, focused primarily on his Christian faith.

———, *The Literary Legacy of C. S. Lewis* (Harcourt Brace Jovanovich, 1979). An early assessment of Lewis's literary skill and lasting legacy.

Watson, George, ed., *Critical Essays on C. S. Lewis* (Scolar Press, 1992). Collected reviews of Lewis's academic works including *The Allegory of Love, Preface to "Paradise Lost,"* and *English Literature in the Sixteenth Century, Excluding Drama.*

Willis, John Randolph, S.J., *Pleasures Forevermore: The Theology of C. S. Lewis* (Loyola University Press, 1983). An assessment of Lewis as theologian from a Roman Catholic viewpoint.

Wilson, A. N., *C. S. Lewis: A Biography* (Norton, 1990). Wilson makes serious mistakes in fact and offers dubious interpretations. To be avoided.

A C. S. Lewis Time Line

DAVID MILLS, WITH MICHAEL NEE, JAMES
KURTZ, DAN KLOOSTER, AND SARAH MILLS

THE TIME LINE includes the dates of the major events in C. S. Lewis's life, his books, and selected essays, papers, and sermons. To put his life and work in context, it gives in other columns a selection of facts — selected (from thousands of relevant facts) both to represent the movements and trends of the time of which Lewis would have been aware and to help readers place the events of Lewis's life by including books most readers will have read and events they will recognize. (The column "Science and Technology" is included because that information is the easiest way to convey the changes in daily life from Lewis's birth to his death.)

The dates are taken from the works themselves, biographies of Lewis and others, Walter Hooper's *C. S. Lewis: A Companion and Guide,* general histories, and reference works.

Readers should note that after the first time a name has been mentioned initials are used, so readers finding initials they do not recognize should read up the column till they find the name. Events in Joy Davidman's and Warren Lewis's lives are included in "The Inklings and Others."

David Mills

	C. S. Lewis	The Inklings and Others	World History, Including Letters	English History and Letters	Science and Technology
1874		G. K. Chesterton born			
1886		Charles Williams born			
1891					Zipper invented
1892		J. R. R. Tolkien born			
1893		Dorothy L. Sayers born			
1894				Rudyard Kipling, *The Jungle Book*	
1895		Warren ("Warnie") Lewis born		Rhodes creates Rhodesia; Oscar Wilde, *The Importance of Being Earnest*	X-rays used for first time
1896				Pope Leo XIII declares Anglican ordinations invalid	Helium discovered; wireless patented in England
1897				H. G. Wells, *The Invisible Man*; Bram Stoker, *Dracula*; RK, *Captains Courageous*	
1898	Born (Nov. 29) in Belfast	Owen Barfield born	Sinking of the U.S.S. *Maine* and beginning of Spanish-American War	Henry James, *The Turn of the Screw*; HGW, *The War of the Worlds*; former prime minister Gladstone dies	Curies discover radium

	C. S. Lewis	The Inklings and Others	World History, Including Letters	English History and Letters	Science and Technology
1899			Boxer Rebellion in China	Second Boer War begins, GKC a "pro-Boer"; RK, "The White Man's Burden"	
1900		GKC, *Greybeards at Play* (first book)	Freud, *The Interpretation of Dreams*	Labour Party founded; Joseph Conrad, *Lord Jim*	Brownie box camera introduced
1901			Australian colonies unite, form Commonwealth	Queen Victoria dies; Edward VII crowned	
1902			William James, *The Varieties of Religious Experience*	Beatrix Potter, *The Tale of Peter Rabbit*; A. Conan Doyle, *The Hound of the Baskervilles*; Second Boer War ends; JC, *Heart of Darkness*	
1902-4		CW studies at University College, London			
1903		JRRT wins scholarship to King Edward VII School in Birmingham		Emmeline Pankhurst begins suffragettes; Malcolm Muggeridge, Evelyn Waugh born	Wright brothers fly first airplane; Henry Ford founds motor company
1904		GKC, *The Napoleon of Notting Hill*; CW takes work as clerk in bookshop	Russo-Japanese war begins; Puccini, *Madame Butterfly*	James Barrie, *Peter Pan*; Graham Greene born; Henry James, *The Golden Bowl*	

	C. S. Lewis	The Inklings and Others	World History, Including Letters	English History and Letters	Science and Technology
1905			Workers revolt in Russia; Jules Verne dies; Baroness Orczy, *The Scarlet Pimpernel*	First public cinema showings in London; George Bernard Shaw, *Man and Superman*	Einstein publishes relativity theory; aspirin marketed (as prescription drug)
1906			Paul Cézanne dies; Schweitzer's *Quest for the Historical Jesus*	London, with 4.5 million people, still the largest city in the world (Tokyo had 1.9 million)	Vitamins discovered
1907		GKC, *The Man Who Was Thursday*	Modernism ("the resume of all heresies") condemned by Pope Pius X	Rudyard Kipling wins Nobel Prize in Literature; W. H. Auden born	
1908	Mother dies of cancer	CW begins working as proofreader for Oxford University Press; GKC, *Orthodoxy*	First major oil strike (Iran); General Motors formed	Kenneth Grahame, *The Wind in the Willows*; Boy Scouts founded	First Model T produced
1909			Peary reaches North Pole		Neon lamp, permanent wave invented
1910			Mark Twain, Leo Tolstoy die; 1910 "Edinburgh Conference" (beginning of ecumenical movement); Portugal becomes republic after revolution	King Edward VII dies; George V crowned; post-impressionist exhibition in London	Automatic transmissions invented

	C. S. Lewis	The Inklings and Others	World History, Including Letters	English History and Letters	Science and Technology
1911		GKC, *The Innocence of Father Brown* (first book in series); JRRT begins studies at Oxford	Amundsen reaches South Pole; Chinese republic established; Turkish-Italian war begins	British empire contains nearly one-quarter of the world's land surface and over one-quarter of its population; Shops Act gives worker half-day off in addition to Sundays; HGW, *The New Machiavelli*	Air conditioning invented
1912		CW, *The Silver Chair* (sonnets, first book)	*Titanic* sinks	Scott dies reaching South Pole; House of Commons votes against vote for women	Cellophane invented
1913	Wins scholarship to Malvern College		"Forbidden Palace" in Beijing used for evangelistic meetings; Unamuno, *The Tragic Sense of Life*	D. H. Lawrence, *Sons and Lovers*; *Foundations* published by several Oxford dons; GBS, *Pygmalion*	X-ray tube invented
1914		GKC, *The Flying Inn*	WWI begins; Panama Canal opened	E. R. Burroughs, *Tarzan of the Apes*; England declares war on Germany, Austria-Hungary, Turkey	

	C. S. Lewis	The Inklings and Others	World History, Including Letters	English History and Letters	Science and Technology
1914-17	Tutored by William Kirkpatrick ("the Great Knock"); starts writing to Arthur Greeves				
1915		JRRT takes first-class degree in English, joins army	*The Tramp* (starring Charlie Chaplin), *Birth of a Nation* (films)	Germans try to blockade British Isles; Somerset Maugham, *Of Human Bondage*	
1916		JRRT marries while on leave, fights in Battle of the Somme, evacuated to England with trench fever	Margaret Sanger opens first birth-control clinic; tanks first used in battle	Easter Rebellion in Dublin; Battle of the Somme	Stainless steel invented
1917	Briefly attends University College, Oxford University; volunteers for the army; meets Mrs. Moore	CW marries, is initiated into Order of the Golden Dawn; JRRT writes "Of Beren and Luthien"	Czar abdicates; Bolshevik ("October") Revolution; Rudolf Otto, *The Idea of the Holy*; Degas, Rodin die	British capture Jerusalem; Balfour Declaration	
1918	Injured in battle and sent home		WWI ends, with 8.5 million dead; worldwide flu epidemic (kills 22 million in two years); Billy Graham born	Women over 30 get the vote; Lytton Strachey, *Eminent Victorians*	

	C. S. Lewis	The Inklings and Others	World History, Including Letters	English History and Letters	Science and Technology
1919	Begins study at Oxford; *Spirits in Bondage* (uses pseudonym Clive Hamilton)	DS, *Catholic Tales and Christian Songs* (poems); JRRT takes temporary work in English School at Oxford, is made junior editor of *Oxford English Dictionary*	Herman Hesse, *Demian*; League of Nations founded; Karl Barth's *Commentary on Romans*; Mussolini founds Fascists	Amritsar massacre in India	
1920	Takes first-class degree in Classical Moderations	JRRT appointed reader in English language at Leeds University	First performance of complete "Planets" of Gustav Holst; Wittgenstein, *Tractatus Logico-Philosophicus*; Karol Wojtyla (Pope John Paul II) born	IRA begins guerrilla war; Lambeth Conference issues *Appeal to All Christian People*; Agatha Christie's first mystery novel	
1921	Visits W. B. Yeats; wins Chancellor's English Essay Prize; Kirkpatrick dies		Einstein awarded Nobel Prize in physics; Pirandello, *Six Characters in Search of an Author*	DHL, *Women in Love*; population of England 42.5 million; 7,319 books published in England	Chromosome theory of heredity offered
1922	Takes first-class degree in Literae Humaniores ("Greats"); begins writing *Dymer*; turns down offer of position in Classics department of Reading University	GKC becomes Roman Catholic; JRRT, *A Middle English Vocabulary* (first book); OB joins Anthroposophical Society	Mussolini forms Fascist government in Italy; Attaturk proclaims Turkey a republic	Creation of Irish Free State; James Joyce, *Ulysses*; BBC founded; T. S. Eliot, *The Waste Land*	Insulin first administered to diabetics

	C. S. Lewis	The Inklings and Others	World History, Including Letters	English History and Letters	Science and Technology
1923	Takes first-class degree in English	DS, *Whose Body?* (first Lord Peter book); GKC, *St. Francis of Assisi*	Hitler's "Beer Hall Putsch" fails; Freud, *The Ego and the Id;* Gerschwin's *Rhapsody in Blue; Time* founded	P. G. Wodehouse, *The Inimitable Jeeves;* W. B. Yeats wins Nobel Prize	
1924	Temporary appointment teaching philosophy at University College, Oxford; begins "Great War" with Barfield	JRRT, made professor of English at Leeds	Lenin dies; Thomas Mann, *The Magic Mountain; The Ten Commandments* (film); first Winter Olympics	First Labour government; Conservatives return to power; E. M. Forster, *A Passage to India*	Rocket engine and frozen food invented; insecticides first used
1925	Named fellow in English of Magdalen College, Oxford (five-year appointment); tutors John Betjeman	JRRT comes to Oxford as professor of Anglo-Saxon, edits (with E. V. Gordon) *Sir Gawain and the Green Knight;* GKC, *The Everlasting Man*	Rudolph Steiner dies; Hitler, *Mein Kampf;* Hemingway, *The Sun Also Rises;* Pavlov publishes "Conditioned Reflexes"		
1926	*Dymer* (uses same pseudonym); meets J. R. R. Tolkien	GKC begins *GK's Weekly;* DS, *Clouds of Witness*	Trotsky expelled from Moscow; Turkey abolishes polygamy	General Strike; A. A. Milne, *Winnie the Pooh*	Television invented; Goddard fires first liquid fuel rocket
1927	Joins *Kolbítar* ("Coalbiters") led by Tolkien; takes first walking tour with Owen Barfield	DS, *Unnatural Death*	First talking movie (*The Jazz Singer*); Lindbergh crosses Atlantic; Martin Heidegger, *Being and Time*	TSE baptized in the Church of England; Virginia Woolf, *To the Lighthouse*	First solo flight across Atlantic; first crop-dusting

	C. S. Lewis	The Inklings and Others	World History, Including Letters	English History and Letters	Science and Technology
1928		OB, *Poetic Diction*	Dali/Buñuel, *Un Chien Andalou*; Margaret Mitchell, *Gone with the Wind*; Sigrid Undset awarded Nobel Prize; first Mickey Mouse films from Disney	14,399 books published in England	
1929	Real friendship with Tolkien begins; comes to believe in God; father dies		Beginning of the Depression; A. N. Whitehead, *Process and Reality*		Penicillin discovered; jet engine invented
1930	Moves into the Kilns	CW, *War in Heaven* (first novel), *Poetry at Present*	Nazis gain in election; Dashiell Hammett, *The Maltese Falcon*; Grant Wood, "American Gothic"	DHL dies; EW, *Vile Bodies*; Gandhi begins "Salt March" as protest against British Rule; TSE, *Ash Wednesday*	
1931	Walks along Addison Walk with Tolkien and Hugo Dyson (Sept. 19); a few days later accepts Christianity	CW, *Many Dimensions*, *The Place of the Lion*; WL accepts Christianity	Spain declared a republic; Pearl Buck, *The Good Earth*; *Frankenstein* (film)	Whipsnade Zoo opens; first trolley bus in London; British Commonwealth founded	Empire State Building completed

	C. S. Lewis	The Inklings and Others	World History, Including Letters	English History and Letters	Science and Technology
1932		CW, *The Greater Trumps*; WL retires from army and comes to live with his brother	Franklin D. Roosevelt elected president of United States in landslide; China (with 410 million people) largest nation, United States has 122 and Great Britain 46 million	Mosley starts British Union of Fascists; Aldous Huxley, *Brave New World*	Neutrons discovered
1933	*The Pilgrim's Regress*; Inklings begin*	CW, *Shadows of Ecstasy*; JRRT, "Errantry" (poem); DS, *Murder Must Advertise*; GKC, *The Dumb Ox*	Hitler appointed Chancellor of Germany, Herman Goebbels made minister of propaganda		
1934			Mao leads "Long March"	TSE, *The Rock*	
1935	Asked to write volume for Oxford History of English Literature	DS, *Gaudy Night*, "Aristotle on Detective Fiction" (lecture)		TSE, *Murder in the Cathedral*; Penguin Books founded, introducing paperbacks	
1936	*The Allegory of Love*; meets Charles Williams	CW meets CSL; GKC dies; DS, "The English Language" (article)		King George V dies; Edward VIII abdicates; George VI crowned; A. J. Ayer, *Language, Truth and Logic*; BBC starts regular television service	

*A disputed point. In *The Inklings*, Humphrey Carpenter noted that it might have begun in 1933, but there is no public mention of the group until 1938 (Houghton Mifflin, 1979, p. 67). In his *C. S. Lewis: A Companion and Guide*, Walter Hooper gives the date as 1933 (HarperCollins, 1996, p. 123).

	C. S. Lewis	The Inklings and Others	World History, Including Letters	English History and Letters	Science and Technology
1936-39			Spanish Civil War		
1937		JRRT, *The Hobbit*, "Beowulf: The Monsters and the Critics" (lecture); CW, *Descent into Hell*; DS, *The Zeal of Thy House* performed at Canterbury	Picasso, *Guernica*; Edinburgh Conference on Faith and Order; *Snow White and the Seven Dwarfs* (film)		
1938	*Out of the Silent Planet*	CW, *He Came Down from Heaven*, *Taliessin through Logres*; JRRT, "On Fairy-Stories" (lecture); DS, "Are Women Human?" (address), *Busman's Honeymoon* (last Lord Peter novel), *He That Should Come* (BBC play); Joy Davidman joins the Communist Party	Kristallnacht	Neville Chamberlain promises "peace in our time"	Ball point pen, Teflon invented
1939	*Rehabilitations and Other Essays*; *The Personal Heresy* (with E. M. W. Tillyard); meets Monsignor Ronald Knox	CW, *The Descent of the Dove*; CW moves to Oxford, joins Inklings; DS, "The Devil to Pay" performed at Canterbury	Germany invades Poland, starting WWII; *The Wizard of Oz* (film); John Steinbeck, *The Grapes of Wrath*	T. H. White, *The Sword in the Stone*; TSE, *The Family Reunion*, *The Idea of a Christian Society*	

	C. S. Lewis	The Inklings and Others	World History, Including Letters	English History and Letters	Science and Technology
1940	*The Problem of Pain* (dedicated to the Inklings)	CW lectures in English faculty; DS, *Begin Here,* "Creed or Chaos?" (address); JD, *Anya* (first novel)		Churchill becomes prime minister; Graham Greene, *The Power and the Glory;* W. H. Auden accepts Christianity; London blitz; TSE, *East Coker* (first of the *Four Quartets*)	Invention of radar; penicillin developed as antibiotic
1941	Four talks on "Right and Wrong: A Clue to the Meaning of the Universe?" on the BBC; "The Weight of Glory" (sermon); *The Screwtape Letters* appear in a religious newspaper	DS, *The Mind of the Maker,* "The Man Born to Be King" broadcast, "The Other Six Deadly Sins" (address); CW, "The Way of Exchange" (pamphlet)	Japan attacks Pearl Harbor; Rudolf Bultmann invents term "de-mythologizing"		

	C. S. Lewis	The Inklings and Others	World History, Including Letters	English History and Letters	Science and Technology
1942	Gives more BBC talks on "What Christians Believe" and "Christian Behaviour"; *The Screwtape Letters*; *A Preface to "Paradise Lost"*; *Broadcast Talks* (first and second set of BBC talks); first meeting of Socratic Club; begins (about this time) spiritual direction under Fr. Walter Adams, SSJE (Cowley Father); meets Dorothy L. Sayers	CW, *The Forgiveness of Sins* (dedicated to the Inklings), *Witchcraft*; DS, "Why Work?" (address); JD marries William Gresham			
1942-44				William Temple Archbishop of Canterbury	
1943	*Perelandra*; *The Abolition of Man*; *Christian Behavior* (third set of BBC talks)	CW, *The Figure of Beatrice*, receives honorary M.A. from Oxford; DS, *The Man Born to Be King*	Jean-Paul Sartre, *Being and Nothingness*		

	C. S. Lewis	The Inklings and Others	World History, Including Letters	English History and Letters	Science and Technology
1944	Gives last set of BBC talks, "The Christian View of God"; "The Inner Ring" (oration); "Transposition" (sermon); "The Death of Words" (article); *Beyond Personality* (last set of BBC talks)	David Gresham born; DS, "Toward a Christian Aesthetic" (lecture)	D-Day	TSE, *The Four Quartets*	
1945	*That Hideous Strength*; *The Great Divorce*; "The Grand Miracle" (sermon); begins tutoring Kenneth Tynan	CW, *All Hallows' Eve*; CW dies; EW, *Brideshead Revisited*; JRRT appointed professor of English language and literature at Oxford, "Leaf by Niggle" (story); DS proposes translation of Dante's *Divine Comedy*; Douglas Gresham born	U.S. drops atom bombs on Japan; end of WWII, with about 50 million dead	Labour government elected; George Orwell, *Animal Farm*; GG, *The Heart of the Matter*	
1946	*George MacDonald: An Anthology* (editor); passed over for professorship of English at Oxford			Bank of England nationalized; BBC resumes television broadcasts with 12,000 viewers; H. G. Wells dies	

	C. S. Lewis	The Inklings and Others	World History, Including Letters	English History and Letters	Science and Technology
1947	*Miracles; Essays Presented to Charles Williams* (editor)	DS, new production of "The Man Born to Be King" broadcast, *Unpopular Opinions*	India becomes independent nation, divided into India and Pakistan; Albert Camus, *The Plague*; Bertrand Russell awarded Nobel Prize	Coal industry nationalized	Transistor invented
1948	*Arthurian Torso* (editor); defeated in Socratic Club debate by G. E. M. Anscombe	CW, *Seed of Adam and Other Plays, Arthurian Torso* (unfinished "The Figure of Arthur"); JD and her husband become Christians	State of Israel founded; World Council of Churches formed	Railways, power, and gas industries nationalized; National Health Service founded; EW, *The Loved One*; TSE, *Notes Toward a Definition of Culture*, awarded Nobel Prize	Velcro invented
1949	*The Weight of Glory and Other Addresses*; Chad Walsh's *C. S. Lewis: Apostle to the Skeptics* (first book on Lewis)	DS, translation of Dante's *Hell*, publication of *Creed or Chaos?*; JRRT, *Farmer Giles of Ham*, finishes *The Lord of the Rings*	Communists take over China; NATO founded	GO, *1984*; Irish Free State severs all ties with England, becomes Republic of Ireland; TSE, *The Cocktail Party*	
1950	*The Lion, the Witch and the Wardrobe*; "What Are We to Make of Jesus Christ?" (article); first letter from Joy; begins writing to "Mary" (the American Lady)	DS, husband dies	Pope Pius XII declares Mary's bodily assumption into Heaven a dogma that Catholics must believe	GO dies; Bertrand Russell awarded Nobel Prize	DNA discovered

	C. S. Lewis	The Inklings and Others	World History, Including Letters	English History and Letters	Science and Technology
1950–53			Korean War		
1951	*Prince Caspian;* finishes writing first six Narnia Chronicles; defeated in election for professor of poetry by Cecil Day-Lewis.	Mrs. Moore dies; DS, *The Emperor Constantine*	J. D. Salinger, *Catcher in the Rye*	Churchill returns as prime minister	
1952	*Mere Christianity; The Voyage of the "Dawn Treader";* meets Joy; Fr. Adams (spiritual director) dies; tries to write a book on prayer	Collins withdraws offer to publish *The Lord of the Rings*		George VI dies; Queen Elizabeth II crowned; Dylan Thomas, "Do Not Go Gentle into That Good Night"	
1953	*The Silver Chair;* finishes *The Last Battle*	WL, *The Splendid Century* (first of six books); JD moves to England with her two sons	Stalin dies		Oral contraceptive invented; measles and polio vaccines discovered

	C. S. Lewis	The Inklings and Others	World History, Including Letters	English History and Letters	Science and Technology
1954	*The Horse and His Boy*; *English Literature in the Sixteenth Century, Excluding Drama*; named professor of medieval and Renaissance English at Cambridge University; "De Descriptione Temporum" (inaugural address); "George Orwell" (review)	JRRT, *The Lord of the Rings* volumes 1 and 2 published; DS, *Introductory Papers on Dante*; JD divorced, *Smoke on the Mountain: An Interpretation of the Ten Commandments* (with foreword by Lewis)		British troops withdraw from Egypt; food rationing ends; Billy Graham's first English crusade; William Golding, *The Lord of the Flies*	
1955	*The Magician's Nephew*; *Surprised by Joy*; "On Science Fiction" (talk); "On Obstinacy in Belief" (paper); "Lilies That Fester" (article)	JRRT, *The Lord of the Rings* volume 3 published; DS, translation of Dante's *Purgatory* (dedicated to CW)			

	C. S. Lewis	The Inklings and Others	World History, Including Letters	English History and Letters	Science and Technology
1956	*The Last Battle* wins Carnegie Medal as best children's book; *Till We Have Faces*; marries Joy in civil ceremony; Joy diagnosed with cancer; "Sometimes Fairy Tales May Say Best What Needs to Be Said" (article); "The Shoddy Lands" (story)		Soviet Invasion of Hungary	Suez Canal crisis	
1957	Marries Joy in Christian ceremony	DS, *Further Papers on Dante*, dies; OB, *Saving the Appearances*	USSR launches Sputnik; Treaty of Rome begins Common Market; AC wins Nobel Prize	John Osborne, *Look Back in Anger*	
1958	*Reflections on the Psalms*; attacked by Norman Pittenger in *The Christian Century*; "Ministering Angels" (story); records "The Four Loves" for Episcopal Radio–TV Foundation	CW, *The Image of the City and Other Essays* (edited by Anne Ridler)		Charles made Prince of Wales	
1959	"Modern Theology and Biblical Criticism" (address)	JRRT retires professorship; WL, *Louis XIV*	Fidel Castro comes to power in Cuba		

	C. S. Lewis	The Inklings and Others	World History, Including Letters	English History and Letters	Science and Technology
1960	*The Four Loves; Studies in Words; The World's Last Night and Other Essays;* new edition of *Miracles* with revised chapter 3 responding to Anscombe; travels to Greece with Joy; Joy dies (July 13)		17 former colonies in Africa become independent states; OPEC formed		Mini-computer, pacemaker invented; first laser built
1961	*A Grief Observed* (published under pseudonym N. W. Clerke); *An Experiment in Criticism*		U.S. invades Bay of Pigs; East Germany erects Berlin Wall; Soviets put first man in space		Crick and Watson discover structure of DNA
1962	*They Asked for a Paper: Papers and Addresses;* "Sex in Literature" (article)	JRRT, edition of *Ancrene Wisse;* OB, *Worlds Apart;* WL, *Levantine Adventurer* (last book)	Second Vatican Council opens; Andy Warhol, *Marilyn Diptych;* Cuban missile crisis; Alexander Solzhenitsyn, *One Day in the Life of Ivan Denisovich*		
1963	"We Have No 'Right to Happiness'" (article); dies (Nov. 23) at Kilns	Harry Blamires, *The Christian Mind*	John F. Kennedy assassinated; Beatles' first album	France vetoes Britain's application to join Common Market; Beatles become famous; J. A. T. Robinson, *Honest to God*	Audiocassette invented

	C. S. Lewis	The Inklings and Others	World History, Including Letters	English History and Letters	Science and Technology
1964	*Letters to Malcolm: Chiefly on Prayer; The Discarded Image: An Introduction to Medieval and Renaissance Literature; Poems*		Pope Paul VI and patriarch of Constantinople abolish mutual anathemas of 1054		Chemotherapy for cancer developed
1965	*Screwtape Proposes a Toast and Other Pieces*		U.S. escalates presence in Vietnam		
1966	*Studies in Medieval and Renaissance Literature; Letters of C. S. Lewis; Of Other Worlds: Essays and Stories*	JRRT receives Benson Medal from Royal Society of Literature		EW dies	
1967	*Christian Reflections; Spenser's Images of Life; Letters to an American Lady*		Six Day War between Israel and Arab countries; Martin Luther King assassinated		First human heart transplant
1969	*Narrative Poems; Selected Literary Essays*		Astronauts land on the moon		
1970	*God in the Dock*		Apollo XIII flight		
1972		JRRT awarded CBE			
1973		WL, JRRT die			
1974	Wade Center founded at Wheaton College				
1997		OB dies			

The Source of C. S. Lewis's Use of
the Phrase "Mere Christianity"

WALTER HOOPER, editor of many of C. S. Lewis's works, has found the Puritan divine Richard Baxter's *Church-history of the Government of Bishops* (1680) to be the source of Lewis's use of the phrase "mere Christianity."

> You know not of what Party I am of, nor what to call me; I am sorrier for you in this than for my self; if you know not, I will tell you, I am a CHRISTIAN, a MEER CHRISTIAN, of no other Religion; and the Church that I am of is the Christian Church, and hath been visible where ever the Christian Religion and Church hath been visible: But must you know of what Sect or Party I am of? I am against all Sects and dividing Parties: But if any will call *Meer Christian* by the name of a *Party,* because they take up *with meer Christianity, Creed,* and *Scripture,* and will not be of any dividing or contentious Sect, I am of that Party which is so against Parties: If the name CHRISTIAN be not enough, call me a CATHOLIC CHRISTIAN; not as that word signifieth an hereticating majority of Bishops, but as it signifieth one that hath no Religion, but that which by Christ and the Apostles was left to the Catholic Church, or the body of Jesus Christ on Earth.

Permissions

The editor and publisher gratefully acknowledge permission granted to reprint the following materials:

Excerpts from *The Abolition of Man; Christian Reflections* (world outside U.S.); *The Great Divorce; The Horse and His Boy; The Last Battle; The Lion, the Witch and the Wardrobe; The Magician's Nephew; Mere Christianity; Miracles; The Pilgrim's Regress* (world except North America); *The Problem of Pain; The Screwtape Letters; The Silver Chair; The Voyage of the "Dawn Treader";* and *The Weight of Glory and Other Addresses* by permission of HarperCollins Publishers, England.

Excerpts from "Bluspels and Flanansferes" from *Rehabilitations;* "De Descriptione Temporum" from *They Asked for a Paper; They Stand Together;* and *Letters: C. S. Lewis to Don Giovanni Calabria* by permission of Curtis Brown Ltd., London, on behalf of C. S. Lewis PTE Ltd. and Martin Moynihan.

Excerpts from *English Literature in the Sixteenth Century, Excluding Drama* (1954) and from *Preface to "Paradise Lost"* (1942) by permission of Oxford University Press.

Excerpts from *Essays Presented to Charles Williams* reprinted by permission of Charles Williams and the Watkins/Loomis Agency.

Excerpts from *The Four Loves* by C. S. Lewis, copyright © 1960 by Helen Joy Lewis and renewed 1988 by Arthur Owen Barfield, reprinted by permission of Harcourt Brace & Company (world except UK and Canada) and HarperCollins Publishers, England (UK and Canada).

Excerpts from *God in the Dock* reprinted by permission of Curtis Brown Ltd., London, on behalf of C. S. Lewis PTE Ltd. and Martin Moynihan (U.S. only) and HarperCollins Publishers, England (world outside U.S.).

Excerpts from *A Grief Observed* reprinted by permission of Faber & Faber (excluding U.S.) and HarperCollins Publishers, England (U.S. only).

Excerpts from *Letters of C. S. Lewis* by C. S. Lewis and W. H. Lewis, copyright © 1966 by W. H. Lewis and the Executors of C. S. Lewis and renewed 1994 by C. S. Lewis PTE Ltd., reprinted by permission of Harcourt Brace & Company (world except British Commonwealth) and HarperCollins Publishers, England (British Commonwealth).

Excerpts from *Letters to Children* by C. S. Lewis, edited by Lyle W. Dorsett and Marjorie Lamp Mead. Copyright © 1985 by C. S. Lewis PTE Ltd. Reprinted with the permission of Simon & Schuster (U.S. and Canada) and HarperCollins Publishers, England (British Commonwealth).

Excerpts from *Letters to Malcolm: Chiefly on Prayer* by C. S. Lewis, copyright © 1964, 1963 by C. S. Lewis PTE Ltd. and renewed 1992, 1991 by Arthur Owen Barfield, reprinted by permission of Harcourt Brace & Company (U.S. only) and HarperCollins Publishers, England (world outside U.S.).

Excerpts from *Of Other Worlds, Essays and Stories* by C. S. Lewis and Walter Hooper, copyright © 1966 by the Executors of the Estate of C. S. Lewis and renewed 1994 by C. S. Lewis PTE Ltd., reprinted by permission of Harcourt Brace & Company.

Excerpts from *On Stories and Other Essays on Literature* by C. S. Lewis and Walter Hooper, copyright © 1982 by C. S. Lewis PTE Ltd., reprinted by permission of Harcourt Brace & Company (world except UK and Canada) and HarperCollins Publishers, England (UK and Canada).

Excerpts from *Out of the Silent Planet, Perelandra,* and *That Hideous Strength* by permission of Random House UK.

Excerpts from *Present Concerns* by C. Lewis, copyright © 1986 by C. S. Lewis PTE Ltd., reprinted by permission of Harcourt Brace & Company.

Excerpts from *Surprised by Joy: The Shape of My Early Life* by C. S. Lewis, copyright © 1956 by C. S. Lewis PTE Ltd. and renewed 1984 by Arthur Owen Barfield, reprinted by permission of Harcourt Brace & Company (U.S. and Philippines) and HarperCollins Publishers, England (world outside U.S.).

Excerpts from *Till We Have Faces — A Myth Retold* by C. S. Lewis, copyright © 1957, 1956 by C. S. Lewis PTE Ltd. and renewed 1985, 1984 by Arthur Owen Barfield, reprinted by permission of Harcourt Brace & Company (world except Canada and British Commonwealth) and HarperCollins Publishers, England (Canada and British Commonwealth).